CHICHESTER INSTITUTE OF
HIGHER EDUCATION

AUTHOR

LEISINGER

TITLE

ALL

301·32

D0272907

25P95

About Island Press

Island Press is the only nonprofit organization in the United States whose principal purpose is the publication of books on environmental issues and natural resource management. We provide solutions-oriented information to professionals, public officials, business and community leaders, and concerned citizens who are shaping responses to environmental problems.

In 1994, Island Press celebrates its tenth anniversary as the leading provider of timely and practical books that take a multidisciplinary approach to critical environmental concerns. Our growing list of titles reflects our commitment to bringing the best of an expanding body of literature to the environmental community throughout North America and the world.

Support for Island Press is provided by The Geraldine R. Dodge Foundation, The Energy Foundation, The Ford Foundation, The George Gund Foundation, William and Flora Hewlett Foundation, The James Irvine Foundation, The John D. and Catherine T. MacArthur Foundation, The Andrew W. Mellon Foundation, The Joyce Mertz-Gilmore Foundation, The New-Land Foundation, The Pew Charitable Trusts, The Rockefeller Brothers Fund, The Tides Foundation, Turner Foundation, Inc., The Rockefeller Philanthropic Collaborative, Inc., and individual donors.

All
Our
People

All Our People

Population Policy with a Human Face

Klaus M. Leisinger and Karin Schmitt

Foreword by Robert S. McNamara

Washington, D.C.   Covelo, California

This publication was made possible through the generous support of the Pew Global Stewardship Initiative, with additional funding provided by Turner Foundation, Inc., and The Rockefeller Philanthropic Collaborative, Inc.

COPYRIGHT © 1994 BY ISLAND PRESS

ALL RIGHTS RESERVED UNDER INTERNATIONAL AND PAN-AMERICAN COPYRIGHT CONVENTIONS. NO PART OF THIS BOOK MAY BE REPRODUCED IN ANY FORM OR BY ANY MEANS WITHOUT PERMISSION IN WRITING FROM THE PUBLISHER: ISLAND PRESS, 1718 CONNECTICUT AVENUE, N.W., SUITE 300, WASHINGTON, DC 20009.

ISLAND PRESS is a trademark of The Center for Resource Economics.

Library of Congress Cataloging-in Publication Data

Leisinger, Klaus M.
    All our people : population policy with a human face / Klaus M.
Leisinger and Karin Schmitt ; foreword by Robert S. McNamara.
      p. cm.
    Includes bibliographical references (p.) and index.
    ISBN 1-55963-292-5 (cloth : acid-free paper).—ISBN
1–55963–293–3 (paper : acid-free paper)
    1. Population policy. I. Schmitt, Karin. II. Title.
HB883.5.L45 1994
363.9—dc20   93-50647
                                        CIP

Printed on recycled, acid-free paper

Manufactured in the United States of America

10 9 8 7 6 5 4 3 2 1

Contents

Part IV The Effects of Rapid Population Growth   46

Part V The Demographic Transition Theory   98

Part VI Requirements for an Ethically Acceptable Population Policy   116

Part VII Overview and Conclusion   191

Contents

Foreword

In September 1968, in my first speech as President of the World Bank, speaking to the Finance Ministers of the world at the annual meeting of the Bank and the International Monetary Fund, I said: "The rapid growth of population is one of the greatest barriers to economic growth and social well-being of [the people] of our member states."[1]

That was my view in 1968. It is my view today. In the intervening 26 years, the world's population has grown faster than ever before, from 3.4 billion to more than 5.6 billion, an increase of more than 60 percent. Growth rates are still extraordinarily high, almost 3 percent a year in Africa, nearly 2 percent in Asia and Latin America. Even if the fertility rates continue their present decline, 3 billion people will be added to the global population over the next 30 years.

Is this a cause for concern?

For many, the answer is not immediately clear. In spite of the increase of 2 billion in the last quarter-century, during the same time there have been remarkable advances in economic and social welfare in the developing countries, where 80 percent of the world's population lives. Consumption per capita has risen by almost 70 percent, infant mortality rates have fallen, literacy rates have increased, average nutritional levels have improved, and life expectancy has risen.

In spite of such progress, the number of human beings suffering from hunger has increased to more than 1 billion, and the number of illiterates has risen to over 900 million. Maternal mortality has increased: 500,000 women now die each year from pregnancy and childbirth-related causes. Infant and child mortality remain at totally unacceptable levels: 40,000 children—at least half of whom could be saved—die each day.

So I return to the basic question: Is the increase in human numbers and its environmental and developmental ramifications a cause for concern?

I argue that it is; that the interests of both developing and industrial countries—particularly the interests of women and children in the developing world—demand immediate action to accelerate the reduction in population growth rates.

When the World Bank began to discuss population issues systematically in the late sixties, and made its first family planning loan in 1970, there was broad agreement among most scholars that rapid population growth had generally negative consequences for development. The arguments were not as simplistic as those of Malthus, who in the late eighteenth century argued that food production would not keep pace with population growth. Nor did they project such catastrophic consequences as did Paul Ehrlich in *The Population Bomb* (1968), Jay Forrester in *World Dynamics* (1971), and Donella Meadows and her coauthors in the Club of Rome's report *The Limits to Growth* (1972)— the latter predicting that the world had only about 100 years remaining before its economic and/or biosystems collapsed. Instead, my associates and I in the Bank believed that lack of capital and of surplus labor in the rural areas were major constraints to human advance in developing countries—and that rapid population growth aggravated both these handicaps.

By the late seventies, this argument began to be questioned. What might be characterized as "revisionist" thinking came into vogue. It was suggested that if decisions regarding family size were made at the family level, based on market signals (such as the value of additional children as farm labor), these decisions would maximize not only individual welfare but social welfare as well, unless there were clear market failures.

The pendulum appeared to swing back in the mid to late eighties. A major report by the World Bank in 1984 emphasized that there were indeed institutional and market failures and that high population growth rates could, and were, severely inhibiting economic growth and human development throughout most of the developing world.[2]

In the 10 years that have passed since the publication of the World Bank report, we have learned much more about the adverse consequences of rapid population growth: Degrading poverty in developing countries will be aggravated and will affect even greater numbers, if not ever greater percentages, of their inhabitants. The role and the status of women and the health and opportunities of both them and their children will be adversely affected. Furthermore, rapid population growth rates will increase the danger that the present paths of economic development—in industrial and developing countries alike—are unsustainable and risk the destruction of the earth's physical environment.

Given the severity of the environmental and poverty problems facing developing countries and the global community, reducing population growth rates below currently projected levels is a necessary, humane, and low-cost step that will contribute to their solution. Reducing fertility will allow political leaders more time to come to grips with the immense pressures on natural resources, and it will permit governments of developing countries to devote more resources to human development by increasing investment in education, health, welfare, and job creation.

The analysis in the pages that follow echos many of my concerns about the issues of population growth and social and economic development. It is my hope that this very thoughtful and well reasoned volume will contribute to a better understanding of the complex issues involved. Readers of this book will not only come away with a better awareness of the size and scope of the problem, they will learn about the causes and consequences of population growth. This study also makes a valuable contribution in analyzing the ethical issues involved in the population debate and the need to address issues of consumption as well as absolute numbers. In addition, readers will learn about the necessary preconditions for lowering birth rates and, most important, why there are some good reasons to be hopeful that population growth rates may be reduced.

Klaus Leisinger and Karin Schmitt have made a valuable contribution to the argument that more needs to be done to slow population growth. Their work makes it clear that reducing population growth rates will require concerted efforts among individuals and institutions in many countries both rich and poor. In this context I strongly endorse the authors' view that rich countries should contribute substantially to the international efforts to create the necessary conditions for slowing rates of population growth so as to improve the lives of people—especially poor people—in the world. Any such increased contribution should not be viewed as a humanitarian gesture, although that it surely is, but as an act of enlightened self-interest: one intended to reduce pressures on our small, crowded planet with its finite resources.

Robert S. McNamara

Part I

Introduction

Value Judgments in the Population Policy Debate

Gut Reactions: No Basis for Population Policy

While you are reading this sentence, world population will grow by about 20 people. Never before in human history has our planet been home to so many people: today there are more than 5.6 billion of us. And never have there been so many new additions to the human race year after year—about 90 million in 1993 alone. That means more than 250,000 per day . . . about 10,500 per hour . . . almost three per second. In the nineties, world population will increase by some 90–95 million per year, even though birth rates in most developing countries have dropped rapidly since the eighties.[1]

Although world population has increased without interruption, it used to grow much more slowly than it does today. For example, it took approximately 200 years for the world population of 500 million in the middle of the seventeenth century to double to 1 billion. The doubling time has been drastically reduced since then. In 1927—less than 100 years later—there were 2 billion people. And by 1974, not even 50 years later, world population had doubled to 4 billion.

Children born today are likely to know a world as adults of some 10 billion people. The young age structure of world population, with a third the world under the age of 15, has more or less set the course of population growth for the next 25 years.

Many people in western industrial nations have gut reactions to these projections. Yet similar gut reactions do not seem to arise, at least not enough to result in a change of habits, about their own destructive life-style. People rarely if ever ask whether the United States or Germany, for example, are

1

overpopulated in light of the energy- and waste-intensive consumption patterns of most of their residents.

Current environmental problems give some indication of what could happen if the whole world lived like Americans and Germans do today. Our lifestyles cannot be followed everywhere and therefore are not sustainable. But stronger than the insight into needed changes on our part is the temptation to propose birth control in developing countries as a patent remedy for our planet. Although our gut reactions may motivate the current population debate, they should not be allowed to distort the facts, particularly when the limitation of the human right to reproductive freedom is invariably discussed in this context.

Individual values and interests always exert an enormous influence on the assessment of facts. Popular opinion holds that science is neutral and objective. What objectivity means here is that the scientist should provide disinterested information about facts and not permit his or her subjective values to intrude. Description, interpretation, explanation, and prediction are scientific activities that should be free of subjective values and interests. But "disinterested" sciences have never existed and never will. Gunnar Myrdal and others have repeatedly pointed out that we never observe reality without a preconceived opinion, and that we inevitably judge and weigh facts, define problems, or propose solutions on the basis of a particular class of values.[2]

This certainly holds true for the way the population problem is defined. And this in turn has a direct effect on the type of solutions proposed. When "population bombs" or the "yellow threat" are referred to, a terminological decision has already been made with respect to the merit or the demerit of population growth.[3] An apocalyptic book on demographic problems is prone—not surprisingly—to make radical recommendations. These are not, however, sustainable solutions to complex problems.

Just as in the case of world peace, which the world spent 40 years trying to resolve with the arms race, there is no technical answer to the problem of "population growth." If the superpowers try to secure peace using only science and technology, the results will aggravate the situation; vast amounts of resources will flow into arms and thereby be diverted from meeting the needs for a decent human life. Unfortunately, predominantly technical solutions remain in demand in many areas where a more holistic approach would be appropriate—despite the fact that only rarely do technical solutions exist for social and political problems such as overly rapid population growth.

How Many People Is "Too Many"?

Rapid population growth on its own cannot be evaluated as either positive or negative for the social and economic development of a country. The risks implied by a certain population level and growth rate must be assessed by looking at the numbers in relation to arable land, natural resources, and infrastructure. Only then can any conclusions be drawn about "overpopulation" and "underpopulation," or "overly rapid" and "overly slow" population growth. And even then, those conclusions will be affected by the values and interests of the person evaluating the evidence, as just noted.

In some regions (such as the Sahel) the current population level is already too high given existing resources, and a "negative growth rate" is needed to improve the quality of life. In other cases, however, resource-richer societies face relatively few problems for the foreseeable future in spite of population growth rates of more than 2 percent.

In general, population growth is "overly rapid" if it leads—even where people live at subsistence levels—to an overuse of existing natural resources, or if there is not enough capital to finance the investments needed, for example, for basic educational and medical services.[4] Due to local and global environmental pressures, a growth rate of 2 percent or higher (a doubling of population within 35 years or less) must be considered as "high" in this context.

But a population can also be perceived as being "too small" and its growth rate "too low." Hundreds of millions of people struggle under such adverse living conditions that one in three children dies before the age of five, and mortality rates in general due to hunger, inadequate sanitation and hygienic facilities, and internal and external strife are very high. People in such situations generally count on their own children for support (and not only in their old age, as they may be barely able to scratch out a livelihood earlier), so four or five children frequently offer too little social security. In cultures where women have a very low status and where only boys are seen as an asset to a family, seven or even eight children may seem barely enough to ensure old-age security.

A national population might also seem too small to a government blessed with a low population density and a surplus of fertile land but bordered by a country armed to its teeth that suffers from a shortage of land due to a rapidly growing population, especially if the neighbor is constantly looking across the border—sometimes gently, sometimes aggressively. Such a government might decide that its own population growth is "too slow" and that a higher growth rate would increase its geopolitical weight and therefore the long-term security of its citizens.

Since "too many" is not an absolute measurement but something that must be seen in relation to the existing natural resources or maximum carrying capacity of an ecological system, the calculation must be made separately for each individual country. We do not know how much is "too many" for the entire earth. Increasingly, however, there are social and ecological signs that lasting development for all people cannot be reconciled either with rapid population growth among the poorest third of the world or with a continuation of the energy and resource consumption patterns of the wealthiest 10–15 percent of the world. Global population issues also apply to us, the wealthy minority living in industrial countries.

The Limits of Consumption

The debate over population policy today is subject primarily to the value judgments of western industrial countries. Our nuclear family is regarded as an ideal worth striving for, while the extended family in Africa or Latin America, with its large numbers of children, is basically viewed as a model for "underdevelopment." We usually have a very difficult time even attempting to look at the world through the eyes of a different culture. And the tenor of the population policy discussion implicitly supports and seeks to maintain the current global economic distribution of power.

Many people in rich industrial countries see rapid population growth as a threat to their prosperity. They fear future shortages due to the limited world supply of nonrenewable resources, or the collapse of vital ecosystems due to high levels of pollution. Although a growing world population is indeed an important factor in this scenario, the historical and continuing high consumption patterns of the rich are equally to blame. The overwhelming majority of global pollution and the total consumption of nonrenewable resources such as petroleum to date can be traced to the minority of people in industrial countries—not to the majority of people in the developing world. There would certainly already be too many people in the world today if everyone on earth lived as the average American, German, or Swiss now does, for important ecological systems would collapse. If instead everyone produced, consumed, and created only as much waste as the majority of people in the so-called Third World, a world population three times the present size could live on existing natural resources—albeit at a very modest level.

Two population groups are responsible for a large part of the current destruction of the environment: the wealthiest billion people, with their frightening ability to consume resources and produce waste, and the poorest billion, who overuse and destroy their already scarce resources due to sheer necessity and a lack of alternatives.[5] For people in industrial countries to hand down population policy recommendations while perched on the warm cushion of northwest European or North American prosperity not only holds explosive political implications, it is not even legitimate.[6] We must at the same time make a plea for change in our resource-intensive life-style and production methods. Without new values guiding policy on energy consumption, resource use, and waste production in industrial countries, any population policy debate will be hollow and hypocritical.[7]

A change of course in the environmental behavior of the rich minority would contribute at least as much—indeed, in the short term, even more—to the sustainable development of the entire planet as would lower birth rates in poor countries.

The Authors' Subjective Values

To assess the influence of population growth on "development" or on the "chances for development" of a country, definitional problems must first be resolved, since the concept of "development" is ambiguous and involves subjective evaluations, as the Brandt Commission noted: "Development will never be, and never can be, defined to universal satisfaction. It refers, broadly speaking, to desirable social and economic progress, and people will always have different views about what is desirable."[8]

What is desired, by whom, for whom, at whose expense, and within what time frame are all subject to many different evaluations even within western societies. It is even more difficult to find a consensus when we go outside our own culture: quality of life—beyond satisfying basic needs—is defined quite differently by a Philippine farmer than by a Russian miner. An Indian in the Amazon strives toward different material and immaterial goals of self-realization than a nomad in the Sahel zone, a fisher in Papua New Guinea, or a rice farmer in Bangladesh.

And the comparison with those of us in industrial countries? Does the second or third luxury car, the golf vacation in Hawaii, or jetting around the world add more to the quality of life than, say, a successful Nepalese business-man's meditative retreat to a Buddhist monastery?

In addition, the desires and aspirations of women usually differ from those of men. And substantial differences exist among women as well—between a casteless widow in rural southern India, for example, and an educated woman in New Delhi who works in the government. By the same token, large differences exist between the desires and aspirations of young and old members of a society as well as among the members of different social groups.

"Development" from the Authors' Point of View

Today a relatively strong basic consensus exists that "development" consists of more than the mere replication of the path to industrialization that has given people in industrial countries a comparatively high and broad level of prosperity.

Human "development" means, first and foremost, the satisfaction of the basic needs of all the members of a society and the reduction or eradication of absolute poverty, preventable human suffering, and social inequalities with respect to income, property, and opportunities. But it also means greater availability of goods and services and an increase in economic productivity through improved technologies and production methods while preserving natural resources for present and future generations.

Indispensable for a lasting economic as well as a socially and environmentally sound development are peace, respect for human rights, and the preservation of human dignity. This, in turn, makes a reduction of the prosperity gap between the rich and the poor countries of this earth necessary, along with the resolution of diverse political, economic, religious, ethnic, and other competing interests.

Human development must be based on a participatory structure, involving the greatest possible participation of all social classes (particularly those at the bottom of the social ladder) in the analysis of the political, economic, and social problems to be solved, in decisions regarding the actions to be undertaken, in the implementation of projects and programs, and in the economic and social results of their labor. This applies particularly to women.

When it comes to the question of which practical development strategy should be adopted in a specific country, the choice will again be subject to value judgments: Evaluations must be made on which means are effective and justified, when, and why; which concrete social, technological, and economic conditions are needed if appropriate development visions are to be realized; and how much weight should be given to the values of economic efficiency and growth, especially when they conflict with other values.[9]

Controversial Modernization Ideals

It is commonly recognized that "development" is a multidimensional process in which noneconomic forces are at least as important as economic ones. In this context it has often been argued that certain sociocultural attitudes, values, traditions, and institutions obstruct development while others promote it. The first are usually called "traditional" and the second, "modern."

There has been considerable debate not only about the causal links between "modernity" and "development" but also about the traditional/modern dichotomy as a reflection of western values and about the justification of "supported" and "directed" cultural change.[10] Is there a "universal" set of psychosocial qualities—that is, attitudes, values, and modes of conduct—that identify people as "modern"? And if such a syndrome of individual "modernity" does exist, what are the social forces that move people from being traditional to being modern? Should traditional patterns of thought and behavior that stand in the way of economic efficiency and growth be changed? Thus arises the moral dilemma—from which there is no easy escape—for those who believe in the value of a traditional collective identity but who are also committed to social justice and economic equality for the impoverished two-thirds of humanity.

Causal Links Between "Modernity" and "Development"?

Since the rise of newly industrialized economies in Asia, many social scientists have attempted to identify the cultural background of economic development in this area. Emphasis on the role of resources (technology, capital, and labor outputs, for example) in economic growth has been replaced by a focus on value orientations, attitudes, and behaviors (human quality inputs) as preconditions to the effective use of resources. The view that "development" is the product of modernization has failed to do justice to the traditional values that were the basis of those achievements: a diligent work ethic, discipline, efficiency, and so on.

"Modernity" and "traditionalism" are frequently confused or identified with "development" and "underdevelopment," using industrial western societies as the basis of comparison. The division of values into "modern" versus "traditional" often reflects an ethnocentric perspective idealizing the nineteenth-century values of individualism, laissez-faire, competition, technocracy, and resource exploitation that characterized the industrialization of the West. Yet industrial nations today face mounting crises due, ironically, to their "success" in solving earlier problems. And we have evidence that "modernity"—far from necessarily promoting structural development—emphasizes individual consumption and deters sustainable development. Therefore, we have to agree with Max Weber, who doubted the possibility of creating meaningful life-styles for the masses in the secular culture of our "modern" age.[11]

Modernization, production, and an increase in a country's financial capacity may not lead to a better standard of living for most poor people in developing nations. Development strategies that aim at gradually displacing the traditional sector with a modern, industrial sector have proved to be inappropriate when based on capital-intensive, large-scale, heavy industrial complexes or showcase projects that have little effect on job creation, productivity, or poverty alleviation. If development endeavors fail to reach the poor they can hardly produce genuine "development." A more promising approach in many cases may be a strategy emphasizing the evolution of traditional sectors with intermediate technologies that build local communities because they are locally produced, labor-intensive, repairable, fueled by renewable energy, and ecologically sound.[12]

Last but not least, understanding and defining human desires and needs— for an adequate income, for instance, and creative opportunities, a sense of belonging and purpose, participation, and responsible government—and applying human values to development and modernization should be the test of whether a country's development is successful. Similar criteria can be applied on an international level to evaluate development: respect for other nations, sustainable use of natural resources, solidarity, and mutual trade growth.

Toward Another Concept of "Modernity"

Social modernization is not a type of Westernization or Europeanization implying values that yield cash rewards. It is a concept based on collectivity, security, and cooperation. It is not a static pattern but a dynamic historical process. It is the development of social coordination and political democratization interrelated with traditions.

"Modernity" need not be understood as an advance over the premodern— such an idea unduly privileges the current historical moment. The main carrier of modernity's dynamic is dynamic justice, which enables people to criticize, question, and change existing social arrangements that are to their disadvantage. While today's social arrangements are based on patterns of asymmetric reciprocity, real modern ones would be based on the notion of "one humanity" in order to conquer pollution and poverty, ignorance, disease, and so on.

Individual modernization is a personal resource enabling adaptation to change by increasing a person's attitudinal flexibility. The process of modernization depends on conditions such as formal education, mass media, and unimpeded communication, and it applies to women as well as men. Central among the qualities of individual modernity are informed participant citizenship, a sense of personal effectiveness and responsibility, independence in relation to traditional sources of personal influence, and cognitive flexibility. Individual modernization also manifests in actual behavior, giving meaning and support to changes in the political and economic institutions involved in the modernization process.[13]

Cultural Change

We are faced with problems for which old concepts are of little help. If we use them anyway, the results may be disastrous. A case in point is the habit that otherwise serious thinkers have of speaking of patriarchal societies as "traditional" and, when this meets with raised eyebrows, of explaining: "It is because they desire to preserve their culture." Is it hopelessly ethnocentric to recommend cultural change in societies that repress women by a "culture" of male dominance? Perhaps it is, and yet such a change is requested here.

The traditional gender-based division of labor, for example, limits women to jobs that are regarded as low status and excludes them from decision-making processes. This stops a country from using the full range of available talent and labor force, and does not select the best or most qualified person for a particular job. Socialization and enculturation processes ensure the continuity of this system and the inferiority of the female position, with an accompanying limited mobility. Women are taught to be submissive and passive, and the highest social position of a female is tied to maternity. These values hinder women from aspiring to or preparing for other social roles and options. Thus not all cultural values are moral values that deserve to be preserved.

All around the world, people are breaking away from authoritarian rule because they see that where political choice works—however messily— citizens seem to live better, with more chances to choose their personal futures. Who, then, would object when women want to think for themselves and have a voice in their own destinies and that of their societies?

Social Costs of Modernization

The transition from a traditional society requires a host of changes in the policies and actions of those involved in the governing process as well as a change in individual attitudes and belief systems. Thus the movement toward modernity has political, socioeconomic, and emotional dimensions. Change may cause tension, stress, and strains between the ethos of those who deal in choices and the values associated with modern systems and those who wish to maintain the status quo. In these cases, modernity of individuals might not lead to societal development in underdeveloped or developing countries; it might instead lead to the emigration of the modernized individuals.

Development is a two-edged sword, bringing benefits to some and producing losses for others. Hence, the known and welcome gains (improvements in standards of living, reductions in mortality and morbidity, education, increased freedom of choice, and so on) must be weighed against the destructive edge of the sword.[14] Depending on a specific society's sociocultural structure, this can be, for example, loss of solidarity among the members of a community, increased dependence on anonymous state institutions, social alienation, and role ambiguity, as well as destruction or dilution of cultures. Whether the positive consequences outweigh the losses depends to a considerable degree on the values of the person making the judgment.

The clash between the elements of modernity and the guardians of tradition largely depends on the scope and direction of change, the strength of emotional attachment to the past, and the skills and communicative ability of the modernizing political elites.

Governance and the Capacity to Govern

"Governance" has been defined by the Club of Rome as "the command-mechanism of a social system and its actions, which endeavours to provide security, prosperity, coherence, order and continuity to the system. It necessarily embraces the ideology of the system, which may (democratic) or may not (authoritarian) define means for effective consideration of the public will and accountability of those in authority."[15]

There are plenty of age-old as well as new miseries to tackle: the shocking contrasts of poverty and affluence, human hunger in the face of technological plenty, ecological degradation, injustice and bigotry, eruptions of long-suppressed ambitions for cultural and national identity in Eastern Europe and elsewhere, the probability of unprecedented migrations of people, and so on. The main threats to world security are likely to arise from turbulence and terror in poorer countries, driven by resentments about economic unfairness and cultural conflict. In these conflicts, 85–90 percent of the victims are civilians, mostly old people, women, children.

We need the international machinery to anticipate, deter, and resolve conflicts around the world, along with education, which affects the behavior of whole populations. Issues such as these are a collective responsibility. Our "nobody-in-charge" world system requires a more consensual style of leadership, featuring less complacency, command, and compliance and more responsibility, consultation, and compromise.

The hope for healthy growth with fairness and for regional security arrangements lies not in the developing countries clubbing together to confront the world's richer minority, nor vice versa. It rests instead on cooperation between these groups. The challenge of creating better standards of living amidst more freedom, peace, justice, and security are enormous, but so are the opportunities—where the capacity for good governance exists.

We are not, of course, arguing that industrial countries are by definition outstanding champions in governance, which would be impossible to say in light of "modern" poverty, record levels of public debts, the disturbing phenomenon of jobless growth with high levels of unemployment, or the "ethnic cleansing" occurring in the center of Europe. It is not only in the developing nations of Asia, Africa, and Latin America where we have witnessed ruthless exploitation of people and corruption midst the most pitiable poverty—and it is not there where the most spectacular waste of resources and the most apocalyptic devastation of the natural environment takes place. Nevertheless, the lack of good governance in the countries that contain the great bulk of the world's population bears the risk of increasing their dependence on a few rich nations, and also the risk of generating resentful behavior that threatens the delicate establishment of a network within the global community.

The governance issue is a complex one. As the World Bank put it: "This complexity arises from the unique imprint of history, geography, and culture on each country's institutions and rules, and the multidimensional nature of governance as a concept. Thus each country is at a different level of political, economic, and social development reflecting a wide array of historical, geographic, and cultural factors."[16] The Bank goes on, however, to note some clearly definable main symptoms of poor governance:

- failure to make a clear separation between what is public and what is private and, hence, a tendency to divert public resources for private gain;
- failure to establish a predictable framework of law and government behavior conducive to development, or arbitrariness in the application of rules and laws;
- excessive rules, regulations, licensing requirements, and so forth, which impede the functioning of markets;
- priorities inconsistent with development, resulting in a misallocation of resources; and
- excessively narrowly based or nontransparent decisionmaking.

Such "problems" may be due to lack of institutional capacity or to political volition, or to both, and may be of varying severity. When they are sufficiently severe and occur together, however, they create an environment hostile to development.

Two fundamental tasks are at the forefront for developing countries: an expenditure structure for their limited public resources that is oriented toward people's problems, and an appropriate economic policy that promotes and does not hinder growth.

The Satisfaction of Basic Needs as a Priority

Since at least 1976, when the International Labour Organization elevated the "satisfaction of basic needs" to a doctrine of development policy, national and international corresponding strategies have been common sense.[17] The "satisfaction of basic needs" means that the private minimum requirements of food, clothing, and shelter are being met and that the minimal household necessities are being provided. Basic needs also includes a supply of healthy drinking water, sanitary facilities, public means of transportation, and health and educational facilities. Finally, it includes the fulfillment of more qualitative needs such as a healthy, humane, and satisfying environment, as well as people's right to participate in decisions that affect their lives, livelihoods, and individual freedoms.[18]

The success of development strategies oriented toward the satisfaction of basic needs is widely undisputed and is even recognized by institutions that tend to be more conservative, such as the World Bank.[19] Establishing priorities for government funds in relation to existing problems and reallocating budgetary items to basic needs programs instead of to armaments has desirable effects not only from the development perspective but also in terms of financial policy. According to the U.N. Development Programme (UNDP), some $50 billion could be freed up to fight human suffering in this way.[20]

Socially and Ecologically Sound Market Economies

Although economic and social progress is always the result of the combined effect of a variety of current and historical factors, experience shows that a market-oriented economy is a key factor. Long before *glasnost* and *perestroika,* a study by the Munich Institute for Economic Research showed that "more market" leads to better economic and social results for all segments of a population.[21]

Economic growth cannot—there is no longer any doubt—be dictated into existence through higher government expenditures and government intervention in the economy. Constant government intervention, administrative investment obstacles, bureaucratization, and legal uncertainty have a negative effect on the individual motivation to produce, invest, and take risks, and thereby also on economic growth as a whole. A secure legal framework, free trade, and free consumer choice promote economic growth in developing as well as industrial countries.

Further measures, such as efforts to decrease high inflation rates, the opening of local markets (as soon as and to the extent that circumstances allow it), or the introduction of a fair tax system, would also create more favorable conditions for economic and social progress. The fact that a market economy—as an expression of "economic democracy"—tends to be accompanied by political pluralism can also be viewed as an additional advantage.

The market, however, cannot do everything. And economic growth per se is no guarantee of a socially just distribution of resources—particularly in poor countries. It is worth noting, therefore, that market economies have various legal (such as anti-trust laws) and social (employee protection, for example, and social security) safeguards that cannot be assumed to exist in poor countries.

Since the only ones who can profit from a market economy are those who have the necessary purchasing power to act as consumers or who possess products or skills that can be successfully offered on the market, the concept of a "social market economy" gains significance for developing countries. It tries to connect the principle of a free economy with that of social equity.[22] The phrase, coined by the German political economist Alfred Müller-Armack in the post-World War II era, describes a synthesis between economic liberalism and democratic socialism—a concept closely related to the spirit of those times. Within this, the "subsidiarity principle" has a special significance: It gives preference to the self-initiative of individuals or groups over state intervention. But labor unions, consumer protection institutions, and economic and political participation play an important role as well.

Many developing countries must deal with the problems of absolute poverty and great inequities with respect to property, income, and opportunity. Wherever monopolies and cartels, land ownership structures, tenancy systems, and other institutional frameworks favor a tiny portion of the society, the market mechanism does not lead to socially acceptable results. The trouble, however, stems not from the system of a free economy but from the fact that so many are not included in it. In these cases, structural reforms are necessary, along with appropriate control by the forces of society and by the state, so as to guarantee that the basic needs of the whole society are met. In other words, a market economy—particularly in developing countries—requires state intervention to correct the ill effects of the market and cushion its unwanted social consequences through social safety nets. As participation and flexibility are important, UNDP notes, "people should guide both the state and the market, which need to work in tandem, with people sufficiently empowered to exert a more effective influence over both. [M]arkets should serve people—instead of people serving markets. After all, markets are only the means—people the end."[23]

There are also ecological reasons to improve the market economy. An unregulated market economy uses the resources of the general public without passing on to the user costs that are proportionate to the loss of resources. An example to illustrate this: when Paul Ehrlich pointed out to a Japanese journalist that Japan's whaling industry was eradicating not only whales but also the source of its own prosperity, the journalist's reply was probably correct from an economic point of view. But it was highly unsatisfactory from a holistic point of view: "You mistakenly take the whaling industry to be an organization interested in the preservation of whales. In fact it represents a huge capital force that is trying to make the largest possible profit. If it causes whales to become extinct in 10 years but makes a 15 percent profit until that time, whereas you would make only a 10 percent profit with a sustained fishing rate, then it is obvious that the whales will be made extinct in 10 years and the capital will then be used to exploit a different resource."[24] The cost of making the whales extinct, however this is quantified, obviously does not enter into the balance sheet of the Japanese whaling business; instead, it is passed on to current and future generations.

A state that is trustworthy and "strong"—because it is democratically legitimized—is necessary in order to balance the conflicts of interest that arise in a socially and ecologically sound market economy (for example, performance incentives versus redistribution goals) and to implement an appropriate social and environmental policy that does not undermine competitiveness, investment capacity, or future economic growth.

International Solidarity and Support of Local Initiatives

As indicated earlier, good governance is required not only from politicians in developing countries but also from those in industrial countries, because the international environment must be favorable as well. Far more money flows between industrial and developing countries as trade and capital than as development assistance. Thus the trade, financial, economic, and environmental policies of industrial countries are issues of international governance as well. No national development policy—no matter how good—can succeed if the available financial means shrink because, for example, the prices of a country's exports are subject to a constant process of erosion, while those of necessary imports only continue to rise. Wherever local political and economic mismanagement and unfavorable external factors converge, the consequences are particularly dramatic, as the current conditions in several sub-Saharan countries clearly prove.

In any successful international development policy, efforts to diversify the production structure of countries with an imbalanced dependence on certain commodities must be matched by attempts to raise export prices. Paths to this goal include the local processing of raw materials, greater participation in the transport and international marketing of these commodities, and a reduction of industrial countries' protectionistic barriers to trade, as well as improvement of existing compensation mechanisms (such as STABEX). The World Bank estimates that reducing trade protectionism would yield approximately $55 billion in additional export earnings for the so-called Third World—as much as it receives today in development assistance.[25] Cutting agricultural protectionism in particular would have considerable positive consequences, since it keeps the world market prices for many developing-country products artificially low.

The June 1992 U.N. Conference on Environment and Development in Rio put the seal of approval on our growing understanding that "sustainable development" for the entire globe requires the North to show consideration for the South, particularly regarding environmental policy. The Brundtland Commission defined "sustainable development" as development that satisfies the needs of the current generation "without compromising the ability of future generations to meet their own needs" and as "a process of change in which the exploitation of resources, the direction of investments, the orientation of technological development, and institutional change are made consistent with future as well as present needs."[26] The commission added that a standard of living that goes beyond elementary basic needs can be sustained only if consumption takes long-term carrying capacity into account.

Most people in industrial countries have production, consumption, and waste patterns that fail to account for either potential shortages or future generations and their needs. This life-style cannot be universalized. And it violates a basic ethical maxim of western Christian thought: Kant's categorical imperative to "make the maxim of thy conduct such that it might become a universal law."[27] It is also incompatible with the philosophy of "sustainable development." Since in addition to searching for new technologies and appropriate economic and legal frameworks, sustainable development requires changing thought and behavior patterns—or in more concrete terms, altering the consumption mentality—short-term improvements in this respect are unfortunately not to be expected.

Finally, the continuation and, wherever possible, expansion of development cooperation is part of good governance, so that the translation of political will into action does not fail due to a lack of resources. Even with budgetary priorities commensurate to the problems and with appropriate economic and financial policies, many developing countries will continue to need the financial and technical support of economically advanced countries. In a situation where "[t]he nation-state now is too small for the big things, and too big for the small," as UNDP put it recently, new patterns of cooperation and solidarity are needed to prevent a further deterioration of today's global social and ecological status quo.[28]

Conclusions

Since as Paul Streeten once suggested, one cannot be objective, practical, and idealistic at the same time, we will explicitly state what in our view would be desirable.[29]

Economic, social, political, and ecological changes that reduce poverty, injustice, inequality, and human suffering and that bring about a sustainable increase in the quality of life are steps that we view as desirable for people in poor countries. Where there is a conflict between a short-term increase in the quality of life and a mid- and long-term increase, the mid- and long-term increase should take precedence.

Changes that result in an increase in the economic and political participation of all social classes are also desirable. The burdens of bringing about desirable changes should be distributed in a socially just way.

While the value premises described here are subjective, they are not arbitrarily selected. They express the goals and the expectations pursued in most of the development plans of various countries.

The economic, social, and ecological effects of rapid population growth that work against these goals are judged to be "negative" effects, and thus lead to development policy recommendations that aim to reduce birth rates.

All people—those in rich as well as those in poor countries—carry a responsibility that there will be a future where a decent life is possible, both for us and for generations to come. Those of us in industrial countries, however, due to our greater political and economic power and our immense technical and scientific capabilities, have an even greater duty to show solidarity with global efforts for peace, justice, and the preservation of the Creation. Our action should not be postponed because:

> Every minute lost, every decision delayed, means more deaths from starvation and malnutrition, and means the evolution to irreversibility of phenomena in the environment. No one will ever know for sure the human and financial cost of lost time.[30]

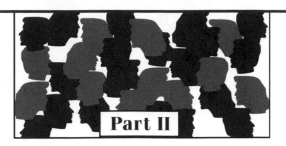

Part II

Data and Facts on Population Growth

World Population and its Growth

Only 350 years ago, around the end of the Thirty Years' War, world population was just 10 percent the size it is today. By 1800, less than 200 years ago, approximately 1,000 million people inhabited the earth—the first billion. (See Table II-1.) By that time, three out of four people lived in what we refer to today as the Third World.[1] It then took only 130 years for world population to double. By 1960, just 30 years later, the 3 billion mark was passed. Fifteen years later, in 1975, world population had grown to 4 billion. And sometime in the spring of 1987, only 12 years later, the fifth billion inhabitant of the earth was born.

In 1994, more than 5.6 billion people live on this planet. Between 1970 and the year 2000, the earth will have had to cope with a population increase of more than 50 percent. (See Figure II-1.)

Such a high population level is a phenomenon without historic precedent: For 99.9 percent of the time humankind has existed, world population was less than 10 million—roughly as many people as live in New Delhi or Jakarta today.

This absolute growth in numbers is of greater significance for the analysis of various consequences than the rate of growth: For China, an annual growth rate of 1.3 percent means that each year more than 15 million additional people need to be provided for. For Zambia, today's growth rate of 3.1 percent represents a considerable burden, but in concrete terms it means "only" 265,000 additional people per year.

Of the more than 3.2 billion people projected to be added to world population between 1990 to 2025, at least 3 billion—94 percent—will live in

Table II-1

The Growth of World Population

	Year	Time Period
Historical		
1 billion	1800	entire human history
2 billion	1930	130 years
3 billion	1960	30 years
4 billion	1975	15 years
5 billion	1987	12 years
Projection		
6 billion	1998	11 years
7 billion	2009	11 years
8 billion	2020	11 years
9 billion	2033	13 years
10 billion	2046	13 years

Source: Population Reference Bureau: 1991 World Population Data Sheet. Washington, D.C. 1991.

developing countries that already have extensive social and economic problems and that are in the poorest position to cope with such a large increase in numbers over such a short period of time.[2]

The Limits of Long-range Population Projections

Population projections are not predictions of inevitable developments. They simply indicate how many people will live in a country or a region if the economic, social, ecological, and political assumptions on which the projections are based actually occur. In other words, population projections depict a future population scenario based on hypothetical social changes. The most important influences on the future population size of a country are:

- present population size and age distribution,
- assumed birth rate,[3]
- assumed life expectancy, and
- assumed time needed to attain a stationary population.[4]

Future life expectancy figures, for example, are based on the assumption that this demographic component will not vary a great deal from the past. But since no one today can predict the economic, social, ecological, and technical events in the middle of the twenty-first century, and since the degree to which AIDS will influence population development in sub-Saharan Africa, for exam-

Figure II-1

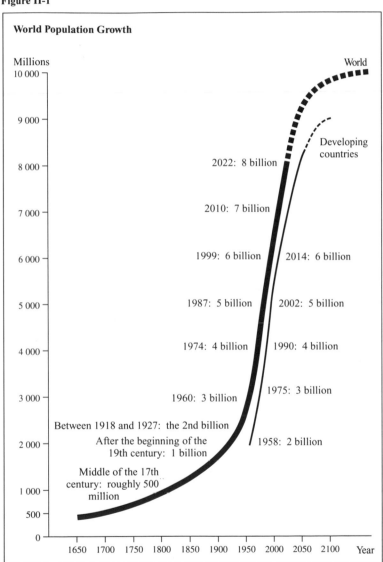

Source: UNFPA: The State of World Population 1988. New York 1988.

ple, is unknown, projections beyond this period of time are of limited relevance. As demographer Nathan Keyfitz has noted: "Demographers can no more be held responsible for inaccuracy in forecasting population 20 years ahead than geologists, meteorologists, or economists when they fail to announce earthquakes, cold winters, or depressions 20 years ahead."[5]

We distinguish between "low," "medium," and "high" population projections. The UN Population Fund (known as UNFPA) notes that: "The low projection offers the possibility of only six decades of continued increase, and a decline to more manageable levels thereafter. But during those six decades of growth human numbers, consumption and technology could still do massive and irreversible damage to local and global ecosystems. The high projection offers the prospect of indefinite population growth, with the inevitable accompaniments of overcrowding, pollution and continuing poverty on a huge scale."[6]

Today the "medium" projection is considered the most probable. It assumes that the world's population increases from 5.48 billion in 1992 to 10 billion in 2050, and reaches a plateau of just over 11.6 billion in 2150.[7] The "high" projection of 20.7 billion appears to be fairly improbable.[8]

In all probability, world population will have doubled in size by some time in the next century, if—yes, *if*—nothing unforeseen occurs that would have dramatic consequences. In order to keep the "unforeseeable" factor as small as possible, political, economic, social, and ecological assumptions are made that most closely approximate the potential future reality.

Many population projections of the past have proved to be blatant miscalculations because they were based on unrealistic assumptions. In 1951, in their first projection, U.N. population experts predicted a world population of 3.3 billion for the year 1981. The actual total in 1981 was 4.4 billion![9] This miscalculation can be traced to insufficient knowledge regarding the population of China at the time and pessimistic assumptions regarding the decrease in infant and child mortality in developing countries.

In 1981, the United Nations estimated that world population would reach 22 billion by 2025 and that there could be an increase to approximately 150 billion by the year 2125—assuming that the number of children that a woman has during the course of her life (the total fertility rate) remained at the level it was in 1975. At that time women bore an average of 3.9 children; today this figure is only marginally lower, at 3.3 children per woman.[10] While such statements may trigger a dramatic response in the general public, they are not suited for serious discussions of population policy. Today, no institution that values its own credibility would dare to make such projections public.

Substantial errors are often still made in assumptions regarding initial population size. Overly low or overly high estimates for China or India in 1960 almost inevitably lead to correspondingly inaccurate projections for the year 2000. Such errors occur despite more sophisticated census methods: In the spring of 1992, the governmnet of Nigeria announced, following a census, that the country's population was not 120 million, as anticipated, but actually below 89 million.[11] Even industrial countries with well-equipped statistical infrastructures have made major miscalculations: The extent and duration of the U.S. "baby boom" after World War II, for example, was completely unanticipated by population scientists.[12]

We simply do not know whether world population will stabilize at some point at a level of 10, 12, or 15 billion. World Bank projections in 1984 varied by up to 3 billion—depending on whether they were based on the most or the least favorable assumptions.[13]

Many projections currently in use do not take into account, for example, any ecological bottlenecks, even though these have been apparent for a long time, for example in the Sahel zone of Africa.[14] Projections made in an ecological vacuum have substantial shortcomings.[15] Assumptions regarding existing social conditions and political decisions have a considerable influence on projections: Will China maintain its current population policy, or will it be changed and, if so, how? Will the birth rate in sub-Saharan Africa drop substantially if there is a lasting modernization of traditional African society? Will there be regions in which the mortality rate will increase again dramatically due to famine, diseases, wars, or ecological catastrophes? If so, how will the affected societies react? Answers to questions such as these shape population projections; erroneous assumptions can lead to considerable discrepancies between projections and reality.

Current projections of future world population are still based on the assumption that no epidemics will spread in a way that drastically affects growth, as happened with the plague in medieval Europe. World wars or even other global collapses of law and order are excluded. Finally, it is assumed that our global environment will not deteriorate substantially. Although it would indeed be absurd to include wars in population projections, increased mortality rates due to the AIDS epidemic are beginning to be taken into account in certain African countries.[16] And today a growing number of people fear that in various regions (the Sahel, for instance), important, life-sustaining ecosystems could collapse if the population exceeds a certain level. This, however, has not (yet) led to revised population projections.

Carl Haub of the Population Reference Bureau in Washington, D.C., has developed three criteria as a rule of thumb for the reliability of population projections: A projection becomes more realistic

- the shorter the time period for which it is being made,
- the larger the geographical area for which it is being made, and
- the lower the current birth rate and the higher the current life expectancy of the people in the area.[17]

Over a period of 10 years, for example, projections reflect the observations of the immediate past—that is, the likelihood of error is relatively small because the age structure, mortality and birth rates, and likely migration patterns are known. Potential deviations accumulate as the time period considered increases, and predictions take on an increasingly speculative character. Likewise, projections for an entire continent (Africa) are more reliable than for a single country (Uganda) because overestimates, underestimates, and other errors offset each other. Finally, countries with high birth rates and high mortality rates have a much greater potential for demographic change than those that are approaching the biologically inevitable limits of human life and that already have low fertility rates.

At least the last of these three criteria suggests that population projections for developing countries are encumbered with a greater likelihood of error than those for industrial ones.

The greatest value of population projections lies perhaps in the fact that we respond to alarming predictions and can thereby introduce changes that prevent the predictions from becoming reality. The proclamation of doom was the cause of its prevention in the Old Testament example of the Prophet Jonah. The people of Ninive took Jonah seriously and were moved to change their ways, which saved them. For philosopher Hans Jonas, prophesies of doom are intended to provoke change and, in doing so, to prove themselves to be wrong.[18] The discussion in this book of the possible negative effects of overly rapid population growth—and of the negative effects of unchanged consumption and production patterns—has the same goal.

Population in Industrial and Developing Countries

In mid-1994, approximately 5.6 billion people live on the earth.[19] While the current rate of growth of world population (1.6 percent annually) is lower than in earlier years, population growth in absolute numbers is higher than ever due to the larger size of the population base. Of the 90–95 million people per year by which the earth's population will increase in the nineties, four out of five will be born in developing countries—already home to four out of five people today.[20] Of the 910 million people by which the world population will grow between 1990 and 2000, 62 million will be born in industrial countries, and 848 million in developing ones. (See Table II-2.)

Table II-2

Distribution of World Population, Industrial and Developing Countries

Year	World Population in Millions	Industrial Countries		Developing Countries	
		(Millions)	(Percent)	(Millions)	(Percent)
1950	2,516	832	33.1	1,684	66.9
1985	4,842	1,177	24.3	3,665	75.7
1990	5,282	1,211	22.9	4,071	77.1
2000	6,192	1,273	20.6	4,919	79.4
2025	8,479	1,380	16.3	7,099	83.7

Sources: United Nations: World Population Prospects as Assessed in 1984. New York 1986 (for 1950 data); World Bank Population and Resources (eds.): Europe, Middle East, and North Africa Region Population Projections. 1990–91 Edition (WPS 601). Washington, D.C. (for the later data).

The "rich" countries' proportion of world population will continue to decrease over the next decades compared with that of "poor" countries, which ideally will increase the political weight of the developing world. Soon, more people will be living in countries such as Nigeria, Indonesia, and Bangladesh than in the United States or the former Soviet Union. India will replace China as the earth's most populous country.[21]

Population in Developing Countries: Regional Distribution and Growth

Generalized demographic statements for the so-called Third World obscure considerable regional differences.[22]

Sub-Saharan Africa

On no other continent are fertility rates as high as in Africa.[23] And nowhere are the problems caused by this so great.[24]

With the exception of a few countries (such as Zimbabwe), there are only weak indications of a lasting decline in the birth rates in sub-Saharan Africa.[25] (See Table II-3.) While population growth clearly slowed in all other regions during the past 20 years, it increased in sub-Saharan Africa from an already high 2.8 percent in the seventies to approximately 3.1 percent between 1985 and 1990. (See Table II-4.)

In 1950, the people of Africa represented just under 9 percent of world

Table II-3

Cumulative Number of Children in Various Countries in Sub-Saharan Africa, Late Eighties

Country	Year	Cumulative Fertility of All Women (ages 45–49)
Botswana	1987	5.8
Burundi	1987	6.9
Ghana	1986	7.25
Kenya	1988	7.5
Liberia	1986	6.4
Mali	1987	7.06
Senegal	1986	7.0
Togo	1988	7.28
Uganda	1988–89	7.77
Zimbabwe	1988	6.87

Source: E. Van der Walle and A.D. Foster: Fertility Decline in Africa: Assessments and Prospects. World Bank Technical Paper No. 125, Washington, D.C. 1990, p. 4.

Table II-4

Changes in the Population Growth Rate in Various African Countries, 1965–2000

Country	Average Population Growth (percent)		
	1965–80	1980–91	1991–2000
Mozambique	2.5	2.6	2.9
Tanzania	2.9	3.0	3.0
Ethiopia	2.7	3.1	2.7
Somalia	2.9	3.1	3.1
Chad	2.0	2.4	2.6
Malawi	2.9	3.3	3.1
Burundi	1.9	2.9	2.9
Zaire	3.1	3.2	3.0
Uganda	3.0	2.5	3.3
Sierra Leone	2.0	2.4	2.6
Mali	2.1	2.6	3.1
Nigeria	2.5	3.0	2.8

Sources: World Bank: World Development Report 1992. Oxford University Press, New York 1992, p. 268 (for 1965–80 data); World Bank: World Development Report 1993. Oxford University Press, New York 1993, p. 288 (for later data).

population; now the figure stands at 12 percent. By the year 2000 it will be 14 percent and by 2025, approximately 19 percent. This means that Africa's contribution to global population growth will increase by 58 percent between 1990 and 2025. By the end of this century, almost 900 million people will live in Africa.[26] Nigeria alone will in all probability double its population during the next 20 years.[27] Never before has any region of the earth grown this fast.

Diverse reasons for this unusual development can be found. By and large, the high birth rates in African societies are the result of the demographically explosive combination of almost 100-percent marriage rates at a young age and the extensive unavailability of any means of contraception. In addition, a number of important socioreligious and cultural variables can be cited, such as specific concepts of "masculinity" in patriarchal societies and flows of income within families. (See Part III.)

In some Arab states in North Africa and in the Middle East, similar demographic conditions are found. Population growth rates in these countries have also increased from 2.8 percent (1975–80) to 3.0 percent (1985–90). Various cultural and religious factors favor a young marriage age, the traditional extended family is still intact, and modern methods of family planning are rarely used—in some Islamic countries they are even prohibited.[28]

Asia

Asia, where the two most populated countries on earth are located (China and India), is home to approximately 59 percent of the world. The continent increases by some 56 million people each year, accounting for 61 percent of world growth. In 2025, its annual addition is expected to be 48 million people. As a whole, population growth in the Asian developing region has been decreasing since 1975, from 1.9 percent to a current level of 1.7 percent per year. (See Table II-5.) Recently, however, it seems to be increasing again since there are indications that birth rates in China rose slightly.

Demographic changes in China, because it has so many people, are of the greatest significance for all of Asia. Due to the traditional Chinese preference for large families, it is feared that an easing up of the Chinese population policy emphasis on "one-child families" will lead to a considerable increase in birth rates.[29] Between 1984 and 1987 the Chinese birth rate increased by more than 20 percent, primarily due to the younger marrying age and a younger age structure of the population.[30] An even greater increase is expected from a further lowering of the average age of marriage. This would substantially change the population statistics for all of Asia. India's population growth rate is also expected to remain high. The global population weight of China and India will therefore continue to increase during the next 25 years.[31]

Table II-5

Changes in the Population Growth Rates in Various Asian Countries, 1965–2000

Country	Average Population Growth (percent)		
	1965–80	1980–91	1991–2000
China	2.2	1.5	1.3
India	2.3	2.1	1.8
Indonesia	2.4	1.8	1.4
Bangladesh	2.6	2.2	1.9
Pakistan	3.1	3.1	2.8
Nepal	2.4	2.6	2.5
Myanmar	2.3	2.1	2.0
Thailand	2.9	1.9	1.4
Sri Lanka	1.8	1.4	1.1

Sources: World Bank: World Development Report 1992. Oxford University Press, New York 1992, p. 268 (for all 1965–80 data and later data for Myanmar); World Bank: World Development Report 1993. Oxford University Press, New York 1993, p. 288 (for all later data except Myanmar).

Efforts to decrease birth rates in the populous countries of India and Pakistan have not met with much success to date. The population of India (approximately 897 million in 1993) will increase to 1 billion by the turn of the century, barring any social or ecological disasters. And the population of Pakistan (123 million people, with a growth rate of 3.1 percent in 1993) will double in less than 23 years.[32] Recent studies indicate that Bangladesh has made impressive progress in its efforts to decrease birth rates—despite unfavorable social conditions.

On the whole birth rates in most Asian countries are decreasing.[33] A significant downward trend in population growth there is thus expected during the next 10 years. Nevertheless, even with declining population growth rates, Asia will be home to approximately 5 billion people in 2025—as many people as inhabited the entire world in 1987. For many countries this means that the population density per agriculturally productive acre will increase to an alarming degree.

Latin America

Declining birth rates and therefore also a declining population growth rate have been observed during the past few years in Latin America. (See Table

Table II-6

Changes in the Population Growth Rates in Various Latin American Countries, 1965–2000

Country	Average Population Growth (percent)		
	1965–80	1980–91	1991–2000
Brazil	2.4	2.0	1.4
Mexico	3.1	2.0	1.9
Venezuela	3.5	2.6	1.9
Costa Rica	2.7	2.7	2.0
Panama	2.6	2.1	1.7
Bolivia	2.5	2.5	2.4
Guatemala	2.8	2.9	2.9
Ecuador	3.1	2.6	2.1
Peru	2.8	2.2	1.9
Colombia	2.4	2.0	1.5

Sources: World Bank: World Development Report 1992. Oxford University Press, New York 1992, p. 268 (for 1965–80 data); World Bank: World Development Report 1993. Oxford University Press, New York 1993, p. 288 (for later data).

II-6.) But the continent's population will still increase from a 1993 level of more than 460 million to approximately 682 million people by the year 2025.

In addition to countries such as Guatemala or Nicaragua, which have high rates of population growth, the Latin American region also has countries such as Uruguay, Chile, and Argentina that consider themselves to be underpopulated and are striving for an increase in numbers.

Projected Growth

Doubling times and population sizes for the different continents can be calculated on the basis of their respective population growth rates. (See Tables II-7 and II-8.) Short-term successes in family planning will have little impact on mid-term developments because population growth in developing countries is the consequence of specific demographic characteristics.

Special Demographic Characteristics of Developing Countries

The special demographic characteristics of most developing countries are:

- high fertility (that is, many births per woman of childbearing age),

Table II-7

Doubling Time for Various Populations (Based on 1993)

Region	Annual Growth Rate (percent)	Doubling Time (years)
World	1.6	42
Industrial Countries	0.4	162
Third World (excluding China)	2.3	30
Third World (including China)	2.0	35
Africa	2.9	24
Asia (excluding China)	2.1	34
China	1.2	60
Latin America	1.9	36

Source: Population Reference Bureau: 1993 World Population Data Sheet. Washington, D.C. 1993.

Table II-8

World Population in 1993 and 2025 by Region

Region	Population in 1993 (millions)	Average Growth per Year (percent)	Projected Population in 2025 (millions)
World	5,506	1.6	8,425
Industrial Countries	1,230	0.4	1,360
Third World	4,276	2.0	7,065
Africa	677	2.9	1,552
Asia	3,257	1.7	4,946
Latin America	460	1.9	682

Source: Population Reference Bureau: 1993 World Population Data Sheet. Washington, D.C. 1993.

- distinctly lowered mortality rates among children under the age of five, and
- distinctly younger age structures than in industrial countries (see Figure II-2).

The total fertility rate—the number of live births an average woman would have during her lifetime if her childbearing behavior were the same as a cross-section of women at the time of observation—is currently approximately 3.7 in developing countries.[34] The U.N. medium population projection is based on the assumption that this will drop to 3.3 births per woman by the year 2000; this in turn assumes that the percentage of couples using modern contraception methods increases from 51 to 59. Judging from the current situation, this is realistic. For the past 10 years a declining trend in birth rates has been observed almost everywhere in the world.

Figure II-2

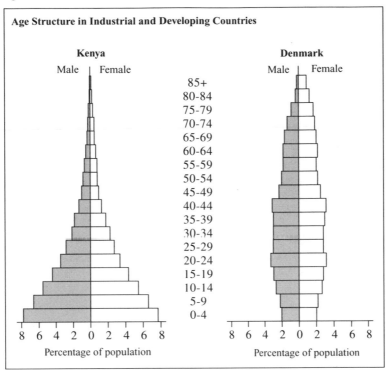

Age Structure in Industrial and Developing Countries

Source: J.A. McFalls: Population. A Lively Introduction.
Population Reference Bureau, Washington, D.C. 1991, p. 22.

Mortality rates, particularly for infants and children under the age of five, have dropped dramatically during the past 25 years: in low-income countries, from 124 per thousand live births in 1965 to 71 in 1991. In the middle-income countries, the rate went from 97 to 38 during the same time.[35]

The average age of the entire world population is still very low: approximately 23 years.[36] This masks considerable variation within regions. (See Table II-9.)

The age structure of a population will be of greatest significance during the next 25–50 years. Information on this allows a prediction of how many women will be entering their childbearing years soon, and from this the likely number of future births can be determined. The high birth rates of the past 20 years and the marked decrease in mortality mean that more women than ever before will reach childbearing age in the near future. While approximately 21 percent of the population in industrial countries is younger than 15 years of

Table II-9

Average Age of the Population According to Region

Region	Average Age
Industrial Countries	32.5
Europe	33.9
Developing Countries	21.0
Africa	17.3
Latin America	20.8
South Asia	20.3

Source: WHO: World Health Statistics Quarterly, Vol. 40, No. 1, 1987, p. 13.

age, the figure in the developing world (excluding China) is about 39 percent.[37] This means that almost half the people living in the developing countries today have not yet reached their reproductive years. The young age structure of the population in developing countries can actually offset the effect of declining births per woman.

Even under the utopian assumption that birth rates in all developing countries would drop over the next three to four years to a level at which only the respective parents would be "replaced" (known as replacement-level fertility), absolute population growth would remain large. Population numbers in most cases would still double due solely to the momentum of all those young people having their two-children families. In other words, the growth of world population could probably only stabilize at approximately 10 billion people even if dramatic results were achieved through efforts to reduce birth rates.

This is the reason why the "time factor" is of such great significance for all population policy measures. Whether fertility decreases sooner rather than later makes a big difference. In the case of Kenya, for example, with its current population of about 28 million, it would mean at least 50 million fewer people by the year 2050.[38]

It is not an exaggeration, therefore, to speak of the nineties as a critical decade, as UNFPA Executive Director Nafis Sadik does:

> The choices of the next ten years will decide the speed of population growth for much of the next century; they will decide whether world population trebles or merely doubles before it finally stops growing: they will decide whether the pace of damage to the environment speeds up or slows down. The next ten years will decide the shape of the 21st century. They may decide the future of the earth as a habitation for humans.[39]

Urbanization

The rapid growth of cities in developing countries represents a special problem. Nowhere is the consumption of water, air, and soil as high and nowhere is the environment as heavily burdened with waste and sewage as in cities. The undesirable social and ecological consequences are so serious that it would almost be better to discuss the topic of urbanization in the section on "The Effects of Rapid Population Growth" rather than here.

Enormously rapid urbanization has many explanations: There is the "pull" of the economic benefits of concentrated settlements and the related productivity advantages.[40] But this is aided by the "push" of the increasing impossibility of providing growing populations in rural areas with satisfying prospects for life.

In most developing countries, urban numbers are growing almost twice as rapidly as the overall population. Estimates indicate that in the next 30–35 years the urban populations of developing countries will rise from approximately 1.5 billion to more than 4 billion people. Because people in poor countries no longer have emigration opportunities and because many of them can no longer earn a livelihood in rural areas, and since many of them take the deceptive bright city lights to mean increased opportunities and a better life, urban areas will continue to grow at an alarming speed.

The parts of these cities that will grow most rapidly will be the already huge impoverished areas—the *favelas,* shantytowns, and slums. The number of urban poor in developing countries is expected to grow from 330 million in 1990 to about 1 billion.[41] For every 100 households that were set up in urban areas of developing countries in the eighties, 72 were located in slums. In sub-Saharan Africa the figure was even higher: 92 percent.[42]

The extent of urbanization is a relatively new phenomenon. Since humans developed forms of community life, there has been a tendency toward the construction of settlements and a common infrastructure. Although large cities always distinguished themselves as cultural, scientific, and economic centers, no more than 6 percent of the world population lived in cities or even towns with more than 5,000 inhabitants until after 1850.[43]

Today, 39 percent of the population of countries with low per capita incomes live in cities. In countries with middle incomes, the figure is 62 percent.[44] (See Table II-10.) Urban populations have doubled in more than 85 countries during the last 10 years.[45] Industrial countries never had to confront such urbanization rates: Between 1800 and 1910, the population of greater London increased almost sevenfold, from 1.1 to 7.3 million people, while that of Paris grew from 550,000 to 3 million. Many cities in developing countries have had to deal with comparable increases in just one generation.[46]

Table II-10

Urbanization in the Third World

	Urban Population			
	Percentage of the Entire Population		Annual Growth Rate in Percentages	
	1965	1991	1965–80	1980–91
Low-Income Countries	17	39	3.5	—
Mozambique	5	28	10.2	10.1
Tanzania	5	34	11.3	10.1
Sierra Leone	15	33	5.2	5.3
Nigeria	17	36	5.7	5.8
China	18	60	2.3	—
Kenya	9	24	8.1	7.8
Middle-Income Countries	42	62	3.4	3.2
Upper-Middle-Income Countries	44	73	4.1	3.0

Sources: World Bank: World Development Report 1991. Oxford University Press, New York 1991,
         p. 306 f (for 1965–80 data); World Bank: World Development Report 1993. Oxford Univer-
         sity Press, New York, 1993, p. 298 f (for later data).

The largest cities in the world are increasingly located in developing countries. The Brazilian industrial center of São Paulo, which in 1950 was still
smaller than Naples, is likely by 2000 to be the second largest city in the
world, with 26 million residents. It would then have more than twice as many
inhabitants as Sweden. London, which was the second largest city in the world
in 1950, will by the end of this decade not even be among the top 25.[47]

By the end of the nineties, almost twice as many people will live in the
cities of developing countries as in the cities of industrial ones. The proportion
of the urban population in the developing world is expected by then to be 45
percent, which would mean more than 2.2 billion people.[48]

Whereas much public attention is given to "green" issues such as destruction of the rain forests, soil degradation, or declining biodiversity, "brown"
issues such as air pollution, water pollution, and inadequate sanitation are
sorely neglected. And yet these problems are costly, as Michael Cohen shows
for different cities:

• Bogotá: About 2,500 tons of solid waste is left uncontrolled every day.
Some is partially recycled informally while the rest is left to rot in small
dumps or in canals, sewers, or streets.

- Bangkok: Nearly 33 percent of the city's potential gross product is lost because of congestion-induced travel delays; this could rise to 60 percent if no remedial measures are taken. Air pollution is causing irreversible brain damage and loss of I.Q. in children.
- Accra: 70 percent of health care expenditures are linked to environment-related diseases—as they are in all of Ghana. The expenditures include productivity losses and health resource costs such as doctors, nurses, technicians, administration, equipment, and drugs.
- Jakarta: The equivalent of 1 percent of the city's gross domestic product—more than $50 million—is spent each year by households to boil impure water.
- Mexico City: An average of 2.4 work days per person is lost and 6,400 deaths are caused every year by abnormally high levels of suspended particulates. Annual health costs from air pollution are estimated to exceed $1.5 billion.
- Lima: Unsolved sanitation problems recently triggered an outbreak of cholera that spread quickly into neighboring countries.[49]

The intense spatial concentration of people already places such a burden on the air (see Table II-11), water, and soil that industrial-country cities could be considered "health resorts" by comparison.[50]

The U.N. Environment Programme and the World Health Organization estimate that 625 million people in developing countries are exposed to concentrations of sulphur dioxide that are hazardous to their health. Due to lead pollution caused by traffic emissions in Mexico City, intolerably high concentrations of lead were found in 7 out of 10 newborns.[51]

Public investments in additional housing, sewage treatment facilities, roads, other means of transportation, and infrastructural facilities or municipal services did not keep pace with the increases in the urban populations during the past three decades in almost any "Third World" cities. Thus nearly 1.2 billion people—approximately 60 percent of the urban populations of poor countries[52]—live in slums or make-shift settlements in very confined spaces and without proper drinking water supplies, hygienic and sanitary facilities, electricity, and other basic requirements for an acceptable standard of living. And this in spite of the fact that urban dwellers enjoy a higher political priority than rural populations almost everywhere in the developing world. From today's perspective, there are no apparent reasons to believe that the volume of public investment and services in these cities will change substantially in the next 10 years.

Urbanization also has a strong influence on nutritional security: People in cities have no basis for subsistence and are therefore dependent either on rural

Table II-11

Air Pollution in Selected Cities

City	Number of Days above WHO-Maximum Values[a]	
	Sulphur Dioxide[b]	Soot[c]
Delhi	6	294
Xian	71	273
Peking	68	272
Teheran	104	174
Bangkok	0	97
São Paulo	12	31

Source: UNEP/WHO: Assessment of Urban Air Quality. Nairobi 1988, as cited in L.R. Brown et al.:
State of the World 1990. W.W. Norton & Co., New York 1990.

[a]Average of measurements taken at different points between 1980 and 1984.

[b]The WHO maximum value corresponds to a daily average of 150 micrograms per cubic meter; it may be exceeded on no more than seven days per year.

[c]The WHO maximum value corresponds to a daily average of 230 micrograms of soot and 150 micrograms of smoke per cubic meter; this value may also not be exceeded on more than seven days per year.

food production surpluses or—as has been the case in many countries in recent years—on imported grain. The latter requires foreign currency, which is already in short supply, and has additional undesirable effects that will be analyzed in other sections.

Part III

Determinants of High Fertility

In analyses of the determining factors of a society's fertility, a number of complex biological and technical issues are normally discussed.[1] This will not be the case here. Instead, the social, economic, and sociocultural conditions that cause certain societies to prefer high birth rates will be considered.

Religious and Sociocultural Norms

Children are a source of joy in all societies and cultures—human beings to whom love is extended and from whom love is received. An impoverished condition can actually strengthen this emotional value: it is perceptible not only in a material sense but also in a feeling of helplessness and, particularly, worthlessness. These feelings can create a strong desire to have many offspring. For poor people, children are often the only thing they have on earth and the sole source of their sense of self-esteem.

This genuinely human emotional dimension must be taken into account if discussions of population policy are to be relevant. A mere rational discussion of economic, social, or ecological effects does not do justice to this dimension of human life.

The emotional enrichment through children is, however, an incomplete explanation for high birth rates, since more children do not necessarily mean more love or a higher potential for affection within a family. Whenever additional children bring with them a worsening of the quality of life for existing children, they can certainly mean greater suffering for a family.

Every society has social, religious, and cultural norms and precepts that have a significant influence on the frequency of births.[2] Cultural influences

35

were already very strong in pre-modern Europe[3] and still are today. A study in India found that in a situation where material and social conditions are comparable, cultural variables (such as religion, caste, or family type) are a major influence on reproductive behavior.[4]

Cultural forces that limit birth rates include sexual taboos (against sex during breast-feeding, for example), extended postpartum abstinence (a separation of three to five months between a young mother and her husband is customary in many cultures), prohibition of remarrying for widows (for instance, in India), taboos on pregnancy among women whose children already have their own offspring, and others.[5] Cultural factors also determine how long a mother breast-feeds and therefore influence the length of the natural infertility during lactation.

In addition to these, a number of factors promote fertility to a considerable extent—whether they be social factors, such as the marriage at an early age, or specific religious and cultural rules.[6] Failure to consider these forces, usually for ethnocentric reasons, often leads to incorrect conclusions and hence inappropriate recommendations.

In various religions, a large number of children is considered proof of God's favor.[7] Predominantly Moslem societies in North Africa and in the Middle East, for example, have higher birth rates than other countries with a similar economic and social status.[8] But here, too, it is necessary to differentiate among the various forms of the Islamic religion: birth rates decrease in the Java region of Indonesia,[9] for instance, where women have more rights and better educational opportunities; in other Islamic regions, such as Pakistan and various Arab countries,[10] where women are strongly discriminated against, birth rates remain high.[11] Where religious recognition of high birth rates is accompanied by a low economic status for women, fatal demographic consequences can develop. Data gathered in a mother and child health project in Mali recorded families with Islamic patriarchs who had fathered up to 30 children with two to four women.[12]

Wherever the Almighty God or the gods are thought to have a preference for high fertility, high birth rates are not so much the result of rational decisions made by the parents as a "gift of God" or an act of divine providence that is to be accepted with pride and thankfulness. That is also the reason why, for example, many African societies have no concept of an "adequate" or deliberately "desired" number of children. The larger the number of children, the greater the benevolence of the gods.[13] This results in a high level of social and moral prestige for men and women with many children.[14] The fact that childlessness is portrayed as a punishment of God in the Old Testament should also be mentioned in this connection.

Another cultural force sustaining high fertility has been described by John C. and Pat Caldwell:

> The major influence on behavior is not, however, the gods but the living dead or ancestral shades that survive for four or five generations, especially if the proper rites have been performed, and then disappear. The fact that one's living ancestors will one day become such powerful shades strongly reinforces the earthly power of old people. These concepts were reinforced by a belief in reincarnation, whereby the dead were born again to their descendants. Among Christians and Moslems, the latter belief appears to be eroding, although children are still given the names of grandparents or great-grandparents, and a man will often address his son as his father. Among the Kikuyu of Kenya, and widely across the continent, a child who dies is regarded as a temporary visitor, and the next child is given the same name and regarded as a reincarnation of the same ancestral spirit. Should this child also die, its death is regarded as evidence that the ancestor does not want to return.[15]

In various religions, the complex relationship between the living and their ancestors requires that certain rites during burial ceremonies or sacrificial offerings be performed by the children of the deceased (often explicitly by sons) if the soul of the deceased is to find peace.[16] Against this background, a deliberate limitation of fertility can be associated with a lack of respect for the dead. They, in turn—so it is believed—can express their displeasure with the living by afflicting them with diseases or even greater misfortunes.[17]

Infertility or few children—whether as a result of conscious family planning or of disease-related problems—is then perceived by a large part of society as individual misfortune or as a serious deviation from the religious or social norm, and can result in considerable sanctions.[18] Where the decision to have children is determined by religious, cultural, and social factors,[19] national family planning policy—particularly if it receives foreign funding and support—may be regarded as an immoral intrusion on the intimate sphere of the family and may be rejected.

For reasons that will be discussed in greater detail later in this section, societies in which patriarchal structures or other types of male dominance prevail and in which a pronounced division of roles by gender exists tend to have higher birth rates than societies with relatively egalitarian relationships.[20] Acceptance of family planning is also influenced by whether the pregnancy decision is reached through force (threat of punishment), reward (higher status in the family hierarchy), negotiation (appeal to customs and traditions), or various types of manipulation rather than through joint, responsible deliberations by both husband and wife.[21]

These religious and sociocultural determinants provide some explanation

Table III-1

Preferred Number of Children in Various Countries

Region/Country	Preferred Number of Children
Africa	
Benin	7.6
Cameroon	8.0
Ivory Coast	8.4
Senegal	8.3
Asia	
Bangladesh	4.1
Nepal	3.9
Pakistan	4.2
Sri Lanka	3.7
Latin America	
Colombia	4.0
Paraguay	5.2
Peru	3.8
Mexico	4.4
Europe	
Portugal	2.4

Source: World Fertility Survey, quoted in R.E. Lightbourne: Individual Preferences and Fertility
         Behavior. In J. Cleland and J. Hobcraft (eds.): Reproductive Change in Developing Coun-
         tries. Oxford University Press, Oxford 1985, p. 184.

for the considerable divergence in views regarding the "ideal" number of children in various regions of the developing world. (See Table III-1.)

Socioeconomic Determinants of High Fertility

Help in the Household and in the Field

A number of studies indicate that in addition to deriving emotional benefit from children and from adherence to religious norms, families enjoy considerable economic and social advantages from high birth rates. For individual families in rural areas, there are several convincing reasons for having many children.

Although it is difficult to make exact, general estimates of the extent of children's economic contributions to households, there are many indications that the amount of assistance is significant.[22] The importance of children as workers is greater in rural areas and where technological conditions are primitive than in the cities, and is also more significant for the lower classes than for the middle and upper classes.[23]

Children are important helpers above all for their mothers, because the tasks they typically perform tend to be on the women's list of chores: gathering firewood, fetching water, cleaning, clearing land, planting, fertilizing, and weeding, as well as other agricultural tasks including tending and feeding cattle.[24] In addition, older children can help care for younger siblings. This list of chores changes as children grow older and begins to include increasingly specialized and demanding tasks, as J.L. Collins shows with the example of an Indian society in the Andes. (See Table III-2.)

By performing these tasks, children ease the strain on their parents and let them do other or additional tasks. They rarely "get in the way" because a large part of women's work in rural areas, in traditional crafts, or in trade can easily be combined with looking after children, particularly if other members of the extended family or older siblings can take over child care responsibilities from time to time.

According to the World Bank, six- to eight-year-old boys and girls in the villages of Nepal work three to four hours a day, while in Indonesia (Java), children work eight to ten hours. Many children in Bangladesh work even longer.[25] The proportion of children in the work force is significant in various countries: In 1985, at least 36 percent of the 10- to 14-year-old boys in rural Pakistan were in the work force, while in the cities the figure was almost 18 percent.[26] In Egypt, 29 percent of the 10- to 14-year-old rural population was in the labor force.[27] In Côte d'Ivoire, the figure in 1986 was far over 50 percent of the boys and girls, and in Peru, it was more than 60 percent.[28] Chernichovsky arrived at comparable figures for rural Botswana.[29]

In an analysis of rural areas in the Philippines, E.M. King and R.E. Evenson found that children earned up to 20 percent of the family income and accounted for approximately one-third of the household production.[30] According to other sources, older children contribute just as much as adults do to the household income.[31] Normally, children's wages are considerably lower than adults', which may explain their attractiveness as laborers.

Children thus become a positive economic factor.[32] In many instances, however, they also increase adults' comfort, particularly for older men in the family, who can delegate tasks to the children that they consider too bothersome or as an insult to their honor. Adults who gain time in this way can do other work and perhaps earn additional income.

Table III-2

Productive Activities Performed by Children, by Age at which Activity Begins

Age Group	Activities
5 to 9 Years	Herding sheep, camelids (with older children)
	Carrying water
	Watching younger siblings in proximity of parent
	Short errands
	Collecting dung, dried grass, or firewood for fuel
	Sweeping
	Guarding food being dried
	Food preparation (chopping, peeling, some grinding)
9 to 12 Years	Spinning, knitting, crocheting
	Milking cows
	Gathering reeds and other forage for animals
	Herding cows, pigs
	Watching younger siblings alone
	Longer errands
	Purchasing in the market
	Help washing clothes
	Food preparation (more difficult grinding, tending fire, gathering herbs)
12 to 15 Years	Selling in market
	Travel to regional urban centers on errands
	Fertilizing
	Planting
	Harvesting
	Weaving, sewing
	Weeding
	Cooking, preparing earth ovens for cooking in field
	Food processing (drying, freeze-drying)
15 Years and Older	Chopping wood
	Construction and repair of fences, walls, and houses
	Full agricultural labor (contribution valued as adult)
	Cutting reeds in lake
	Shearing
	Migration

Source: J.L. Collins: Fertility Determinants in a High Andes Community. Population and Development Review, Vol. 9, No. 1, 1983, p. 72.

Social Security Value of Children

The significance of "old-age security" for family size decisions has been controversial for many years.[33] Empirical evidence can be found both for it having considerable influence and for it being a net neutral or discouraging force.[34] In our opinion, the influence of this factor is significant for a number of plausible psychological and institutional reasons.

Many developing countries have no reliable public or private social security schemes such as retirement or welfare funds. Nor are there adequately functioning capital markets or bank infrastructures in which a person could squirrel away potential savings. Moreover, many of these countries suffer high rates of inflation, so that savings accumulated by an individual cannot offer any long-term security.

An additional problem is that the government is seldom perceived as the trustworthy protector of the public good or the guardian of law and order, but instead as a threat to individual welfare. Rarely is there a guarantee that legal claims can actually be brought to bear due to an unpredictable legal framework as well as the laxity, arbitrariness, and corruption of government employees and others with political power. Political unrest or violent changes of government do their part to convince people that in the end they can rely only on themselves and their relatives.[35] Where the state is regarded so suspiciously by its citizens, parents have to depend on their children in the event of invalidity or old age: they have no other choice.

It is therefore not surprising that in surveys in Indonesia, Korea, Thailand, the Philippines, and even in Turkey, 80–90 percent of parents interviewed said they would eventually be supported by their children in old age.[36] And a survey in rural south-central India shows that old-age security significantly influenced family size decisions.[37]

Increasing Economic and Political Influence

In the cultural understanding of many countries, a family's political weight increases with its size. And this, in turn, implies certain economic advantages.[38] In this context, the traditional rights to use land that enhance a family's status in many sub-Saharan societies in Africa must be mentioned. The amount of land allocated to a family for economic use depends on the number of children in that family. Increased economic influence, in turn, leads to greater political influence.

These economic, social, and other advantages on the family level occur to varying degrees in different societies and lead to differing decisions regarding the desired number of children. (See Table III-3.)

Table III-3

Desired Number of Children and Actual Fertility Rates in Selected
Countries, Late Seventies

| | Desired Number of Children | | | |
| Region/Country | Women Interviewed at Ages | | All Women Interviewed | Total Fertility Rate |
	15–19	45–49		
Africa				
Benin	7.2	8.0	7.6	7.3
Cameroon	6.5	8.6	8.0	6.4
Ghana	5.2	7.3	6.0	6.1
Ivory Coast	7.5	9.6	8.4	7.2
Kenya	6.6	8.7	7.2	7.9
Senegal	8.3	8.4	8.3	7.1
Mauritania	8.3	9.4	8.8	7.5
Asia				
Bangladesh	3.7	5.0	4.1	5.4
Pakistan	4.0	4.5	4.2	6.0
Sri Lanka	2.6	4.8	3.7	3.7
Indonesia	3.3	5.4	4.2	4.0
Thailand	2.9	4.4	3.6	4.3
Latin America				
Colombia	2.7	5.7	4.0	4.6
Ecuador	3.1	5.6	4.0	5.2
Peru	3.1	4.6	3.8	5.3
Costa Rica	3.5	6.1	4.7	5.5
Mexico	3.8	5.8	4.4	5.7

Source: World Fertility Survey, quoted in R.E. Lightbourne: Individual Preferences and Fertility
    Behavior. In J. Cleland and J. Hobcraft (eds.): Reproductive Change in Developing Coun-
    tries. Oxford University Press, Oxford 1985, p. 184.

Data gathered by the World Fertility Survey in various countries with
respect to the number of children desired by women in relation to actual
fertility rates leads to the following observations:

- Substantial differences exist between younger and older women in terms
  of the number of children they desire: younger women, without exception, want fewer children.
- In sub-Saharan Africa, the desired number of children is substantially
  higher than in the developing countries of Asia or Latin America.
- Actual fertility rates are for the most part higher than would have been
  necessary to attain the desired number of children.

It is, however, to be noted that a number of potential biases are associated with estimates of "wanted fertility." John Bongaarts has shown that desired family size, while it is the most preferred fertility indicator, significantly overestimates true "wanted fertility." One of these biases he identified is rationalization: "A significant proportion of women who have had unwanted births make an upward adjustment in their stated desired family size so that it is closer or equal to their actual number of children. This post facto revision of family size preference is called 'rationalization.' There is substantial evidence for rationalization, although its extent is difficult to measure precisely."[39]

While the wish to increase the economic and political influence of a family may result in high birth rates, the powerlessness of the poor suggests also another, more psychological aspect, according to Frances Moore Lappé and Rachel Schurman:

> As long as poor men are denied sources of self-esteem through productive work, and are denied access to the resources they need to act responsibly toward their families, it's likely they will cling even more tenaciously to their superior power vis-à-vis women. For many men, this may mean showing their virility through siring large numbers of children. Men who are forced to migrate for work, for example, may decide to start up a second family, further increasing the number of children. In many cultures, men unable to bring in enough income to support dependants feel inadequate to maintain a permanent household. The sad irony is that self-blame for this failure, lowering self-esteem, can result in a behaviour pattern of moving in and out of relationships and the fathering of even more children.[40]

The Subordination of Women and High Birth Rates

Women are often in a strongly subordinate position to men with respect to status and decisionmaking regarding family affairs, including their own fertility. Their scope for action is limited to domestic affairs like cooking, housekeeping, and childrearing. Having in many cases no possibility of generating their own income, they remain dependent on male members of the family. A wife's position is inferior to all other (also female) members of her husband's house. She can only get some security and acceptance by producing many children—especially sons.

The subordination of women to men, the consequent lack of communication between husband and wife, and women's limited access to education, employment, and alternatives to motherhood have in the past been the main obstacles to the diffusion of family planning and the reduction of fertility.[41]

If women wish to limit their pregnancies, they have to get consent from their husbands, who often do not agree due to their preference for more sons as economic assets. Women's attitudes toward and practice of contraception are highly influenced by their husbands' attitudes. The effect of availability of and accessibility to family planning services, although significant, is often weaker than the cultural forces that limit a woman's freedom to choose fewer births. Therefore family planning programs in developing countries, in addition to providing contraceptive knowledge and supplies, must address men's attitudes toward family size and contraception.[42]

Son Preference

Discrimination against females begins with birth. A baby girl is often considered as a liability for the family unless she is the first daughter after several surviving sons. Therefore, a woman has to keep having children until she gives birth to a son, regardless of the possible jeopardy to her health. In India, the preference for sons is so strong that amniocentesis is sometimes used to determine the sex of the fetus in order to abort it if it is female. Clandestine or unsafe induced abortion is estimated to result in the death of nearly 500,000 women in developing countries annually and to 25–50 percent of all maternal deaths in Latin America.[43]

In countries where girls commonly move to their in-laws' house when they get married, daughters have no "economic value," and therefore the incentive for parents is strong to bear sons for their future support. In Bangladesh, where females remain dependent on men during their whole life—first on their fathers, or in his absence on other male members of the family, and after marriage on their husbands—sons play a vital role, especially in case the father dies. In the Islamic law of inheritance, a widow is deprived of a major share of her husband's property if she has only daughters. Without a male heir, the brother of the deceased inherits the property. If a father-in-law is still alive when the husband dies, all the property goes to him. Such practices naturally motivate women to give birth to more children with the hope of having a son, which can lead to a doubling of the required number of children.[44]

Child Mortality

In spite of many improvements during the last 30 years, infant and child mortality rates are still very high in many countries, making a large number of children desirable. In virtually all 40 least developed countries[45] of the world, every fifth or sixth child dies before reaching the age of six, and in many cases it is even every third child. (See Table III-4.) So one additional child is a relatively low "insurance premium" wherever the additional costs of that child to the household are low and where there is an absolute need for old-age security.

Table III-4

Mortality of Children under Five Years of Age per 1000 Live Births, 1960 and 1990

Country	1960	1990
Mozambique	331	297
Afghanistan	381	292
Angola	345	292
Mali	369	284
Sierra Leone	385	257
Bhutan	298	189
Nepal	298	189
Bangladesh	262	180

Source: UNDP: Human Development Report 1992. Oxford University Press, New York 1992, p. 135.

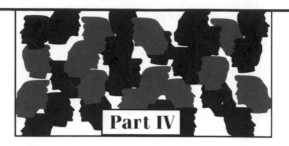

Part IV

The Effects of Rapid Population Growth

Introduction: Controversial Theories

There is no overall accepted population theory but rather a multitude of frameworks and theories originating from sciences such as biology, economy, social psychology, ecology, and so on. The controversy over population growth rests on the question of whether population control is the crucial factor for development planning. The economic and the general effects of population growth have been a subject of debate for more than 30–40 years; in fact, population growth was already an issue nearly 200 years ago, popularized through the writings of Thomas Malthus.

The Population Theory of Thomas Malthus

In his "Essays on the Principle of Population as it Affects the Future Improvement of Society" in 1798,[1] Thomas Robert Malthus initiated a systematic discussion of the effects of population growth on the well-being of humanity in general and on the economic development potential of a country in particular.[2] The population theory proposed by Malthus and published in seven revised editions was based on the assumption that "population has this constant tendency to increase beyond the means of subsistence" and "that population, when unchecked, goes on doubling itself every twenty-five years."[3]

In an article on population that appeared in the 1824 edition of the *Encyclopaedia Britannica,* Malthus asserted that the population of the North American colonies, and later that of the United States, doubled in no more than 25 years. This illustrated the tendency for rapid geometric increase when the checks to population were minimal or when there was no motivation to employ preventive checks.[4] According to Ansley Coale, Malthus employed a surprisingly modern type of demographic analysis, including stable population techniques, to prove that such a rate of increase had occurred by procreation, after due allowance for migration.[5]

Malthus claimed that the world's population was increasing geometrically while food supplies were increasing arithmetically,[6] leading eventually to legal sanctions limiting family size as well as to "positive checks" to population growth such as "severe labour and exposure to the seasons, extreme poverty, bad nursing of children, great towns, excesses of all kinds, the whole train of common disease and epidemics, wars, plague, and famine"[7]—in other words a "die-back" of the population.

With this essay, the young Malthus contradicted the theory of William Godwin that was popular at the time, namely that a growing population was the surest sign of the happiness and welfare of a people. In advancing such a gloomy theory at a time of general optimism, Malthus demonstrated a secularised Calvinist world view, somewhat analogous to Augustine, that although men should try to control their sinful nature,[8] they will never achieve this goal and will in time be subject to a collective hell.

Malthus basically believed that population control should be attained not through contraception, because sexual intercourse that precludes procreation degrades the dignity of human nature, but through preventive checks such as "moral restraint" and "restraint from marriage."[9] "Promiscuous intercourse, unnatural passions, violations of the marriage bed, and improper arts to conceal the consequences of irregular connexions, are preventive checks that clearly come under the head of vice."[10] He was rather realistic, however, in his judgment of members of his sex: according to him, "moral restraint"—which he regarded as the primary preventive check to rapid population growth—was not particularly prevalent among the male segment of the population.

Malthus was convinced that even peaceful political development would be threatened by overly rapid population growth because hunger and suffering induced by poverty would result in constant political change and incessant fighting. Legitimated by social Darwinism, the Malthusian perspective suggested that a society's economic crises and social instability derived from uncontrolled increases in dependent and marginalized people.[11] He therefore considered support for the lower classes, as provided in England at the time on the basis of the "poor laws," counterproductive in terms of population policy. His assumption was that if parents were not held responsible for all the costs arising from the existence of their children, they would have no incentive to limit the number of offspring: "Among the lower classes of society, where the point is of the greatest importance, the poor-laws afford a direct, constant and systematic encouragement to marriage, by removing from each individual that heavy responsibility, which he would incur by the laws of nature, for bringing beings into the world which he could not support."[12]

This argument is one that has resurfaced recently in demands for an "internalization of external costs" in the population policy debate, as some extreme elements of political parties object to giving aid that supports families that choose to have many children—in spite of currently undisputed commitments to development assistance and to the promotion of appropriate social policies in developing countries.

Malthus's thesis that population multiplies faster than food supply was based on the assumption that soil quality would decrease with increasing use. While the spectacular productivity gains since the end of World War II fostered the belief that technology will always outpace demographic expansion, today's damages to our life-support systems have taught us that, in the end, Malthus was right. Many of the postwar productivity gains were achieved by exploiting land in ways that yielded quick but short-lived results. Putting marginal lands into production boosted yields temporarily, but eventually eroded soil and robbed land of its vitality.[13]

The scientific neutrality of Malthus's population theory was and still is disputed. Some view his statements as a means to the end of explaining the poverty of the English working classes as a result of their overly high population growth rate, thus portraying their condition as something brought on themselves. The Industrial Revolution had at that time not brought about any measurable social, political, or economic improvements for the majority of the workers in the rapidly growing cities of England's industrial regions. The forms of poverty during Malthus's time that were becoming increasingly visible required an explanation, which was then eagerly accepted.[14]

Another aspect that is justifiably criticized (at least on the basis of the early editions of Malthus's writings) is that the right to live rests on a concept of property that is not further questioned, on a division of humanity into those who have property and those who do not—into the wealthy, who have a moral right to their inheritance, and the poor, who have only to fulfill their purpose for living as expendable laborers.[15]

Several aspects of the Malthusian theory, therefore, remain justifiably controversial. With respect to the effect of rapid population growth on the totality of production factors, however, his ideas remain relevant to this day. Now that we have seen the earth from space, as a beautiful yet limited planet, many people have finally become aware of the finite nature of our resources. The "law of minimums" developed by Justus Liebig more than 100 years ago states that the ability of a species to thrive is limited by the one respective vital factor that is present in the most minimal amount. The factor that will prove to be the limiting one for us humans—water, air, land, or a protective atmosphere—is not yet known. It is, however, certain, according to our current state of knowledge, that many of our environmental resources are limited, at least in the long term. This means that—as Malthus also saw it—we are being squeezed between two dynamic factors: a growing population and a shrinking basis for life.

Pronatalistic Population Theories and Their Weaknesses

Even though the current tenor of the population policy debate emphasizes the development-inhibiting effects of rapid population growth, fairness requires mentioning the arguments of those who view population growth—albeit at moderate levels—as favorable for the economic and social development of a country. In part, this theory has existed for several decades and incorporates early schools of thought that many consider outmoded today;[16] in the eighties, however, U.S. authors such as Julian Simon seized on or expanded this belief.[17]

In a recent publication, for example, Simon maintains that natural resources are becoming less important for economic development. Under conditions of need, such as in overpopulation, unlimited amounts of human-made resources, he argues, are created that improve the human condition, and more human minds and knowledge can lead to progress. For Simon, population growth is beneficial, not detrimental, to society, even if it is caused by extended mortality.[18]

Supporters of this theory generally cite five effects of population growth as positive.

Stimulation of Demand

According to proponents of pronatalistic population theories, a larger population creates a greater demand for goods and services by the sheer necessity of meeting its basic needs. This, in turn, creates impulses for the growth of the respective national economy.[19] The conclusion that rapid population growth increases the demand for goods and services is based on the assumption that high birth rates do not have any negative effects on the purchasing power of a population.

This assumption, however, can be refuted on the basis of several concrete examples.[20] The negative effects of rapid population growth on income are discussed in greater detail in the next section of this chapter.

The theory that more people equals greater demand, which equals stimulation for economic development, is closely linked to the argument that a high population growth rate results in advantageous technological change.

Advantages of Mass Production

In most sectors, the product-unit costs depend primarily on the produced quantity of a certain product. Therefore, the advantage of mass production is reduced costs per unit produced, because the mostly high costs for basic investments (buildings, machinery, environmental protection, and so on), which are necessary for the efficient manufacturing of goods regardless of the quantity that is to be produced, can be defrayed by a larger production quantity. Moreover, there are greater opportunities for the division of labor and, therefore, also for an increase in productivity. This is particularly true in the production of automobiles and steel and the manufacturing of various capital goods, but also, for example, for pharmaceutical production. Many economists attach great significance to these "economies of scale" for the economic development of a country.

Of course, it is true that countries such as Brazil, China, India, or Indonesia have better basic conditions for their own industrialization due to their large internal markets (provided their people have the necessary purchasing power) than do small countries such as Burundi, Sierra Leone, or Togo.[21] In light of the great successes of Singapore, Hong Kong, and Switzerland, however, it is clear that a large population is much less important than, for example, a high level of education, disciplined and industrious workers, and free trade that allows for unrestricted export of domestic goods. Larger economic markets resulting from free trade create the same opportunities as mass production, as well as cost savings. Several leading international institutions for economic cooperation rightly point to the immense damage to developing countries caused by the protectionism of the industrial world.[22]

From a development policy point of view, the cost advantages of capital-intensive mass production—while no doubt important for business and for international competitiveness—should always also be weighed against the level of total employment achieved. The high global levels of unemployment and underemployment[23] and the fact that employment's growth will continue to lag far behind that of output and the labor force[24] suggest that "production by the masses" instead of "mass production" is a far wiser recommendation. Further advantages of "smaller" technologies are their less harmful environmental impact and lower energy consumption.

Impetus for Technical Progress

Everyone is familiar with the saying "necessity is the mother of invention." Albert O. Hirschmann, Julian Simon, and others assumed this to be true when they argued that population growth and its related problems would lead to transformations of thought and behavior patterns and of the state-of-the-art technology.[25] Both of these—and this is largely uncontested—have positive, long-term effects on development.

If a sufficient number of people are motivated—so Simon argues— conditions and institutions can and do change.[26] Esther Boserup already alluded to this in her analysis of traditional agriculture almost 30 years ago.[27] Historical evidence shows that in times of great population pressure, there is not only more labor, more investment, and therefore more production in traditional agriculture, but also more "inventions"—such as the terracing of mountain slopes, new irrigation channels, and more clearing of hitherto unused land.

Julian Simon also argues—and empirical observations supporting this view have been made in sub-Saharan Africa—that agricultural families would respond to the needs of additional children with increased labor (such as clearing more land for cultivation), improved methods (irrigation, weeding, and crop rotation, for example), and increased production.[28] The resulting increase in income can in fact be higher than the costs arising from the additional children, as long as the children are available as free laborers.

The experience of the last 30 years, however, has given little cause for optimism about future technical progress due to pressures resulting from poverty or population growth. Indeed, to the contrary: as will be discussed in greater detail in the next section, the current ecological situation in many parts of developing countries suggests that this argument must be used with great caution. Farmers in sub-Saharan Africa already have to resort to marginal soils if they wish to cultivate additional land. In many cases—particularly in the Sahelian zone—farmers overuse marginal soils by using inappropriate production methods.[29] Similar developments can be observed in regions of Latin America and Asia, where rain forests are being cleared to cultivate additional land.[30]

Another counterargument is that not every innovation can be achieved with labor-intensive means and existing human resources; in most cases, capital is needed. In fact, very large financial resources might even be required for the efficient research and development of new technologies that can make a significant contribution to a lasting reduction of mass poverty. It has not been possible to raise resources on this scale due to the low savings capacity of people in poor countries. Not even the transfer of some $50 billion a year for development cooperation has changed this.

Finally, it borders on cynicism to assume that the billions of people who live in absolute poverty today would have to suffer even more before changes in thought and behavior patterns and innovations can be achieved. Lichtenberg, in response to the saying just mentioned, noted: "If necessity is the mother of efficiency or of invention, then it is a question of who is the father, or the grandfather, or the mother of necessity."[31] The answer might very well be rapid population growth.

Incentives for the Construction of Infrastructure

The term "infrastructure" means the total of all investments made primarily by the public sector, which are the prerequisite for the integration and development capacity of a national economy. Included are transportation facilities (roads, bridges, railways, airports, harbors, and so on), institutions for the communication of news (postal systems, telecommunications), electrification or the provision of other energy sources, water supply, educational and health institutions, sewage and waste treatment facilities, and other buildings and organizations that represent the foundation of the economic activity of a country. Without an appropriate infrastructure, no economic activity can be developed that goes beyond the level of traditional agriculture and the corresponding small trades.

Simon, in particular, has drawn attention to the fact that state investments in infrastructure can only be expected once a minimum population density has been attained.[32] He incorporates irrigation systems into his analysis and describes the advantages of electrification and controlled irrigation for rural development.[33] A minimal transportation infrastructure is also expected to result from a minimum population density. This makes sense in terms of population policy because without reliable supplies of agricultural inputs and without the possibility of transporting harvest surpluses to city markets, agricultural productivity is destined to remain at a very low level. Another positive factor is that prices attained in cities are higher[34]—at least in those cities with market prices, not those set by the government.

Many of today's rural development problems are caused by the lack of roads, schools, and hospitals. The question is whether rapid population growth is a prerequisite for the construction of the infrastructure necessary for development. The thrust of the causal relationship between more infrastructure and higher population density remains unclear. Existing infrastructure attracts people in the same way that urban areas tend to produce a greater demand for new infrastructure.

In addition, there is empirical evidence that although a growing population can result in public investments, the net effect of population growth on income and the standard of living can still be negative.[35]

The advantages described by Simon are not advantages of a high population growth rate but of agglomerations. Theoretically, however, agglomerations could also be achieved through an appropriate settlement and migration policy. Experiences to date with migration forced by the state (for example, in Tanzania, Ethiopia, and, to a lesser extent, Indonesia) and the fact that land flight has already resulted in excessive urbanization—with all its negative consequences—seem to indicate that this path cannot generally be recommended.

As we can see in many developing countries today, there are big agglomerations without any infrastructure or with a totally inadequate one. It is therefore unrealistic to think that population growth results in infrastructural improvements. Rather, rapid population growth tends to inhibit the savings capacity and the capital formation of a country that would be needed for infrastructural and other state investments.

Finally, even in the case of low population density, a minimal infrastructure is required to meet the basic needs of the rural population. Meeting this goal is difficult not due to a low population density but rather due to a lack of resources or—if one considers the elaborate military infrastructure that can often be found in poor countries—of political will.

Younger Population Structure

A final argument in support of the theory that rapid population growth can have development-enhancing effects refers to the structure of the work force. Rapid population growth—as has already been mentioned—results in a very young age structure. This in turn means that large numbers of young workers enter the labor force every year. It is assumed that these younger workers will be more open to technical and organizational change and that they will have a better or more modern education than their parents did.

According to UNESCO, one-quarter of the adults in the world still do not have adequate reading and writing skills,[36] although the basic level of education in developing countries has improved substantially during the past 30 years. In 1960, only 10 percent of all adults in the 34 poorest countries could read and write; 15 years later that number had more than doubled, to 23 percent.[37] Today, the literacy rate in most poor countries is about 50 percent, although the rates for women are substantially lower than for men.[38] The percentage of children in secondary school has increased considerably during the past 20 years—in countries with the lowest income (not including China and India), it increased from 9 percent in 1965 to 25 percent of the respective age group in 1988.[39]

In development policy literature, the entry of more modern thinking, well-educated workers into the labor force and the exit of older, traditionally thinking, poorly educated workers tend to be viewed as positive.[40] Although it enhances the quality of the national economy, this is only partially related to rapid population growth: in light of high urban and rural unemployment and underemployment, relatively many well-educated young people remain unemployed or must accept jobs for which they are overqualified. The resources invested in the education and training of these young people—often at great sacrifice to the entire family—are not put to optimal use or are even completely wasted. The frustration of the unemployed and underemployed also poses a constant threat to the internal peace of economically underdeveloped countries.

In light of the existing shortages of appropriately trained teachers, inadequate school and university materials, and a lack of schools in rural areas, overly rapid population growth has other undesirable effects because additional students further deplete the existing resources for education and training and the quality of education consequently declines. The UNESCO World Education Report clearly points toward a worsening of the student-teacher ratio.[41]

Simon Kuznets argued—albeit many years ago—that the number of geniuses increases proportionately to a country's population growth.[42] While B. Fritsch fears that a further uncontrolled increase in world population could have catastrophic consequences, he also alludes to this. According to his calculations, 0.15 million cubic meters of additional brain mass are made available each year due to the current high rate of population growth; approximately 3.5 million geniuses are supposedly to be found among the newborns.[43] To Julian Simon, the human being is the "ultimate resource" for all progress.[44] A human's creative power, intelligence, energy, will, and imaginative ability to solve problems and to achieve progress for society are, in Simon's opinion, the reason that catastrophic scenarios do not become reality. That is why he does not view population growth or even rapid population growth as a problem but rather as an opportunity for the development of a society.[45]

Human beings are always a source of creativity. This particular basic assumption of the authors who see development policy advantages in rapid population growth remains uncontested here. Creative potential is an asset for every society in the North or the South of this planet. But the sad reality in the overcrowded slums of Calcutta, Nairobi, Rio de Janeiro, and many other cities does not allow much hope that a potential genius will be able to unfold in spite of malnutrition at an early age or inadequate schooling. In order to maintain and expand creative potential to the greatest possible extent, the quality of life of all human beings must be improved. As the next section indicates, this is made much more difficult and in some cases even impossible by rapid population growth.

The Negative Effects of Rapid Population Growth

To a certain degree, every country, region, or family has the capacity for an increase in numbers. Where this "certain degree" lies differs from country to country (and region to region or family to family), and varies in terms of time frame. It also depends on the size of the initial population and on existing resources (such as land, capital, raw materials, and level of education). The quality of the local development policy is a deciding factor in how population growth affects social, economic, and environmental systems.

Regardless of how good the development policy may be, population growth that goes beyond this "certain degree" has undesirable effects.[46] Numerous empirical studies arrive at different conclusions—depending on methodology, size of the target population, place, and time.[47] It would therefore be possible to cite counter-examples for most of the following. Still, this would not change the tenor of the conclusion that high birth rates have a variety of undesirable effects on the natural resource base as well as on socioeconomic development, both at the family level and at the societal and global levels.

Disadvantages at the Family Level

The greatest and most direct disadvantages of high birth rates occur at the family level, starting with a deterioration of the health of the mother and child. (See Figure IV-1.)

Health Risks for Mothers

At least 500,000 women—99 percent of them in poor countries—die every year as a result of complications in connection with pregnancy and birth.[48] This corresponds to a jumbo jet with 250 female passengers crashing every four hours a day. Maternal mortality is 125 to 250 times higher in poor countries than in wealthy ones; even that understates the gap, as a large number of such deaths are never recorded in official statistics.[49] (See Table IV-1.)

A large part—if not the largest part—of maternal mortality can be traced back to unwanted pregnancies that could have been avoided through family planning. Three-quarters of the mothers die during delivery due to unstoppable hemorrhaging, blood poisoning, and complications of birth.[50] Abortion is also a frequent cause of death.[51] Many women who do not die of such problems suffer permanent damage to their health.

There is a direct and measurable relationship between the health of the mother and the number of births she has, the spacing between births, and the time of the pregnancy in her life: the greater the number of children she has,

Figure IV-1

Risk Factors for Mothers and Children

Too often. When the intervals between births are too short, the risks to the mother and child are increased.

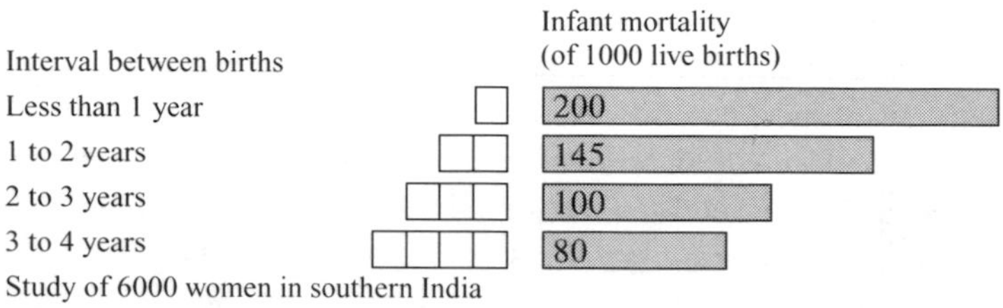

Interval between births	Infant mortality (of 1000 live births)
Less than 1 year	200
1 to 2 years	145
2 to 3 years	100
3 to 4 years	80

Study of 6000 women in southern India

Too many. The health risks to mother and child increase after the fourth child.

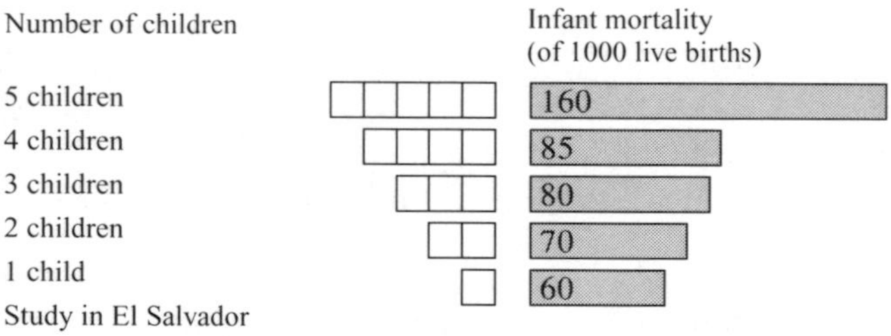

Number of children	Infant mortality (of 1000 live births)
5 children	160
4 children	85
3 children	80
2 children	70
1 child	60

Study in El Salvador

Too young. Infant mortality in children whose mothers are under 20 is twice as high as for children whose mothers were 25 to 30 when they were born.

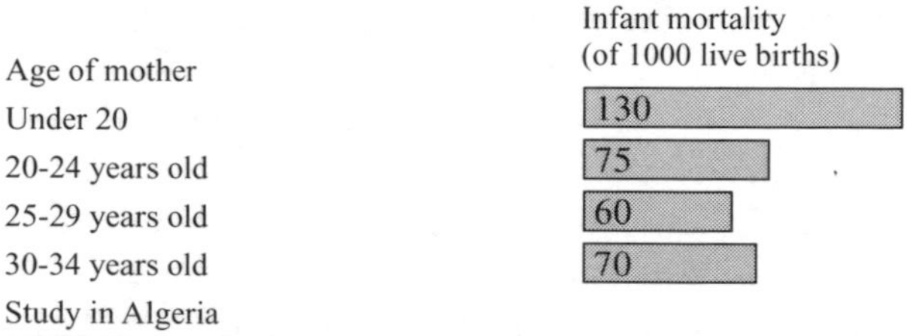

Age of mother	Infant mortality (of 1000 live births)
Under 20	130
20-24 years old	75
25-29 years old	60
30-34 years old	70

Study in Algeria

Source: UNICEF: Information "Birth Control-Family Planning" 1987.

Table IV-1

Births per Woman and Maternal Mortality*a* in Selected Countries

Country	Maternal Mortality per 100,000 births (1980–90)	Births per Woman	
		1970	1990
Switzerland	4	2.3	1.6
United States	8	2.6	1.8
Federal Republic of Germany (former)	8	2.3	1.4
Burkina Faso	810	6.7	6.5
Chad	860	6.1	5.9
Republic of Congo	1,000	5.9	6.0
Somalia	1,100	6.6	6.6
Bolivia	480	6.6	6.1
Bhutan	1,710	5.9	5.5
Republic of China	44	6.0	2.4
India	340	5.7	4.3
Bangladesh	600	6.9	5.5
Pakistan	400–600	7.0	6.5

Source: United Nations: The World's Women 1970–90. New York 1991, pp. 67–70.
*a*Defined by the WHO as "death of a woman during pregnancy or within 42 days following the termination of the same, [. . .] and specifically for reasons related to or complicated by the pregnancy."

the shorter the spacing between births, and the younger (under 18) or older (over 35) she is, the worse the condition of health of the mother (and the child) and the higher the mortality rate.[52] Women under the age of 18 and in particular those younger than 16 have high health risks during pregnancy and birth due to biological (physical) and social (economic circumstances and social security) reasons.[53] Women over 35 have higher pregnancy and delivery risks than women in their twenties due to biological reasons. Studies in Bangladesh indicate that 52 percent of the maternal mortality there could be avoided if women under 20 and over 34 did not become pregnant.[54] And if no further pregnancies were to occur following the birth of the fifth child, maternal mortality in Bangladesh could be reduced by a third.

The increased mortality risk due to overly close spacing between pregnancies can be proved independent of the mother's place of residence (urban or rural), educational level, or household income—in other words, independent of all essential social indicators that are used to measure the quality of life.[55] It is, however, particularly accentuated in lowest-income families and in women whose heavy work burden and poor nutritional condition has lead to a "maternal depletion syndrome" in their bodies—iron deficiency, anaemia, a lack of vitamins, and other deficiencies.[56]

Health Risks for Children

The social environment of poverty and the related lack of hygiene, sanitary facilities, adequate nutrition, and housing also pose a great risk to the health and survival of infants and children under the age of five. High birth rates in this environment increase these risks substantially. Newborns of mothers with maternal depletion syndrome are delivered underweight, weak, and in poor health, and run a much greater risk of becoming seriously ill and dying before reaching the age of five.

A Pakistani study found the mortality risk for a child born within two years of a previous pregnancy is about 30 percent in the child's first month of life, approximately 60 percent until the completion of its first year of life, and, until the completion of its fourth year of life, 50 percent higher than that of a first-born.[57] Other studies have found the risk is particularly high for a newborn whose mother has just experienced an unsuccessful pregnancy or has had to endure the death of her last infant.[58]

Due to shortened lactation periods, premature transitions from baby to adult foods, and a worsening of the nutritional quality as a result of decreased per capita income, the nutritional condition of small children declines as the direct consequence of a growing number of siblings.[59] Another Pakistani study found that in poorer urban areas, children under the age of five with many siblings had a comparatively lower body weight.[60]

Infants of mothers who deliver another child within too short a period of time run high health risks.[61] The "new" child replaces the older siblings in terms of the mother's attentiveness, nutrition, hygiene, and general care. In the course of this competition, last-born girls in families with many children lose their lives with particular frequency. In general the rule is, the greater the number of children in a family, the worse their health, especially in the case of younger girls in families with many children.[62] The opposite outcome—the better health enjoyed by children of smaller families—has been well researched and substantiated.[63]

Infant and child mortality as well as maternal mortality are the social indicators that reflect most clearly the extent of poverty in a given society. In no other set of indicators is the North-South Gap revealed so clearly. The interrelationship between high child and infant mortality and high birth rates is particularly striking in many sub-Saharan countries in Africa, but also in Laos and Bangladesh. (See Table IV-2.)

The key to solving all these problems—in addition, of course, to a general improvement in the living conditions of the poor—lies in family planning.

Table IV-2

Mortality of Infants and Children under the Age of Five and Birth Rates, 1990

Country	Mortality per 1000 live births			Birth Rates[a]
		Children under the Age of Five		
	Infants[b]	Girls	Boys	
Sub-Saharan Africa				
Mozambique	137	194	215	46
Ethiopia	132	185	205	51
Somalia	126	200	223	48
Malawi	149	242	255	54
Sierra Leone	147	236	261	47
Mali	166	209	238	50
Angola	130	207	230	47
Congo	116	172	185	48
Others				
Laos	103	159	179	47
Bangladesh	105	160	142	35

Source: World Bank: World Development Report 1992. Oxford University Press, New York 1992, Tables 27, 28, and 32.
[a]Unadjusted birth rates per 1000 of the population.
[b]Children under the age of one.

The goals of family planning are smaller families and the maintenance of an adequate interval (at least 24 months) between births. The latter has an extremely positive effect on the health of the mother and child—independent of the educational level of the parents, the place of residence (city or country), and the availability of clean drinking water.[64]

Decreasing Quality of Education

Since all the children in a family need to be appropriately fed and clothed, receive adequate health care, and later be educated, families with many children have much higher expenses than those with fewer children. In families with many children, financial resources drop, which often means that attempts are made to cut back on expenses for the children. In poorer households these effects are of course more drastic than in households with higher incomes.

In a study in Colombia, Nancy Birdsall proved that investments per child drop "monotonously" with increasing family size.[65] This effect is particularly pronounced once five or more children are present. Since fewer resources are available for education (tuition, teaching materials, and so on), particularly of the youngest, in multichild households, educational quality and vocational opportunities diminish with growing family size.

Baby-sitting responsibilities for younger siblings that usually fall on girls' shoulders as well as other household duties and money-making activities can also have a negative effect on school attendance.[66]

Land Shortages and Cultivation of Marginal Soils

Shortages of land, particularly of fertile or irrigated land, are a great problem in many parts of the developing world.[67] At the family level, this has particularly tragic effects in areas where people have no choice but to live on what the soil produces for them—which means approximately 60 percent of the people in developing countries.

The amount of land that can be used for agricultural purposes dropped from 0.33 hectares per capita to 0.26 hectares between 1974 and today due to population growth. A further decrease to less than 0.24 hectares per capita can be expected by the year 2000.[68] Every year 1.9 percent of agriculturally arable land per capita is lost.[69] It is becoming increasingly difficult to claim new land due to rapidly increasing soil losses from salinization, erosion, and overuse. Although a 0.5-percent annual increase in agriculturally arable land was still being achieved in the seventies, the growth rate dropped to half that level in the eighties. More intensive farming and a technological breakthrough—in the area of plant varieties for example—conceivably could temporarily help or alleviate this situation, as the Green Revolution did in the seventies by making a substantial increase in crop yield per hectare possible.[70] The principal development problems, however, cannot be solved through technical innovations.

Wherever a family's subsistence depends on their abililty to produce food on their own parcel of land, the size of the area available for this purpose becomes the deciding factor in that family's survival. W.B. Arthur and G. McNicoll proved in Bangladesh that in spite of the political and social structures hindering development, the population dynamic remained the essential element responsible for the decrease in the average cultivable land per family, since it has not been possible to cultivate additional land there since the early fifties.[71] More sons (because usually only sons inherit land) mean an increased fragmentation of the parents' (father's) farm. If the farm is only of a minimal size, a family cannot produce enough to survive. If the family then becomes indebted, due, for example, to a lack of wage labor or because of a bad growing season, they can lose their land permanently.

Millions of farmers in poor countries leave their land every year because it has become too small through inheritance to sustain a family, because it has lost its fertility, or for other reasons. These people, once independent of outside help, are forced to move to the already overcrowded slums of cities, where they become materially impoverished, uprooted, and culturally alienated. They merely swell the masses of unemployed or underemployed and accelerate the ecologically and socially destructive process of urbanization.

The increase in the number of landless people exerts a fatal pressure on the income of day laborers. As a result, rural poverty increases and the per capita consumption of protein and calories sinks. In Bangladesh, it was shown that this has catastrophic effects on the lowest classes. In years of famine, the child mortality rate of this group is 400 percent higher than that of wealthy landowners.[72]

The negative circular interrelationship between rapid population growth and a decrease in soil quality can be illustrated particularly clearly in the Sahel zone. Since more and more people depend on the soil for their survival, fallow periods are shortened, traditional grazing lands are used for planting, and—wherever possible—additional land is cleared for cultivation. Here, again, the poorest groups in a society are most affected by these developments—people who have no other choice when soil quality diminishes but to try to get as much out of the soil as possible. People forced to overuse their already meager resources in a daily struggle for survival cannot afford to think of the long-term ecological effects of their actions in spite of what they know about necessary fallow periods or the effects of regular fertilization.

In this manner a vicious circle is created through the poverty-driven over-exploitation of natural resources, a reduction in soil quality, and intensified poverty, until the soil becomes completely ruined. Then people are forced to resort to other soils in neighboring regions—soils that are either lying fallow for regenerative purposes or are being cultivated by other tribes or family clans. The consequences are conflicts—frequently armed ones—and further stress on existing resources.

In areas where nomads herd their cattle onto the farmland or to the wells of settled farmers—due to decreases in vegetation and in the water supply and in violation of traditional agreements—traditional and historically stable relationships based on trust are undermined and conflicts erupt.[73] Wherever these conflicts are carried out using modern weapons (as in Ogaden), any remaining meager resources are destroyed for "tactical reasons," whether through the burning of fields or the planting of land mines.[74]

Growing Shortage of Firewood

The increasing shortage of firewood[75] could equally well be discussed here or in the sections on "Disadvantages for Society and the National Economy" or "Global and Regional Burdens." Rapid population growth has negative effects for the existing reserves of firewood at all three levels. It is included here because the growing shortage of firewood is felt most directly by potential users.

Of the approximately 1.7 billion cubic meters of wood that were used in 76 tropical countries in 1987, according to U.N. Food and Agriculture Organization (FAO) estimates, 86 percent was used as firewood and 14 percent was used as lumber for industrial purposes.[76] Some 5 percent of the world's energy needs are met by firewood. In some poor countries, firewood accounts for up to 96 percent of total energy consumption. (See Table IV-3.)

While people in developing countries account for only 20 percent of the world's energy consumption, 70 percent of them depend primarily on wood as their energy source for cooking and heating.[77] The German Bundestag's Enquete Commission on "Precautions to Protect the Earth's Atmosphere" arrived at the following conclusions with respect to the relationship between population growth and shortages of firewood or the ecological consequences of the overuse of forests due to the gathering of firewood:

> The demand for firewood in the cities of developing countries is constantly increasing due to high birth rates and the constant influx of people into the urban areas. The inhabitants of these cities also face decreasing forest reserves in the vicinity of the cities, increasing fuel prices, and a lack of alternative energy sources. Whereas kerosene has replaced wood as a cooking fuel in the large cities since the fifties when oil drilling was expanded, increases in the price of oil in the seventies reversed this trend. Niamey, the capital of Niger, and Ouagadougou, the capital of Burkina Faso, have no forests within a 70 km radius. The wooded areas within a 100 km radius of the nine largest cities in India decreased by 15% (Coimbatore) and 60% (Delhi) between the mid-seventies and the early eighties.[78]

The gathering of firewood is a primary cause of the destruction of forests particularly in the dry tropics and in areas where population density is high. Extreme shortages of firewood—the Enquete Commission speaks of a "firewood crisis"—exists above all in the African Sahel zone and in parts of the Indian subcontinent. In tropical and outer-tropical Africa, either on a country-wide or a regional basis:

- 19 countries are experiencing an acute shortage of firewood, which means that even with an overuse of forest reserves and the use of agricultural waste, the demand for firewood cannot be met; and
- 13 countries have a firewood deficit—that is, the demand can be met for the time being only through an overuse of resources and the deficit will change into an acute firewood shortage in the foreseeable future.[79]

In three other African countries, a firewood deficit will occur due to rapid population growth if current trends continue until the year 2000.

Table IV-3

Percentage of Wood in Total Energy Consumption, Selected Tropical Countries

Region/Country	Percent
Africa	
Burkina Faso	96
Kenya	71
Malawi	93
Nigeria	82
Sudan	74
Tanzania	92
Asia	
India	33
Indonesia	50
Nepal	94
Latin America	
Brazil	20
Costa Rica	33
Nicaragua	50
Paraguay	64

Source: Enquete Commission: Precautions to Protect the Earth's Atmosphere. Protection of the Tropical Forests. Economica Verlag, Bonn 1990, p. 306.

More than 50 million people in Africa were not even able to meet their minimum needs of firewood in 1980 without overusing their forests. On a worldwide basis, almost 130 million people are approaching a shortage situation.[80] They can meet their fuel needs only by burning cattle dung or plant residue that could otherwise be used to fertilize their fields. As a result, agricultural production declines unless other measures are taken to maintain soil fertility. Large parts of the Indian subcontinent and parts of Indonesia (Java) and dry regions of Central and South America are also affected by this.

The effects of this crisis are felt most strongly by the poorer classes and, to an even greater extent, by the women and children in them. In rural areas longer distances must be travelled and therefore more time must be spent gathering firewood. This increases the total work load of women and children considerably.

Wind and water erosion is increased by the overuse of soils and the felling of trees and shrubs. The impoverishment of soils worsens the living and production conditions in rural areas, has a negative effect on food and other agricultural production, and contributes to migration from the rural areas. Under arid conditions and at the lowest altitudes, soil erosion has particularly fatal effects because these soils are developed only to a low depth and their regenerative capacities are extremely modest. In these weak, low-performance ecosystems that have developed themselves painstakingly over hundreds or even thousands of years, human intervention can result in irreversible destruction within the shortest period of time.

In places where there is a shortage of firewood, boiled water becomes an expensive commodity. Cooked meals also become more rare; foods with longer cooking times are dropped from the meal plan, even though they may be less expensive and more nutritious (such as legumes). Wherever such changes take place, negative health effects can be expected, in particular an increase in diarrhea, the most frequent cause of death for children under the age of five. For urban populations, the share of family income that must be spent on firewood increases; in some cases it amounts to almost 30 percent of the family income.[81] This detracts from income available for other necessary goods, including food.

According to FAO estimates, approximately 1.2 billion people are using more firewood than can be regrown in their surroundings. Estimates for the year 2000 anticipate a doubling of this figure.[82]

In addition to rapid population growth, two other factors are responsible for the firewood crisis. First there is a lack of firewood-saving stoves and/or ovens. Energy-efficient stoves use up to one-third less wood to achieve the same cooking output. Second, there is a traditional preference for open fireplaces. Firewood-saving stoves—if available at all—have gained acceptance only with great difficulty.

In cities, the common use of charcoal instead of wood aggravates the fuel problem. Charcoal has two advantages over firewood—first it weighs less (and therefore costs less to transport), and second it burns more cleanly, which is a particular health advantage in enclosed kitchens because firewood causes more damage to the eyes and the breathing organs. Charcoal use, however, has the disadvantage that approximately 50 percent of its original heat output value is lost during the current process used to produce charcoal.[83] Improved brick or metal ovens could produce considerable savings in this respect.

Disadvantages for Society and the National Economy

The U.N. Population Fund (UNFPA, from its original name) studied the effects of rapid population growth on the performance of national political institutions in 120 countries and their achievements in the area of development policy. The study concluded that "only a handful of countries with serious demographic pressures had managed to maintain stable constitutional governments with good records on civil and political rights."[84]

Furthermore, "high population growth has made it much more difficult for most governments to keep pace with growing needs for development services such as health and education. The low income countries, excluding India and China, have seen growth in primary school enrollments fall from an average annual rate of 5.6 per cent in 1975–1980 to 2.7 per cent for 1980–1987. According to UNESCO estimates, in 1985 approximately 105 million children 6–11 years old were not in school, and of these over 70 per cent were in the least developed nations. If current trends continue, by the year 2000, the number of out of school children will almost double to approximately 200 million."[85]

The general statement that a high population growth rate makes development more difficult can be proved with studies on, for example, the reduction of capital formation, the strengthening of income inequalities, and the deterioration of food security.

Reduction of Capital Formation

The aggregate savings of a country are its most important source for the financing of investments. Foreign capital—such as that flowing into a country through development cooperation or direct foreign investment—covers only an extremely small share of the need for capital. In light of the international debt situation, it cannot be assumed that this will change in the foreseeable future. This creates a problem for countries with rapid population growth because, as mentioned earlier, they have a young population structure, with approximately half the population 14 years of age or younger.

Even though there are fewer old people in developing countries than in industrial ones, the so-called dependency ratio is high. This measures the ratio between the employable and the unemployable age groups within a population. To give a few examples: in 1991, 16.9 percent of the population of Switzerland was under the age of 14 and 15.6 percent over the age of 64. So a total of 32.5 percent of the population had not yet reached or was no longer in an employable age group. Those aged 15–64 accounted for 67.5 percent of the population—that is, there were more than two members of the employable age group for every one person who needed to be "supported" by the work of the others.[86] For the United States this ratio was similarly favorable: 65.5 percent in the age group 15–64 years and 34.5 percent younger or older.[87]

The situation is totally different in developing countries with rapid population growth: in Rwanda, 48.9 percent of the population is younger than 15 and

0.5 percent of the population is 65 or older. This means that almost half (49.4 percent) is either too young or too old to pursue gainful employment.[88] Even if the income per worker in Rwanda were as high as that in Switzerland, per capita income in Switzerland would be almost one-third higher under otherwise equal conditions due to Switzerland's lower dependency ratio.

A 1:1 ratio (or almost 1:1) between the employable and unemployable age groups can be found in practically all sub-Saharan countries and in many Asian and Latin American developing countries. If the high rates of unemployment and underemployment are also taken into account, the actual burden of dependency on the gainfully employed age groups is even higher. A further complicating factor in many countries, particularly in sub-Saharan Africa, is that the agricultural sector has also not been in a position to create a sufficient number of jobs over the past few years.[89]

This not only creates a greater burden of dependency within the affected families, it also has undesirable effects on the national economy. In developing countries, two to three persons in the employable age group support one schoolchild; in industrial countries, the figure is 4.1 adults—and this at a considerably lower level of unemployment.[90] The higher consumer expenses for a family due to higher dependency ratios reduce its capacity to save as well as its ability to form capital and invest.[91] It is difficult to calculate the precise effect on life savings. Since it can be assumed that children are to a certain degree a substitute for savings for old-age security, it can be argued that children are simply a different type of savings capital and that this must be offset against reduced monetary savings. Such calculations would be very complicated in terms of methodology. If, however, the effects of reduced possibilities for savings at the family level are added together for the entire national economy, this substantially reduces the savings and investment capacities at the aggregate level.[92]

The probability that the decades ahead will be marked by an unprecedented high number of people without productive employment is very high, notes UNFPA: "With 36 per cent of the population under 15 years of age, the labor force in the developing world will grow by 38 million a year during the 1990s. In Mexico alone, a million people enter the workforce annually. In the United States, with a population almost three times greater and an economy almost 30 times larger, the annual addition is only 2 million. Additions to the labor force in developing countries, 732 million over the next 20 years, will exceed the entire 1990 labor force of the industrialized countries of 686 million."[93]

If the adequate amount of capital for investment cannot be saved locally or brought into the countries concerned by foreign aid or private investment, the outlook is bleak: rising social and political turbulence and persistent inequalities will be a further obstacle to any economic development.

Strengthening of Income Inequalities

A broadly based study by the World Bank documented a measurable relationship between population growth rate and the percentage of total income that the lowest 40 percent of income earners can amass: the higher the population growth rate, the lower the income share of the lower classes.[94] Because more and more workers face a job market that has only a limited capacity to absorb them, they depress the wage level. At the same time, interest rates are increasing—for example, in the form of higher land prices or farming rents—due to the increasing shortage of capital. And this in spite of the fact that pressures on wage levels—particularly among the lowest-income groups—are highly undesirable from a development policy point of view.[95]

Because development policy thinking is always permeated by value judgments, any evaluation of growing income inequality is subject to debate. Some development policymakers no doubt see positive aspects in an increasingly unequal distribution of income. They reason that the higher income earners have a higher rate of saving and that these resources are then used for investments in job creation, which in turn will lead to higher employment and therefore, in a second phase, increasing incomes.[96] In our judgment, experiences in development policy over the past 40 years do not support such a positive evaluation of increasing income inequalities.

The frequent flight of capital and the conspicuous consumption of luxury goods by the higher income earners were more common in many countries than reinvestments of profits and the investment of savings in domestic labor-intensive facilities. In spite of high levels of economic growth in the sixties and seventies, more than 1 billion people failed to benefit enough to satisfy their basic needs on a consistent basis. For this reason, the fact that the various effects of high population growth tend to solidify and strengthen existing income inequalities is something that must be viewed as inhibiting development.

Even from the point of view of actual population policy, a worsening of income distribution is counterproductive. There are several indicators that a high degree of fair income distribution is just as important for achieving a reduction in birth rates as the level of per capita income. The examples of Sri Lanka and China (to a lesser extent) verify the significance of income distribution considerations in population policy.[97]

Deterioration of Food Security

Famines have always been part of human history—not only in the developing world, but also in Europe. The Irish Famine is probably the most well known one in modern times, but it was actually only one of many that afflicted Europe well into the Modern Age. Devastating famines that killed millions of people hit Russia (in 1918–1921 and 1932–1934; 5–10 million victims), China (in 1920–1921; approximately 4 million victims), West Bengal (in 1934; 2–4 million victims), and Africa (three famines in the seventies and the eighties, primarily in the countries in the Sahel zone; 2–3 million victims). Paul Ehrlich and his colleagues point out that 200 million or more people have starved to death or died of hunger-related disease in the past two decades, and as many as a billion people are chronically undernourished today, about half of them seriously so.[98] In several major developing regions, including Africa and Latin America, the numbers of hungry people have continued to increase, despite the impressive gains in food production. In 1992, hundreds of thousands died due to food shortages caused by civil wars (for example, in Somalia).[99]

Famines of a spectacular nature represent only the tip of the iceberg, however. In areas where there is no food security, minor influences—a shortfall of rain or a crop yield reduced by a pest—are enough to unleash a catastrophe. Social and political conflicts in the context of chronic food shortages exact an especially gruesome toll because those who become victims of the resulting famine must be added to those who lose their lives in the actual conflict.

To attribute the precarious food situation in many developing countries to rapid population growth alone would be an overly simple explanation. Other important factors include poor natural production conditions, low productivity, and low income—as well as inappropriate institutional, economic, and political conditions (such as unfavorable landownership structures and inequitable access to information, inputs, and farm credit) that determine the extent to which the productive potential can be realized. It is the interrelationship of all these factors—social, political, economic, and environmental—that does not allow any stability of food supply. Rapid population growth does, however, have an undesirable influence on all the factors that stand in the way of nutritional security, as a discussion of purchasing power levels and production levels illustates. (See Figure IV-2.)

The Level of Purchasing Power.   People who have enough money will not starve because they can simply buy the food they need. This principle applies to individuals as well as to entire countries. Because the financial capacity of countries depends, among other things, on the relative prices of their exports (terms of trade), the amount of their debt and debt servicing obligations, and the level of energy prices, general international economic conditions play an important role. Export-strong countries such as Singapore or Hong Kong, where there is virtually no agricultural activity, have sufficient food because they can import it.

Within individual countries, the general level of purchasing power, expressed in terms of average per capita income, is not the only relevant indica-

Figure IV-2

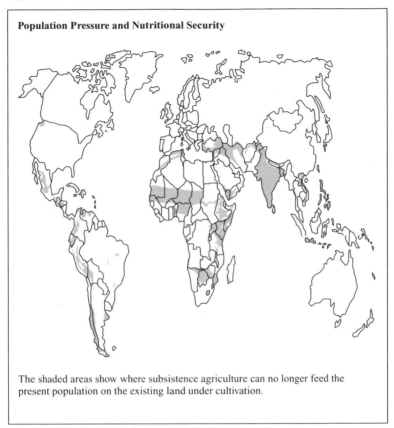

Population Pressure and Nutritional Security

The shaded areas show where subsistence agriculture can no longer feed the present population on the existing land under cultivation.

Source: UNFPA: The State of World Population 1988. New York 1988.

tor: the income distribution structure is of great importance too. Just as in the world economy, the great wealth of a few and the acute poverty of broad masses coexist in various developing countries. Therefore the central goal of any development policy must be to ensure that the minimum purchasing power of lower-income groups allows them to meet their basic needs.

Production Level.   All in all, there is enough food produced in the world so that no one would have to go hungry, much less starve. Still, the problem cannot simply be solved by redistributing all the food from surplus countries to deficit ones because this would cause too many countries to become dependent on others for their food supply, which is not reasonable for several reasons.

The national economies of most developing countries are based either entirely or primarily on agriculture. The majority of the population traditionally is rural. Few income-producing employment opportunities exist outside the agricultural sector. In addition, the work of farmers not only produces employment and income for them, it also creates employment in the processing industry, conserves the environment, and protects against erosion (provided sustainable agricultural techniques are employed).

Food aid and imports undermine a country's own agricultural performance and weaken the budget of the national economy. Due to the current debt level in food-deficient countries, fewer and fewer financial resources are available to import food. A rise in food prices as a result of increased demand from the countries of the former East Bloc also poses a risk for poor countries in the South. At present, worldwide emergency food supplies are already at a lower level than they were only 10 years ago.[100] In addition, climatic irregularities over the past years have led to substantial yield losses even in countries that usually have a surplus. The greenhouse effect could lead to further drastic yield reductions.

The low production levels of countries with a food deficit have a variety of causes. Agroecological factors such as soil fertility, climate, length of the growing season, and so on all influence agricultural productivity to a high degree. But the technology that is used and the availability of yield-enhancing inputs (such as adapted seed varieties, fertilizers, plant protection) and irrigation also determine to what extent the agroecological influences can be balanced. In the end, price policies for agricultural products, the quality of agricultural development policy, and the planting structure (that is, the planting of food for self-sufficiency versus for export) either increase or decrease a country's potential for self-sufficiency.

A minimum level of food security can be achieved through appropriate rural development and agricultural policies in spite of limited resources and poor climatic conditions. By the same token, poor agricultural policies and the absence of social reforms can lead to insufficient food security for lower-income groups in spite of fertile soils and sufficient levels of precipitation. A comparison of the experiences of India or Bangladesh with those of Ethiopia, Mozambique, or Chad provide ample evidence of this.[101]

Dietary structures are also important. Recent world harvests, if equitably distributed and if grain is not diverted to feeding livestock, could supply a vegetarian diet to about 6 billion people.[102] But diets of the sort eaten by many people in affluent countries (with about 30 percent of calories from animal sources) could be supplied to less than half the current world population.

Where people have no choice but to produce food on marginal soils with primitive technology and without adequate advice, food supply barely suffices for survival even in "normal times." Larger warehouses to store food for harder times cannot be built; individual savings and public resources are inadequate to finance substantial improvements to the infrastructure, such as the terracing of mountain slopes or the construction of supply roads. If, in addition, it does not rain at all or rain does not fall at the usual time or in the required amounts, or if pests such as grasshoppers destroy the harvest or political turmoil disturbs the normal agricultural cycle, dramatic shortages can develop within a very short period of time. In countries where the distribution of income and access to the means of production are determined by unjust social and political power structures, no food security can be achieved.

Even if measures to counteract all these limiting factors for agriculture were introduced, overly rapid population growth can in many cases jeopardize the attainment of the goal of food security. To increase food production it would be necessary either to expand agricultural areas or to intensify farming, but this is increasingly difficult in several regions of the developing world. Environmental damage due to population growth pressures has already become a considerable problem. Segments of the rural population in sub-Saharan Africa, for example—people who were once self-sufficient—suddenly found themselves unable to provide their families with enough food as a result of the overuse of their soils. The consequence has been a mass migration to the cities, which in turn has created new food supply problems—problems that can usually only be solved by importing food.

Countries such as Egypt that were traditionally food exporters now have to import up to 60 percent of their food due to rapidly increasing populations and ecological bottlenecks, but also due to an inappropriate agricultural policy.[103] Although food imports from countries that produce surpluses due to highly productive farming techniques, favorable climate conditions, and fertile soils has helped contain acute famines, it has not prevented chronic malnutrition.

FAO estimated that it will be necessary to double agricultural production (not only food production) by the year 2000 in order to meet the needs of growing populations. But the agency added that this would require a virtual "agricultural revolution" through massive investments in new technologies and inputs as well as an increased awareness of the necessity to preserve resources.[104] Even then, 260 million people would still live in a state of serious malnutrition. Rapidly growing populations in countries with weak agricultural and economic performance in general can expect a considerable worsening of their nutritional status. All projections regarding the food situation in developing countries agree on this point—even those that do not take into account the additional problems that will arise due to the increasing environmental constraints (losses of farmland, erosion, limited water resources, declining genetic diversity, and so on).

Thus, according to Ehrlich and his colleagues, "complacency about the security and abundance of the world food supply even in the near future, moreover, is unjustified, especially if the environmental dimensions of the agricultural enterprise are carefully considered. Indeed, the expansion of global grain production (the basis of the human food supply), which kept well ahead of population growth between 1950 and 1985, has failed to do so since then. The 1990 harvest, the largest in history, was lower on a per capita basis than that of 1984."[105]

They conclude their analysis in a rather alarming way:

> Were society to concentrate its efforts on improving agricultural production and distribution systems worldwide, substantially more food could be grown than is grown today—for a while. It is doubtful, however, whether food security could be achieved indefinitely for a global population of 10 or 12 billion people. Rather, it seems likely that a sustainable population, one comfortably below Earth's nutritional carrying capacity, will number far fewer than today's 5.5 billion people; how many fewer will depend in part on how seriously Earth's carrying capacity will have been degraded in the process of supporting the population overshoot. Moreover, we are convinced that 10 billion people cannot be nourished even temporarily unless far greater attention and resources are directed to developing a more productive, environmentally sound agriculture and to improving food distribution.[106]

Global and Regional Burdens on the Environment

As discussed earlier in this book, a certain level of population growth is not necessarily or automatically relevant to the economic, social, or ecological situation of a country. The "population factor" is just one influencing factor among many. It only becomes relevant in interaction with the state of economic development (and therefore the per capita income), the quality of the development policy pursued in the respective country (and therefore also the social, economic, and political conditions), the supply of natural resources, the state of technology (and its ecological efficiency), and given cultural conditions.[107]

The findings of the Brundtland Commission on the subject of sustainable development also hold true here, namely that there are "limitations imposed by the present state of technology and social organization on environmental resources and by the ability of the biosphere to absorb the effects of human activities."[108] Even if the technical and social limitations can be extended through corresponding developments, the need to slow population growth remains because of its undesirable ecological effects independent of the respective state of economic, social, and technical developments.

Global environmental burdens are influenced by three factors:

- income, consumption style, and behavior patterns, as well as the societal framework and the quality of governance;
- state of technology, because this determines the environmental impact of a consumption or production unit and therefore also the extent to which human activity either damages or preserves the environment; and
- population size, as a multiplying factor, which determines the total impact on the environment.[109]

Robert McNamara expressed this relationship as Ed = P × C × D, meaning that environmental damage (Ed) ensues from population number (P) multiplied by the consumption unit per capita (C) multiplied by the environmental damage per unit of consumption (D).[110]

This implies that large populations with low levels of consumption as well as small populations with high levels of consumption can cause environmental damage. As noted in Part I, the group that is clearly much more destructive in ecological terms is the wealthiest billion people. The top consumers and waste producers live in North America, Europe, and the rich countries of Asia, and they break all records of putting pressure on the absorption and regeneration capacity of the global environment. The present condition of the earth and its atmosphere is to a considerable extent a result of the industrial development in today's wealthy countries and of the consumption and waste-producing habits of those who live there.

Serious population policy discussions must take into account these historical facts. The finite nature of global resources cannot be introduced by the North as an argument against population growth in the South as long as the current consumption patterns of people in industrial countries are maintained. Only if and when the North changes its wasteful life-style will the environmental burden be eased enough for the South to develop economically. This in turn will create the local resources to finance the social development that is the precondition of lower birth rates, which will help ease the global environmental burden.

The equation about environmental damage also shows the significance of the state of technology in developing and industrial countries, because the environmental damage per consumption unit depends greatly on the production and waste management technologies used. Therefore, appropriate technical progress must be viewed as an important outlet for reducing or avoiding environmental damage.[111] A consistent transfer to developing countries of technologies known to be ecologically efficient could reduce environmental damage caused by industrialization efforts using outdated technologies. Poverty is often the reason environmentally friendlier technologies and methods available from industrial countries are not imported.

The U.N. Population Fund, which uses a similar equation in its arguments,[112] arrives at the same conclusion: "For any given type of technology, for any given level of consumption or waste, for any given level of poverty or inequality, the more people there are, the greater is the impact on the environment."[113]

Changes in the Earth's Atmosphere and the Greenhouse Effect

According to the information available today, the most significant and potentially far-reaching global environmental threat lies in the changing of the earth's atmosphere and its major consequence, global warming.[114] A natural "greenhouse effect" has always existed—caused by water vapor and the greenhouse gases: carbon dioxide (CO_2), ozone, nitrous oxide, methane, and chlorofluorocarbons (CFCs).

Life on earth as we know it would not be possible without this natural greenhouse effect, which keeps the current average temperature at ground level at approximately +15 degrees Celsius instead of a life-threatening −18 degrees.[115] The industrialization of the past 100 years and other human activities have led to a strong increase in the concentration of greenhouse gases, particularly carbon dioxide, methane, and ozone, in the earth's atmosphere. This additional human-made greenhouse effect considerably increases the natural one. (See Figures IV-3 and IV-4.)

The Enquete Commission of the 11th German Bundestag describes the consequences of this human-induced greenhouse effect:

> The increase in the average global temperature by 0.5° C over the past ten years, as well as the rise in the sea level by 10–20 cm over the same period of time can probably be traced back to the additional greenhouse effect caused by humans. According to the current state of scientific knowledge, the global mean temperature will increase by approximately 5° C (most probable value, estimates vary between 3° and 9° C) over its pre-industrial value, if the emissions of greenhouse gases . . . and volatile chemical compounds . . . continue to increase at the current rate until the year 2100. By that time approximately 4° C of the expected 5° C warming will be realized, because the ocean delays the warming by several decades. The warming in about 100 years would be exactly as great as the warming since the last Ice Age over 18,000 years ago.[116]

Such an increase in the earth's temperature—irreversible for centuries—or even the smaller increase predicted by the Intergovernmental Panel on Climate Change in 1992[117] would have many serious effects, for example:

- a shifting of climate and vegetation zones;
- a rise in the sea level by 30–100 centimeters, with the result that coastal areas and islands would be flooded and people forced to move;

Figure IV-3

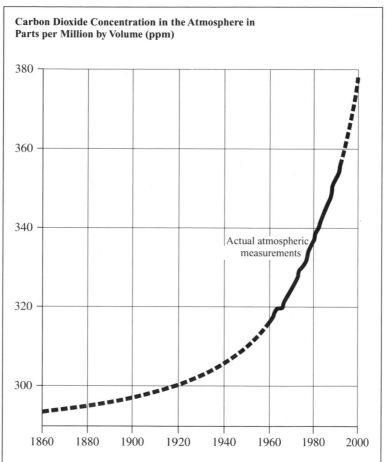

**Carbon Dioxide Concentration in the Atmosphere in
Parts per Million by Volume (ppm)**

Actual atmospheric
measurements

The concentration of carbon dioxide in the atmosphere has risen from roughly
290 parts per million (ppm) in the last century to over 350 parts per million, and
it continues on its exponential growth path. The sources of the carbon dioxide
buildup are human fossil fuel burning and forest destruction. The possible
consequence is global climate change.

Source: D.H. Meadows, D.L. Meadows, and J. Randers: Beyond the Limits.
  Chelsea Green Publishing Company, Post Mills, Vermont 1992, p. 6.

Figure IV-4

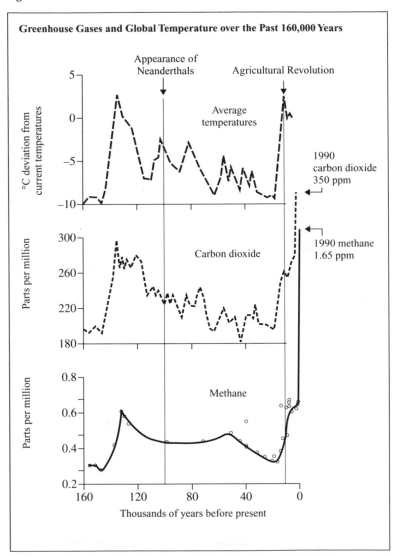

Greenhouse Gases and Global Temperature over the Past 160,000 Years

Source: D.H. Meadows, D.L. Meadows, and J. Randers: Beyond the Limits.
Chelsea Green Publishing Company, Post Mills, Vermont 1992, p. 98.

- widespread climate-induced destruction of forests at medium and higher latitudes (approximately 20 percent of the current surface area);
- reduction of water resources in many areas; and
- worsening of the food situation for large segments of the world due to droughts, floods, bad harvests, increased damage to agricultural crops, and so on.[118]

The human misery that would arise from these changes would be immeasurable—something that has been pointed out for several years.[119] Sixty percent of the world lives in coastal areas and 65 percent of all cities with a population of more than 2.5 million are coastal cities.[120]

With regard to the interdependence of shifting vegetation zones and food security, Ehrlich and his colleagues point out that

the shifts will not constitute a mere redealing of the climatic cards with some areas losing (becoming less productive) and others winning. Rather, if the flow of greenhouse gases into the atmosphere continues relatively unabated in the foreseeable future, agricultural systems will be faced with the stresses of continual adaptation to rapidly changing conditions. As in the case of ozone depletion, successful adaptation will require ample genetic variability and ample scientific talent, as well as flexible management. But even these will almost certainly not be sufficient to prevent serious drops in harvests in some places and at some times, beyond the drops that would occur in response to normal fluctuations in weather.[121]

The U.N. Population Fund describes the likely consequences of a sea level rise:

Deltas are unusually vulnerable to even a moderate amount of sea level rise. Yet these are precisely the areas that feature some of the densest human settlements and most intensive agriculture on Earth. Among such "severe risk" areas are the estuaries of the rivers Hwang Ho, Yangtze, Mekong, Chao Phraya, Salween, Irrawaddy, Indus, Tigris/Euphrates, Zambezi, Niger, Gambia, Senegal, Courantyne and Maruni (in the Guyanas), and La Plata. Given present populations and their growth rates, at least 100 million people would find themselves flooded out or suffering related troubles from periodic storm surges, coastal erosion, and saltwater intrusion into ground water aquifers. Furthermore, the newly created coastal zones would be more crowded than ever.

Still other communities could be threatened in low-lying coastal territories, notably the metropolises of Jakarta, Madras, Bombay, Karachi, Lagos and Rio de Janeiro. If only half of their projected populations eventually become displaced, that will add 40 million people to the refugee total. At the same time a number of developed-world cities will be threatened as well, notably Rotterdam, Venice, New York, Miami and New Orleans. But developed nations have the engineering skills and the finances to hold back the sea with massive dikes, after the manner of the Netherlands; or they could go some way toward moving their cities inland. Neither of these options is open to developing nations.

In broader terms, a one-metre rise in sea level would threaten almost 5 million square kilometres of coastal lands in total. While this is roughly equivalent to the United States west of the Mississippi River, it amounts to only 3 per cent of Earth's land surface. Yet it encompasses a full third of global croplands and is home to well over a billion people already, a figure projected to rise to over 2 billion within a few decades. In addition to areas mentioned above, affected coastal zones could generate another 50 million refugees. Today, 30 million Chinese live in coastal lands a mere half metre above sea level.[122]

The U.N. Environmental Programme lists 10 countries as being most threatened by a rise in the sea level. (See Table IV-4.)

According to various experts, an increase in global temperatures and the consequent reduction in precipitation as well as flooding of coastal areas could reduce the earth's agricultural land by up to one-third.[123] Tropical countries, such as those in the Sahel zone or on the Indian subcontinent—operating already at the limits of their capacity to feed their people—would be at a particular risk. Paul Ehrlich and Gretchen Daily warn of a greenhouse scenario where global grain harvests could be reduced so much that between 50 million and 400 million people could die of starvation.[124] Even those countries that now produce the majority of surpluses for export to developing nations—the United States, Australia, and the European Community—can expect climate-induced reductions in their grain harvests. The economically measurable loss due to a temperature increase of only 2.5 degrees Celsius would amount to $60 billion a year for the United States alone.[125]

According to current knowledge, the greenhouse effect is accelerating for the following reasons:

- 50 percent of the increase is due to energy use, as a result of the emission of the greenhouse gases CO_2 (40 percent) and methane and ozone (10 percent) through the burning of fossil fuels such as coal, petroleum, and natural gas, in the process of transformation (such as production of electricity and district heating) as well as in the energy end-use sectors (households, industry, and transportation);
- 20 percent from chemical products and their applications due to emissions of CFCs, halons, and other compounds that contribute to the depletion of the ozone layer in the stratosphere as well as to the greenhouse effect;
- 15 percent from the destruction of rain forests due to the emission of CO_2 (10 percent) and other greenhouse gases (5 percent) through the burning and the decomposition of the forests and increased soil emissions; and

Table IV-4

Countries Highly Vulnerable to a Sea Level Rise

Country	Population (millions, 1993)	Per Capita Income (U.S. dollars, 1991)
Egypt	58.3	610
Bangladesh	113.9	220
Gambia	0.9	340
Indonesia	187.6	610
Maldives	0.2	450
Mozambique	15.3	80
Pakistan	122.4	400
Senegal	7.9	720
Surinam	0.4	3,350
Thailand	57.2	1,570

Sources: UNEP Country List: Criteria for Assessing Vulnerability to Sea-Level Rise. A Global Inventory to High Risk Areas. Delft 1989. Population numbers from the Population Reference Bureau: 1992 World Population Data Sheet. Washington, D.C. 1992. Per capita income (GNP per capita) from World Bank: World Development Report 1993. Oxford University Press, New York 1993, except for Gambia, Maldives, and Surinam, which are from UNDP: Human Development Report 1993. Oxford University Press, New York 1993.

- 15 percent from agriculture and other human activities, above all through methane due to cattle raising, wet rice cultivation, and fertilization but also, for example, from landfills.[126]

Even though these are only approximate values with considerable uncertainties, they do indicate the areas in which solutions must be sought in order to avoid future global catastrophes. Analysis of the greenhouse effect—no matter how incomplete it may be on the basis of current knowledge—shows that two population groups on this planet play a major role in damage done to the environment: the world's wealthiest and its poorest billion people.

Every growing population consumes energy and nonrenewable resources to an increasing degree. But not all people consume the same amount, because the economic and technical development level of a country as well as country-specific behavior patterns lead to considerable differences: every individual in industrial countries consumes, on average, as much commercial energy as approximately 10 people in the developing world.[127] For this reason, the approximately 1.2 billion people living in industrial countries[128] use 2.8 times as much commercial energy as the approximately 4.3 billion people living in economically underdeveloped countries.

The fact that rapid population growth in developing nations is responsible for only a very small degree of current global environmental problems can be clearly shown in terms of the emissions that change the atmosphere—CO_2, CFCs, halon, and nitrous oxide. The industrial countries, which account for slightly more than 25 percent of the world population, are responsible for some 80 percent of CO_2 emissions. (See Table IV-5.) The so-called Third World, where more than 75 percent of all people live today, by contrast account for only 20 percent of these emissions.[129]

Emissions have accelerated tremendously during the past 50 years, notes the World Resources Institute: "Worldwide consumption of fossil fuels in the period 1860 to 1949 is estimated to have released 187 billion metric tons of CO_2. In the past four decades, fossil fuel use has accelerated and CO_2 emissions in the period 1950–89 totalled an additional 559 billion metric tons."[130]

Per capita emissions of carbon dioxide reached a level of 19.7 tons in the United States in 1989 and 10.5 tons in Germany, while remaining at 0.11 tons per capita in Bangladesh and 0.77 tons in India.[131] This means that Germany—with a population of 80 million—emitted more CO_2 in absolute terms than India with its almost 900 million inhabitants. And that 255 million Americans emitted 7.5 times more CO_2 (4,870 million tons) than all of Africa, with its 650 million people (647 million tons), and more than twice as much as the almost 1.2 billion inhabitants of China.[132] Seven million Swiss emitted 2.8 times as much CO_2 as the 111 million inhabitants of Bangladesh. Similar comparisons can be made between all other industrial countries and all other developing ones.

The enormous potential for savings and environmental protection therefore lies with industrial countries—a savings potential that would allow poor countries to develop their economies and hence to continue increasing CO_2 emissions for many years without raising the global total. Varyingly high levels of CO_2 emissions should by no means be equated with varyingly high standards of living. Technical standards, criteria for efficiency, and behavior patterns play a large role. Switzerland's per capita emissions of slightly below 6 tons of CO_2 per year are less than a third of the U.S. emissions of 16.7 tons. The standard of living in Switzerland, however—according to UNDP's Human Development Index—is actually slightly higher than in the United States.[133]

The differences are even more pronounced for other greenhouse gases. At a level of 130,000 tons in 1989, the United States emitted more than eight times as much CFCs as all of Africa. The Federal Republic of Germany emits 27,000 tons of CFCs, more than twice as much as the People's Republic of China.[134] It should be added, however, that as a result of the Montreal Protocol and the more stringent conditions for implementation set in London in 1990, the threat from production and use of CFCs in industrial countries is smaller in relative terms. (This international agreement stemmed from CFCs' ability to degrade the earth's protective ozone layer, not their role as a greenhouse gas.

Table IV-5

Carbon Dioxide Emissions of Various Countries from Industrial Processes in 1989

Land/Region	Carbon Dioxide Emissions		Population, 1992 (millions)
	Per Capita (tons)	Absolute (1,000 tons)	
Africa	1.03	647,352	654
Burkina Faso	0.07	520	10
Ivory Coast	0.66	7,595	13
Kenya	0.22	5,192	26
Nigeria	0.77	79,263	90
South America	1.91	557,298	300
Argentina	3.70	118,157	33
Brazil	1.39	206,957	151
Bolivia	0.77	5,064	8
Asia	1.93	5,812,064	3,207
Afghanistan	0.40	6,273	17
Bangladesh	0.11	14,114	111
People's Republic of China	2.16	2,388,613	1,167
India	0.77	651,936	883
Japan	8.46	1,040,554	124
Europe	8.74	4,347,794	511
France	6.38	357,163	57
Federal Republic of Germany (former)	10.48	641,398	80
Switzerland	5.94	39,326	7
Soviet Union (former)	13.26	3,804,001	284
United States	19.68	4,869,005	256

Source: World Resources Institute: World Resources 1992–93. Oxford University Press, New York 1992, Table 24.1, p. 346 f.

The negative health consequences of a thinner ozone layer [skin cancer, eye diseases] and the undesirable effects on plant and animal life are well known today.)

UNFPA reports that China intends to increase significantly its stock of refrigerators, presumably using CFCs:

> To date only one Chinese household in 10 possesses a refrigerator. The government plans a nation-wide effort to increase the proportion, along the lines of the Beijing experience during the 1980s where the proportion soared from less than 3 per cent to more than 60 per cent. China has built 12 CFC production plants in

order to accommodate the refrigerator needs of many more of today's 250 million households. The government has been planning that by the year 2000 the nation would expand CFC production 10-fold, which would still leave per capita output at only one fifth that of the United States. But China's vast human numbers—1.16 billion today, growing by 17 million a year—make the CFC impact a critically determining factor.[135]

India plans to provide 300 million refrigerators by early next century, according to Indian press reports. Fortunately, however, both India and China recently signed the Montreal and Helsinki initiatives to reduce CFC production.[136]

The situation is different only for methane, because—in addition to waste production and the production of coal, oil, and natural gas—agriculture (wet rice fields and cattle raising) emits large amounts of methane. Yet with methane emissions of 37 million tons, the United States lies ahead of all of Africa, with 19 million tons. Nigeria's methane emissions, by contrast, amount to 3.7 million tons (mainly from oil production), compared with Germany's 3.6 million tons. Argentina emits 3.8 million tons as a result of cattle raising alone, 1.5 times as much as all of France (2.6 million tons). Brazil's cattle herds emit 8.8 million tons of methane gas per year. Asia's rice fields emit 67 million tons, 2.5 times as much as all of Europe.[137]

The extent of future CO_2 emissions caused by population growth is likely to be large—even when compared with all the other "sins" of industrial countries—and, therefore, considered to be a global threat. Adding all the greenhouse gases together—as the World Resources Institute did—provides a greenhouse index indicating every country's contribution to global warming during a given year; five developing countries are already among the top 10 contributors today.[138] (See Figure IV-5.)

It is striking that the developing countries that already figure high in the greenhouse index are heavily populated nations. Even though their per capita emissions of greenhouse gases are very low compared with those of industrial countries and even though they are not among the top 50 countries in that respect, they appear among the front ranks in terms of total emissions due to their large populations.

If developing countries' CO_2 emissions alone were to increase as a result of anticipated developments in industry and transportation over the next 35 years at the same rate they increased during the past 40 years—in other words, if per capita emissions more than double[139]—a population growth of approximately 3 billion people would produce an additional CO_2 burden of nearly 10 billion tons. Increases in developing countries' CO_2 emissions are to be expected as a result of growth in the number of motor vehicles, in agricultural and industrial production, and in energy production.

Figure IV-5

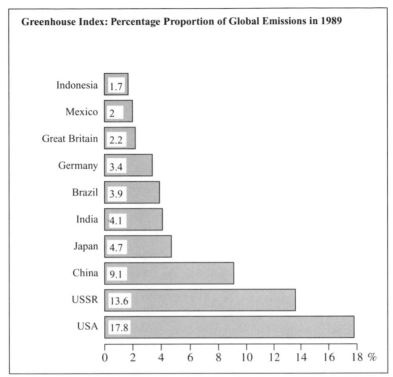

Greenhouse Index: Percentage Proportion of Global Emissions in 1989

Indonesia	1.7
Mexico	2
Great Britain	2.2
Germany	3.4
Brazil	3.9
India	4.1
Japan	4.7
China	9.1
USSR	13.6
USA	17.8

Source: World Resources Institute (ed.): World Resources 1992–93.
A Guide to the Global Environment. Washington, D.C. 1992.

Even if countries such as China or India do not aspire to individual transportation patterns comparable to those in industrial countries today, the number of automobiles in heavily populated developing countries will increase. If the ratio of bicycles to cars in China, which was measured to be 250:1, matched just the current ratio in India (30:1), there would be an additional 8.8 million cars in China. (See Table IV-6.)

Assuming that it will be necessary to intensify agriculture in order to feed increasing numbers of people, the CO_2 burden will increase an estimated 25 percent.[140] The population-induced increase of CO_2 emissions corresponds to roughly half the total emissions today.

Finally, assuming that improvements in the standard of living of people in the most heavily populated countries will be more than modest—which is of course to be hoped—then energy consumption and thus the CO_2 burden will

Table IV-6

Bicycles and Automobiles in Selected Countries, 1985

Country	Bicycles (millions)	Automobiles (millions)	Ratio of Bicycles to Cars
China	300.0	1.2	250.0:1
India	45.0	1.5	30.0:1
Egypt	1.5	0.5	3.0:1
Mexico	12.0	4.8	2.5:1
Tanzania	0.5	0.5	1.0:1
Holland	11.0	4.9	2.2:1
Germany[a]	45.0	26.0	1.7:1

Source: L.R. Brown et al.: State of the World 1990. W.W. Norton & Co., New York 1990, p. 121.
[a]According to more recent statistics, there are over 40 million cars in united Germany.

increase considerably, with all the ecological consequences.[141] The U.N. Population Fund shows the example of India and its electricity needs:

> With a current per capita income of only U.S. $330 a year—about one-sixtieth that of the United States—India's electricity capacity today is only 55,000 megawatts, about twice that of New York State. Although the country possesses meagre coal reserves, it is exploiting them so fast that it now ranks as the world's fourth largest coal burner. In 1950, its coal use was only 33 million tonnes but, by 1989, it had soared to 191 million tonnes. At the same time, production of crude oil, another fossil fuel, rose from 0.3 million tonnes to 30.4 million tonnes; and total power generation increased from 5 billion kilowatt hours to 217 billion kilowatt hours. The government plans a number of energy based initiatives for development; for instance, to supply electricity to half the houses in the country. This goal alone will require the production of an additional 80,000 megawatts of power, compared with the present total capacity of 55,000 megawatts. It is anticipated that this measure, together with other development plans, will shortly induce a doubling of India's carbon emissions.[142]

The three-quarters of the world's population living in developing countries today produce approximately one-third of the world's CO_2 emissions. By the year 2025, they will comprise four-fifths of the world population and will produce an estimated two-thirds of a much greater total amount. A reduction in population growth would have much farther reaching advantages with respect to methane, a potent greenhouse gas, particularly because wet rice fields and cattle herds—two significant sources of food in the developing countries—are responsible for half the methane emissions produced by humans. The Intergovernmental Panel on Climate Change projects a 45-percent increase in meat and milk production by the year 2025, accompanied by a parallel increase in methane emissions.[143]

One important reason why there is no reaction or only belated or slow reaction to global threats such as climate change is that the deterioration process is an insidious one and the signals often incomplete and contradictory. It therefore becomes possible to ignore, suppress, or deny them without any direct consequences. The inertia of the systems with which we are dealing here, however, is very dangerous. Once we all finally understand the seriousness of the situation and are forced to change our course abruptly under the pressure of the problems, we could suffer the same fate as the Titanic: the first warning signals were consistently ignored over a long period of time. But once the iceberg came into sight and the machines were prepared for a turnabout, the catastrophe could no longer be averted because the ship could not carry out the rapid change in course due to its large turning circle.

Three decades ago, K. William Kapp warned against the attitude that "the future will take care of itself" and against the expectation that research and technology would automatically find new energy sources for us.[144] Hopes expressed by renowned scientists in the sixties for the year 2000 with respect to energy production (such as through fusion power plants), cures for diseases (cancer, for example), or even the eradication of world hunger have proved to be unrealistic. In light of the immense potential problems that will arise if the fostered hopes for technical solutions are not fulfilled, it would be more responsible, at least for the time being, to assume the worst and to make corresponding and more responsible plans for the future.[145]

To our knowledge, there is still no full scientific evidence for a long-term global climate change. What is certain, however, is that mean global temperatures have risen since 1880 and that all the warmest years in this century were recorded in the eighties. It is also certain that during the past 160,000 years the concentrations of CO_2 and methane in the atmosphere were never nearly as high as they are today.[146] Linking these two facts together, it would be wise advice to apply the "precautionary approach," as the Rio Declaration on Environment and Development urged in Principle 15: "Where there are threats of serious or irreversible damage, lack of full scientific certainty shall not be used as a reason for postponing cost-effective measures to prevent environmental degradation."[147]

Excessive Exploitation of Nonrenewable Resources

Rapid population growth combined with the efforts of poor countries to raise their standards of living results in increasing demand for raw materials. Renewable resources such as biomass (firewood, and agricultural and animal products), solar, wind, and water energy as well as geothermal energy do exist.

But today there is widespread agreement that renewable raw materials—particularly renewable sources of energy—have by no means been given the political priority they deserve. The suboptimal use of renewable resources exacerbates a problem that has been recognized for nearly half a century: the overuse of nonrenewable resources, with its negative consequences for future generations.[148]

Most of the raw materials that made our industrialization possible are nonrenewable. They are not only the fossil fuels (coal, oil, natural gas), but also important metals and ores such as iron, copper, nickel, cadmium, lead, tin, zinc, tungsten, manganese, cobalt, uranium, and molybdenum. The lion's share of these limited, nonrenewable resources has always been consumed in industrial countries.[149] It was they who plundered the existing reserves beyond all measures, and it would thus be unfair to try to blame the foreseeable shortages of nonrenewable resources on population growth in developing countries. Not only our current prosperity in the industrial countries but also the future development opportunities of the so-called Third World depend heavily on the availability of such resources.

Population growth in developing countries will, nevertheless, lead to an increased demand for resources, even if these people remain at their current low standard of living. The demand will become even greater the more the standard of living improves—as it should, and as it already has for more than 4 billion people in developing countries. Whereas the consumption of these resources can be reduced with economizing measures and through recycling, and although improved technologies will help discover new deposits, the principal problem of the finiteness of these deposits still remains.

Julian Simon, for example, counters the argument that nonrenewable resources will be exhausted through population growth by saying that prices will increase as these goods become scarcer, which will not only lead to a decrease in consumption and demand but will also stimulate the search for substitutes and thereby also stimulate technical progress.[150] He views innovations triggered by shortages as the solution—albeit short-term, as he himself admits—to this difficult situation.

In principle, this argument makes sense, but it must be seen in context. First of all, the current prices of important resources do not nearly reflect all social costs, such as those that will arise for future generations due to shortages or even the absence of these resources. The consolation that shortages will lead to substitutions by way of higher prices may in terms of practical consequences be relevant for industrial countries, with their great potential for research and development. But poor countries, such as those in sub-Saharan Africa, may just be hit by the higher costs and slowed down in their development. They do not have access either today or in the foreseeable future to the capital or accumulated knowledge needed for the research and development of substitutes for goods in short supply. For industrial countries that would be in a position to develop alternatives to resources in short supply, new competitive advantages over developing nations and new dependencies would be created once again in this way.

Destruction of Fertile Soils

Between 7 million and 9 million hectares of arable land—the estimates vary—are destroyed every year as a result of erosion, flooding, salinization, or overuse. A further 200,000 square kilometers lose practically their entire productivity.[151] FAO fears that some 544 million hectares—18 percent of the arable land in the world—could be lost forever if no measures are taken to preserve them.[152] Some estimates suggest that "globally some 24 billion tons of soil are lost annually in excess of the natural rate of soil regeneration, and it has been estimated that the remaining topsoil on Earth's cropland is being lost at an average rate of 7 percent per decade. Even if this estimate were several times too high, current agricultural practices would still be unsustainable in the long term."[153] In areas where soils are not being directly destroyed, the fertility will decline if current patterns of use are continued.

As a result of erosion alone—that is, the removal of the top layer of soil and its organic components through water and wind—29 percent of the food production in rainfed fields is threatened. Soil erosion caused by water is one of the most serious problems in the tropics and takes on a magnitude in many places that can no longer be offset by soil regeneration measures. India loses 16.35 tons of soil substance per hectare a year in this manner, and only 4.5–11.2 tons can be regenerated using appropriate cultivation measures. Sixty-one percent of the eroded materials are deposited elsewhere, 10 percent remain in reservoirs (reducing dam capacities by 1–2 percent annually), and 29 percent (1.5 billion tons a year) are lost forever to the ocean.[154] The U.N. Population Fund points out that "unchecked soil erosion could well cause a decline of 19 to 29 per cent in food production from rainfed croplands during the 25 years from 1985 to 2010."[155]

Erosion can be expected particularly in areas where marginal land is being farmed (on slopes, for instance), where soil is exposed without protection to wind and water (perhaps as a result of cleared forests or the removal of bushes and hedges), and where soils are used beyond their regeneration capacity. The associated losses in productivity are substantial; the reduced capacity of the soil to absorb water and thereby to prevent downstream flooding is enormous.

The overuse of agricultural production areas is a consequence of various factors, one of which is poverty. Impoverished peasants cannot afford the conservation measures needed to protect the soil. Another factor is growing population pressure. The situation in the Sahel zone, where an increased number of people must expand food production to areas suitable only for extensive cattle raising, which in turn forces the cattle farmers to move to areas unsuitable for cattle, is a problem that has been discussed elsewhere in detail.[156]

Various experts on population and environment, such as UNFPA, use the example of Java to portray the consequences of the overuse of agricultural land:

> The population has surged from 51 million in 1950 to 112 million today; 62 per cent of the nation's total population is now located on 8 per cent of its national territory. This rapid buildup in human numbers has served to aggravate soil erosion. In 44,000 square kilometres of upland farming areas, the population density has reached a level of 700 to 900 persons per square kilometre, even 2,000 persons or more in some localities, while the average land holding has declined to a mere 0.7 of a hectare. One third of these upland areas are seriously eroding, and more than 10,000 square kilometres of grainlands have been degraded to the point they no longer support even subsistence farming. This threatens the livelihood of 12 million people, many of whom live in absolute poverty and have no means to engage in soil-conservation practices.[157]

The area of Nepal that borders on India is confronted by similar problems: there, too, continuing population pressure has forced people to use steeper areas for agricultural purposes. In some cases the cultivation of mountain slopes becomes possible only after forests are cleared, which, in turn, causes further erosion. High population growth (2.5 percent in 1992) and existing inheritance laws have caused the average area of cultivation for one household to drop from three to four hectares in the sixties to approximately one hectare today. Already a third of the households are no longer in a position to live off of their own land.

Desertification—or the transformation of agricultural land in semiarid and arid regions into noncultivable land due to overuse by humans—is an even more severe form of land degradation. UNFPA estimates this process to be threatening 45 million square kilometers or a full third of the Earth's land surface—together with the livelihoods of at least 850 million people, of whom 135 million are coping with severe desertification. Already it eliminates 60,000 square kilometers of agricultural land each year, and impoverishes another 200,000 square kilometers, reducing yields and requiring costly remedial measures. The costs in terms of agricultural output forgone are estimated to be in the order of $30 billion a year. One of the main causes of desertification is overgrazing by domestic livestock.[158]

Lee Talbot uses the example of the Masai country in East Africa to illustrate the effects of high population growth on land resources and the introduction of desertification processes: for nomadic cattle farmers, increasing numbers lead to an increase in the size of the cattle herds, which in turn leads to the overuse of grazing areas and thereby to the gradual destruction of the basis for nomadic life.[159] The cattle farmers are forced to migrate onto farmland, which either leads directly to conflicts or forces the resident farmers to resort to lands not suitable for permanent cultivation. Both these options in turn create new burdens for the soils.[160]

Today, desertification processes have advanced everywhere that traditional, soil-preserving farming methods were abandoned due to increasing population pressures and where new methods were introduced that cannot be applied over sustained periods. Inappropriate agricultural policy, disregard for the needs of small farmers, and the absence of resource management and other factors have helped to bring about these problems, and this in regions that already were at a considerable disadvantage in terms of climate and natural conditions. Therefore, population policy measures alone cannot prevent the destruction of fertile soils. A slowing of population growth, however, could give countries a breather and could substantially aid development policy efforts of all kinds.

Destruction of Forests

The fact that the earth's forest reserves are dwindling is nothing new. It was documented in detail more than 10 years ago in the *Global 2000 Report to the President*.[161] But this warning did not help much—all over the world the destruction of forests has continued apace.

The causes are quite complex.[162] The kinds and sources of damage vary in significance from one country to another, and the speed with which destruction progresses depends on the social, economic, and political conditions that prevail in the respective countries (such as support of small farmers, the importance of agriculture for employment and national income, and issues of land reform). Among the most important causes are:

- shifting cultivation mainly or exclusively for subsistence;
- agroindustrial land use for cash crop (such as coffee or palm oil) or fodder (for instance, soybeans or corn);
- extensive animal husbandry, chiefly cattle;
- cutting firewood;
- lumbering; and
- clearing land for mining or power supply (dams).

Along with the damage to soils through overuse, the destruction of tropical forest areas is largely a direct result of growing population pressure and of the consequent need to expand agricultural land; UNFPA estimates set the figure at 79 percent.[163] In the Philippines, for example, the combination of population pressure and scarce land led to the deforestation and settlement of uplands with slopes as steep as 45 degrees. Extreme poverty, insecurity of tenure in their farmlands, and lack of agricultural extension services and credit institutions prevented the settlers from investing in soil conservation. The result has been devastating erosion and a growing water shortage.[164]

Ethiopia, one of the poorest countries in the world, faces the same problems. There, once-fertile plateau land is losing between 1.5 billion and 3.5 billion tons of humus per year.[165] In Kenya, population pressure on arable land and on forests has caused so much erosion that the "potential food output could eventually decline by as much as 50 per cent if soil loss cannot be reversed."[166]

In other regions of the developing world, different causes predominate. In Costa Rica, for example, the production of meat has turned forest areas into pastureland. In West Africa and Southeast Asia, projects of the wood industry are eating up the forest reserves. In Brazil, high unemployment and a widespread scarcity of agricultural land have provided the stimulus for clearing activities. For a growing number of people, deforestation offers the only—and the quickest—way of securing a livelihood.[167]

The frightening dimensions of contemporary forest destruction are indisputable. In the last 45 years, destruction of soil and forests has damaged approximately 11 percent of the earth's vegetation so seriously that the biological functions have been lost.[168] Today, less than half the original stands of tropical forest remain. The destruction of tropical rain forests causes special concern. According to the World Resources Institute, it progressed between 1981 and 1990 at an average rate of about 17 million hectares (about 42 million acres) a year, considerably faster than had been assumed.[169]

Wherever the population growth rate is particularly high (above 2.5 percent a year), wherever a large part of the population lives in absolute poverty, wherever unjust arrangements for landownership and leasehold are to be found or other structures hinder development, the destruction of forests takes on especially dramatic proportions. Here again, therefore, it is not just population growth that creates problems but its combination with other problems of underdevelopment.

The fact that areas that small farmers clear for subsistence can only be used for agricultural purposes for a very short time hastens the process of forest destruction. The fascinating variety of vegetation in tropical rain forests obscures the fact that their soils contain relatively little nourishment and that, as a result, there is a steep drop in yields after as little as two or three years. After that, new forest areas are cleared. If the cycles of rotation were long enough— that is, if the land were permitted to lie fallow for 35–100 years,[170] as was done in traditional patterns of shifting cultivation—then most of the negative consequences of clearance could be avoided. But under the pressure of growing populations, this has become impossible.

In many cases it is impossible to distinguish between clearing for lumber and clearing to obtain tillable agricultural land. Building roads through rain forests not only facilitates access for the felling of certain kinds of valuable wood, it eases the way for landless settlers to press forward and put large areas of virgin rain forest to agricultural use. The case of the Brazilian state of Rondônia has demonstrated that after the construction of a major road, the rate of clearing forest areas rises dramatically.[171]

The large-scale destruction of forests, especially tropical ones, has a number of serious ecological, social, and economic consequences.

Erosion.   One of the most serious consequences of destroying tropical forests, particularly rain forests, is soil erosion. In eroded areas, the process of desertification is able to run its course. A number of conditions related to climate, topography, composition of the soil, and nature of vegetation trigger natural erosion. The human action that intensifies erosion is generally the destruction of stabilizing vegetation.

Wind erosion produces its worst effects in arid and semiarid areas, such as those that have been deprived of their natural cover by overgrazing. More than 22 percent of the land in Africa north of the equator and 35 percent in the Near East is exposed to wind erosion. Under extreme conditions, up to 150 tons of soil can be carried away from a hectare of land in one hour.[172]

Soils on sloping land and in mountainous regions that lose their stabilizing cover of vegetation through improper agricultural methods are exposed to water erosion. Soil is washed away into rivers by precipitation (or glaciers) and accumulates there as silt, which, by raising the water level, causes flooding. Deforestation in the Himalayas, for example, causes a considerably larger runoff than the lower-lying areas in the valleys can accept without damage. The area of India hit by severe flooding has more than tripled since 1960.[173] Flooding was so bad in the fall of 1988 that two-thirds of Bangladesh was under water for several days and the rice crop, among others, suffered such big losses that substantial amounts of grain had to be imported.

Because of strong population pressure and inequitable land distribution, the humid tropics have the highest rate of soil erosion and the heaviest burden of river sedimentation in the world. In this connection, the Enquete Commission of the German Bundestag especially mentioned the Ambuklao and Binga Rivers in the Philippines and the Brahmaputra in India.[174] The Yangtze in China and the Ganges in India are said to carry off about 3 billion tons of soil a year.[175]

Climate Changes.   Tropical rain forests play an important role in regulating both regional climates and the global climate. They maintain the atmospheric balance by producing enormous quantities of oxygen and, through photosynthesis, consuming enormous amounts of carbon dioxide. Soils in temperate forest areas absorb 9.3 million tons of methane a year; those in tropical forests, four times less.[176]

According to Worldwatch Institute, the decline of tropical forests as "storage areas for greenhouse gases" is responsible for 20–30 percent of carbon emissions,[177] 38–42 percent of methane, and 25–30 percent of di-nitrogen monoxide.[178] The potential of these greenhouse gases for altering the atmosphere is well known.[179]

Because the destruction of forests by lumbering and also by the burning of biomass changes microclimates and hydrological cycles, food cycles can be influenced for decades or even centuries.[180] The result of excessive lumbering and burning of biomass is the loss of soil productivity, desertification, and the extinction of species.

Loss of Biological Diversity.   The extent of biological impoverishment all over the globe has been a source of great concern for many years.[181] If the present trend in destruction of biotopes continues, a quarter of all plant species, along with the fauna that depend on them, will disappear within the next century.[182] Human activities and the spread of human beings, as a result of population growth, into hitherto untouched ecosystems are the main reason for the reduction of the biological diversity.[183]

The total number of species on earth is not known. Only about 1.4 million species have been identified, but estimates of the total range from 5 million to 30 million.[184] Today, this natural variety is more threatened than at any time in the last 65 million years. While human beings only see the larger animals and plants and worry about their extinction, 95 percent of species are lost almost without being noticed. Their loss is regrettable for esthetic, ethical, philosophical, and ecological reasons.[185]

The loss of biodiversity is also deplorable from an economic standpoint since it involves the irrecoverable loss of genetic resources whose value for humans and nature has never even been determined. It is pure speculation whether tropical rain forests contain basic materials for decisive breakthroughs in the treatment of diseases that today are regarded as incurable. To date, less than a tenth of 1 percent of naturally occurring species have been used.[186]

The present state of our knowledge does not permit us to judge the indirect value of biodiversity emerging from the varied (and still largely unknown) reciprocal relationships between animals, plants, and micro-organisms as they affect various ecosystems.

According to various estimates, as much as 50–75 percent and perhaps even 90 percent of all species are native to tropical rain forests (which constitute only 7 percent of the earth's surface). Since these forests are currently being destroyed more rapidly than all other habitats on earth, the extinction of species is today greater than ever before in history—possibly one species per hour since the mid-eighties.[187] (See Table IV-7.) Of the 45,000 to 50,000 species of plants in tropical Asia alone, 300 disappear forever each year.

Destruction of Habitat.   Ultimately, the destruction of forests leads to the destruction of habitat and cultures (as is happening with Indian tribes in the Amazon area, for example) and, in the process, to human misery for ethnic minorities who are not part of the modern way of life. A concomitant result is the further suppression of ecologically appropriate forms of land use.

Even if all clearing operations were halted right now—which is not expected—millions of hectares of land would still have to be replanted to meet future needs for firewood and to stabilize the soil and the water supply. Today, however, the tropical forests are still being cleared much faster than nature and reforestation are able to compensate for. Rapid population growth is one of the essential factors in this process.

Water Availability and Quality

The fact that humans use more water than the hydrological cycle can replace was pointed out more than 20 years ago by Paul and Anne Ehrlich—but this did nothing to change people's behavior.[188] The misuse of water constitutes a serious and growing threat to sustainable development because, as stated in the Dublin Declaration from the International Conference on Water and the Environment, human health and prosperity, food security, industrial development, and the ecosystem on which they all depend will be at risk if we do not use our water and land resources more sparingly.[189]

Almost a third of the earth's surface has insufficient precipitation.[190] At present about 2 billion people in 88 different countries are living in regions that suffer from a chronic water shortage.[191] North Africa and the northern regions of East and West Africa face this problem, which is steadily exacerbated by rapid population growth.[192] In the Sahel, for example, it was formerly the custom to use mainly ground water that was near the surface and dependent on variable precipitation; today, more and more use is being made of modern deep wells operated by motorized pumps. The water reserves that can be exploited in this way are, however, often fossilate in nature—that is, they are not resupplied either by rainfall or by river water. On the one hand, a high rate of population growth and intense agricultural development necessitate the exploitation of additional water reserves; on the other hand, tapping

Table IV-7

Destruction of Species in Tropical Forests

	Current Number of Species in Thousands	Expected Decline of Forest Area (percent)		Loss of Biodiversity (percent)	
		Low	High	Low	High
Latin America	300–1,000	50	67	33	50
Africa	150– 500	20	67	13	50
Asia	300–1,000	60	67	43	50
Total	750–2,500	47	67	33	50

Source: Enquete Commission: Precautions to Protect the Earth's Atmosphere. Protection of the Tropical Forests. Economica Verlag, Bonn 1990, p. 497.

into fossilate sources of ground water runs the risk of overusing and exhausting a vital and unrenewable resource.[193]

Several tens of thousands of villages in India suffer from water shortages. Plans to redirect the Brahmaputra for irrigation purposes arouse great fears in Bangladesh. Present water consumption in China and Mexico cannot be sustained with the available water resources. The sinking groundwater level, especially in the vicinity of large cities, is creating more and more problems for agriculture.

Water for Irrigation.   Irrigation is one of the most important factors in agricultural productivity. The Green Revolution, which in various Southeast Asian countries has led to substantially larger yields of the main food crops, rice, and wheat, would not have been possible without regular and controlled irrigation.[194]

The expansion of the irrigated portion of land under cultivation is responsible for about half the increase in food production since 1950. A third of the world's agricultural yield stems from only 17 percent of the land cultivated worldwide—that is, the part subjected to irrigation.[195] The price paid for this is that the share of world water consumption accounted for by irrigation, 65 percent, is very high.[196] Water shortages not only put at risk any further expansion of food production in the developing world, they endanger even the production levels already achieved. Examples of this can be seen in Indonesia, Pakistan, Thailand, and Vietnam as well as—to an especially large extent— Egypt.[197]

Swedish hydrologist Malin Falkenmark predicts that by the turn of the millennium most of the countries in North and East Africa will be engaged in a growing struggle over water.[198] For both its food and energy production,

Egypt is entirely dependent on the water of the Nile, whose sources lie beyond Egypt's borders in countries that themselves depend on irrigation for the intensification of their agriculture. Bigger claims on water by the Nile-riparian states of Ethiopia and the Sudan could have dramatic consequences, including armed conflict. For the whole of the Near East—a region where armed hostilities are in any case a constant risk—as well as for the riparian states of the Ganges (India, Nepal, and Bangladesh), water has become so scarce that the statement "water is peace—no water means war" has acute significance.[199]

Drinking Water. In contrast to water requirements for irrigation, the drinking water supply entails the question not only of adequate amounts but also of quality. In 1985–1988, more than 1.5 billion people throughout the world had no access to clean drinking water[200] and almost 2.2 billion had no sanitary installations at their disposal. Wherever households are forced to take their drinking water from rivers, streams, and lakes—water that is generally contaminated by sewage containing human and animal excrement—diarrhea, cholera, and other stomach and intestinal diseases are widespread. Diseases of this type are responsible for most infant and child mortality.

There have been impressive improvements in the water supply in recent years, but in many countries the situation remains desperate. (See Table IV-8.) Where a lack of clean water goes hand in hand with a shortage of firewood, making it more difficult or more expensive to boil contaminated water, a deterioration of the situation must be expected.

In solving problems related to the shortage of water, a slowing down of population growth is, once again, only one factor among many. Patterns of consumption in agriculture and industry, technology, and appropriate care of the natural environment (forests, soils) are factors of at least equal weight.[201]

Increased Potential for Conflicts

In 1929, W.S. Thompson asked whether the growing number of people who were becoming steadily poorer would in the final analysis wait peacefully for their death from starvation and simply watch a wealthy minority enjoying the good things of the earth.[202] He did not risk an answer at that time and left open the question of whether the unavoidable redistribution of land (which indeed came about as a result of decolonialization) would occur peacefully or through open warfare.

Today, armed struggles over scarce resources have long been a reality. Thus, Senegal and Mauritania fought in 1989,[203] Kenyan and Somali tribes in the early eighties, and Ethiopian and Somalian clans in the seventies and eighties—all over the use of pastureland. The conflict between Ethiopia, the Sudan,[204] and Egypt as well as those between the states on the borders of the Ganges, the Ussuri, and the Tigris[205] were over water resources. Tensions are

Table IV-8

Portion of Population with Access to Clean Water, 1975–80 and 1988–90

Country	1975–80	1988–90
Afghanistan	9	21
Nepal	8	37
Ethiopia	8	19
Zaire	19	34
Kenya	17	30
Tanzania	39	56
India	31	75
Indonesia	11	28
Mexico	62	71
Peru	47	61

Source: UNDP: Human Development Report 1992. Oxford University Press, New York 1992, Table
        4, p. 134.

increasing in the entire Sahel region.[206] More than 99 percent of the 300 wars
that have broken out since 1945 took place in the developing world.[207]

Further conflicts are inevitable if environmental catastrophes, poverty, or
armed hostilities precipitate significant streams of migrants and if the regions
the migrants move to either feel overburdened or are in fact overburdened.[208]
Today there are already at least 10 million environmental refugees. A rise in
the sea level resulting from the greenhouse effect could multiply this number
many times over.

Within the complex network of causes leading to social and political instability, bloodshed, and wars over shrinking resources, a high rate of population growth plays a significant role. The military struggles between Ethiopia
and Somalia, tensions between India and what was then East Pakistan (today
Bangladesh), and fears relating to future fighting over the water of the Nile are
all clearly related to rapid population growth.[209]

Conclusion: Rapid Population Growth Impedes Sustainable and Humane Development

In the vicious circle of social, economic, ecological, and political deterioration, the factor "rapid population growth" represents both a cause and an
effect. For that reason, as already mentioned, the solution of existing problems
and the avoidance of new ones will in all these areas require global changes in
thought and behavior patterns. In the face of continuing rapid population

growth, progress toward sustainable human development—badly needed in the poorest countries, especially among the poorest sections of the population there—will come slowly, if at all. It would take much too long, using development strategies of whatever kind, to ease the bitter misery of millions of people to such an extent that the population would stabilize itself.

High population growth rates mean that more children have to be adequately nourished, educated, and later given productive job opportunities. Since people today in developing countries are already unable to meet their most basic needs,[210] rapid population growth means that the number of people living in absolute poverty will increase. Hence, the obstacles to a successful development policy increase as well. This occurs because development policies have to deal with more people and more resources have to be mobilized; at the same time, rising numbers of people living in absolute poverty represent a factor of deterioration that in turn has negative and cumulative effects on the prevailing system of "underdevelopment."

While the responsibility for the condition of the environment in today's world lies mainly with those in industrial nations, the developing countries are catching up. The local and regional consequences of rapid population growth have already begun to jeopardize medium and long-term economic development and, hence, social development as well. Naturally there is a requirement for more than just population measures. Clear and workable national and international legal requirements; a quantification of the costs of using the environment and transferral of these costs to the users; research, development, and application of new technologies that pollute the environment less and clean areas already polluted; measures to conserve endangered soils; where necessary, a reform of landownership and leasehold arrangements and an overall high political priority for the fight against poverty: all these requirements are well known and form a part of institutional demands.[211]

Direct measures to lower birth rates are also necessary. In many parts of developing countries and indeed worldwide we are under time pressure to avoid greater social and ecological catastrophes. Against this background, a number of questions are raised that are addressed in Part V: What are the preconditions for reducing high population growth in the developing countries? Can we use the historical processes observed in industrial countries to provide lessons for developing countries that are culturally and ethnically completely different? How can we make family planning socially and ethically acceptable to large parts of the population?

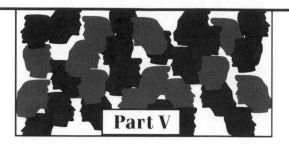

Part V

The Demographic Transition Theory

Much of what is currently discussed or being aimed at in population policies and programs for the so-called Third World is based either explicitly or implicitly on the assumption that these countries could undergo a demographic transition like the one industrial countries went through. This involved a three-phase transition[1] from a "traditional" society with high birth and death rates and hence slow population growth to a "modern" society with low birth and death rates, and thus slow population growth.[2] In between there is a "transitional phase" during which death rates decline substantially but birth rates remain high, the result being high population growth.

"Traditional" and "Modern" Societies

Since the process of social modernization is important for the course of the demographic transition—at least in the classical version of the theory—a short explanation is in order of "traditional" societies and how they differ from "modern" ones.

In his analysis of population policy, Ansley J. Coale defines traditional and modern societies as follows:

> A society was modern, in 1960, if at least 50 percent of the population lived in urban settlements of more than 20,000 persons, if more than 90 percent of the female population at ages 6 to 13 was enrolled in school, and fewer than 30 percent of the labor force was engaged in agriculture, fishing, and forestry. A society was traditional if less than 30 percent of its population lived in urban settlements of more than 20,000 persons, if fewer than 50 percent of females 6 to 13 were enrolled in school, and if more than 60 percent of the labor force was engaged in agriculture, fishing or forestry.[3]

Supplementing this rough portrait, a number of other characteristics are important. In traditional societies, the everyday life of the people and their social relationships are influenced in essential ways by the values, forms of behavior, methods of orientation, prejudices, and standards of legitimacy transmitted by previous generations. People in traditional societies hold fast for long periods of time to patterns of thought and behavior already evaluated (by others in the past) and found to be appropriate. The predominant form of social organization is that of the family and the clan. Daily life is bound up in a network of social values that to some extent are regarded as valid in the absolute sense or involve taboos; fatalistic world views are widespread. The level of technology is very low.

In contrast, "modern" societies, in addition to urbanization, industrialization, and a high level of education for both sexes, are characterized by individual planning and organization of life as well as by democratization and social mobility. Self-determination enjoys growing social acceptance. Modern societies are secular in nature: individuals, social groups, and the state have all freed themselves to a very great extent from ties to the church. Daily life and the events it contains are largely seen from a worldly perspective. The level of technology is high, as are society's opportunities to use technological progress for the enhancement of prosperity.

The definitions of "modern" and "traditional" used here have a marked ethnocentric prejudice. In view of the ecological consequences of the "modern" style of production and consumption described earlier in this volume, it hardly makes sense to talk about a "rational" organization of life by the majority of people in "modern" societies; on the contrary, one is reminded in many ways of the behavior of lemmings.

The critical views of Erich Fromm provide an antidote to any impression of a "healthy" modern world that might arise. In *Anatomy of Human Destructiveness,* Fromm said that traditions, commonly held values, and genuine social ties have largely disappeared in modern industrial societies.[4] Modern mass man is isolated and lonely, even when he or she is a part of the mass. Having no convictions to share with others, only slogans and ideologies taken from the media, the modern person has become an A-tom (Greek and Latin, in-dividual = indivisible), and the only bonds tying these individuals together are common interests—often antagonistic, however—and the connection provided by money.

The modernization process entails a comprehensive transformation of social organization—economically, socially, and politically.[5] Economic changes involve above all the division of labor, production technology, types of goods and services, and, as a result, the overall level of the social product. The most pronounced social changes affect mortality, birth rates, size and structure of the family, residential patterns (such as urbanization), and the educational system. Changes in these various areas have reciprocal and synergistic effects, and affect the political organization of society.

The Three Phases of the Transition

All societies that have survived enjoyed general conditions of life and forms of social organization that permitted them to offset high mortality rates by high birth rates. During the transformation from traditional to modern societies in Europe, birth and death rates changed in a way that led various demographers to formulate a "theory of demographic transition."[6] Frank W. Notestein, one of the fathers of this theory, noted in his analysis of the social parameters and imporant demographic variables in traditional European societies that there were significant parallels to the traditional societies among today's developing countries.[7]

High Death and Birth Rates

Mortality was high in the traditional societies of Europe owing to persistent deficits in the satisfaction of basic needs (food, shelter, drinking water, sanitary facilities, health care, and so on), and life expectancy at birth was well under the age of 50. Members of the lower classes in the traditional European societies of that time, like those in today's developing countries, suffered markedly more from all these problems than did members of the upper classes.

A high birth rate was necessary to keep these societies from going into decline or even dying out. As a result of war, famine, and the plague, absolute population numbers dwindled well into the Middle Ages. It is estimated that the bubonic plague of 1348–1350 took the lives of approximately 25 percent of all Europeans; between 1348 and 1379, the population of England was reduced by almost half as a consequence of the plague.

Since social security depended almost entirely on the continued existence of the extended family with its network of reciprocal obligations, great importance was attached to collective welfare. Individuality was relatively unimportant. This system of values gave rise to strong social pressure to produce as many children as possible in order to ensure the continued existence of the family. Formal education was hardly needed for most jobs in the peasant societies of old Europe. Under these circumstances, school attendance was held to a minimum, particularly for girls.

Economic and social opportunities for women were also limited in traditional European societies to the role of housewife and mother and to those domestic and agricultural tasks that could be performed amidst frequent pregnancies.

Because these traditional forms of social organization had secured survival over the centuries, traditional patterns of thought and behavior enjoyed high social recognition—indeed they were often anchored in religion. Behavior in accordance with prevailing norms aroused approval; offences against these norms excited disapproval or were even punished. All of this gave traditional patterns of thought and behavior a high degree of stability.

The result was that in the first phase of the demographic history of Western Europe, birth and death rates were relatively high and population growth low.

Lowered Mortality and High Fertility

Following the Thirty Years War, Europe enjoyed a period of sustained peace, law, and order. The economy prospered. Where there was a persistent rise in the standard of living for large parts of the population and where political stability provided for internal and international peace, there were durable improvements in the food supply, hygiene, and education as well as in the availability and effectiveness of medical and sanitary facilities. The result was invariably a substantial decline in death rates, especially for small children.

In the early eighteenth century, a variety of innovations in agriculture and the dawn of industrialization increased food supply and the general standard of living to a modest minimum that assured survival. And, with time, the first sanitary and medical improvements brought various epidemic diseases under control.

Although it proved possible to lower the death rate quite rapidly as a result of social changes, the fertility rate did not at first go down. Indeed, in most cases it rose slightly because lowered mortality meant that more women were reaching childbearing age. The traditional forms of social organization still served to give the high birth rate great stability. Consequently, the population rose significantly in this second phase of Europe's demographic history.

Low Death and Birth Rates

In the third phase, birth rates sank gradually to a low level. This phase began toward the end of the nineteenth century in northwestern Europe and, in the years that followed, reached southern and eastern Europe as well as North America, Australia, and New Zealand. As a result, population growth was considerably reduced; in the second half of the twentieth century, it occasionally even became negative as the average number of children dropped below the minimum needed to replace the current population.

During this phase the final transition from the traditional peasant society to the modern, urbanized industrial one took place. A great variety of factors influenced and accompanied this social transformation. The family and the economically productive unit were no longer identical and the extended family was replaced by the nuclear one. Having the workplace outside the home meant that individual as well as collective performance was possible and desirable. The relative anonymity of city life along with the greater social mobility enjoyed there lessened the pressure to observe social norms.

Education and training grew in importance, particularly because technological progress caused a rapid shrinkage in the value of the traditional and informal knowledge acquired through the family. The cost of educating children rose at the same time that children's contributions—both short- and medium-term—to family income declined.

Finally, as a result of lowered mortality, fewer births were needed in order to provide the desired number of surviving offspring. The demographic transition of Europe, which had begun in the middle of the eighteenth century, was concluded in the third decade of the twentieth century—and before 1930 for countries like Germany, France, England, and Wales.[8] (See Figure V-1.)

The Demographic Transition of Europe: A Model for Developing Countries?

The demographic transition theory gained rapidly in attractiveness during the fifties. This stemmed in part from its relative simplicity and in part from the schools of thought that viewed the process of development as "catching up" with the industrialized North. Yet the rapid population growth accompanying modernization in developing countries has called the theory into question. For example, a study in Nigeria found that despite the decreasing infant and child mortality among Nigeria's educated city-dwellers, modern contraceptive methods are not widely accepted, while traditional mechanisms of birth control, such as prolonged postpartum abstinence, are being abandoned. The high value that Nigerian society places on children has not diminished and will probably slow down any decrease in fertility. A true demographic transition is thus unlikely to occur there in the near future.[9]

The temptation and the risks involved in trying to project the demographic future of the developing world based on technological, social, and political conditions in industrial countries at the time of their transition were recognized early, however, and appropriate warnings were sounded.[10] Most participants in the debate agreed that the demographic transition theory could only provide a model for changes in death and birth rates resulting from social

Figure V-1

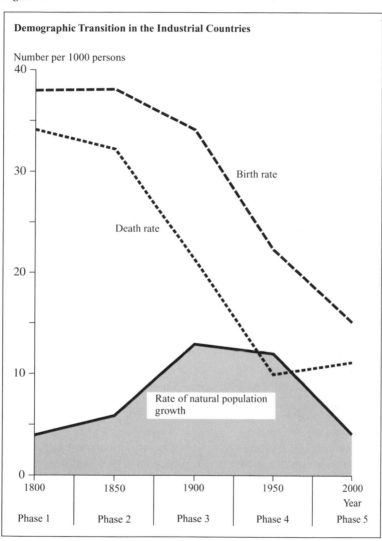

Source: Commission of Inquiry of the German Bundestag (ed.): "Precautionary
Measures for the Protection of the Earth's Atmosphere." Protection of the
Tropical Forests. Bonn 1990, p. 377.

changes and that no mathematically calculable law could be applied without modifications to other times, societies, and cultures.

The theory is not specific enough to permit exact predictions about the length of the transformation phase or to find quantifiable social and economic milestones that, once passed, lead to a reduction of the birth rate. There is also no "magic" numbers for the level of industrialization, gross national product, or literacy rate that triggers the transition. There is still no consensus on the relative weight to be assigned to various factors or on such issues as what additional indicators (such as distribution of income) should be used or which ones should be abandoned (such as per capita gross national product in societies with a very unequal distribution of income).

The demographic transition in Europe was a protracted process, lacking in chronological and structural regularity, that defies simple analysis. Not only were there pronounced regional deviations within various countries of premodern Europe, there were also cases in which birth rates sank before modernization had begun and others in which birth rates even after the beginning of modernization remained high and almost unchanged. Paul Demeny and, later, Ansley Coale pointed out that in various societies of premodern Europe both mortality and fertility rates fell at the same time. In France and in a number of German provinces, the birth rate began to go down even before the death rate.[11]

M.S.L. Cook and Robert Repetto suggested that explanations of demographic transitions during the nineteenth century that omit the influence of economic disparities between households and the economic welfare of low-income households are incomplete. They investigated variations in marital fertility and nuptiality in 48 Hungarian provinces over the period 1880–1910 in order to test competing hypotheses about the socioeconomic and cultural sources of the European demographic transition. Three explanatory models were compared:

- the conventional hypothesis of demographic transition emphasizing urbanization, education, modernization, and the decrease in infant mortality;
- a reinterpretation including cultural and ethnic factors; and
- a hypothesis that emphasizes poverty and economic inequality.[12]

The authors found that neither the conventional model nor the revision adequately explained which cultural and ethnic factors account for differentials and changes in Hungarian fertility during the transition, and that the consideration of economic variables substantially improved the explanation.

The question of whether the "European path" of demographic transformation might be applicable to a society in the developing world or is instead a unique historical and cultural event remains highly controversial.[13] Since a dependable answer would be of the greatest importance for contemporary population policy, we must first examine the differences and similarities between the traditional societies of Europe and those of developing countries today.[14]

Social and Demographic Differences Between Premodern Europe and the Contemporary Developing World

Population Size

For the purposes of a demographic discussion, the most important difference between eighteenth- and nineteenth-century Europe and contemporary developing countries is the initial size of the populations. The population of Europe at the time of the demographic transition was less than 200 million; the population of today's developing countries is more than 4.3 billion. All problems are more difficult as a consequence. This can be demonstrated briefly by a look at the employment problems.

The tumultuous industrialization and the associated supply industry in nineteenth-century Europe were very labor-intensive and hence able to absorb almost all those who left agriculture. In contrast, most of the rural agricultural workers in developing countries today who go to the cities have a very small chance of finding productive employment. The reason lies not only in the larger numbers of job seekers but also in the fact that today's technology is by and large very capital-intensive, particularly when it comes from industrial countries. Other obstacles to a higher employment rate are the lack of international competitiveness on the part of many developing-country industries and the damaging protectionist policies of industrial countries.[15]

Population Dynamics

Another substantial difference between premodern Europe and today's traditional societies in developing countries is the birth rate. Today it is usually much higher.[16] According to the *World Development Report 1984:*

> no country in northwestern Europe had a crude birth rate above forty per thousand in 1800; in several (Denmark, France, Norway, and Sweden) birth rates were nearer thirty per thousand. The crude birth rate in England was thirty-four per thousand in 1850, before marital fertility began to decline, compared with forty-seven per thousand in Colombia in 1960 and more than fifty per thousand in Kenya today. By contrast, in the Indian subcontinent in the nineteenth century, crude birth rates are estimated to have been between fifty and fifty-five per thousand.[17]

Europe in the nineteenth century had a very low rate of population growth (about 0.5 percent), meaning the population doubled in 150 years. The highest figures for the developing world today are in a completely different dimension: Jordan (a 1993 growth rate of 3.6 percent) and Kenya (3.7 percent) double their populations in 19 years; all of East Africa, with its 204 million people, doubles in just 21 years.[18]

Possibilities of Emigration

The population pressure that did develop in nineteenth-century Europe was relieved by the emigration of large numbers of people, a "safety valve" that is no longer available to developing countries. About 50 million people emigrated from Europe to Australia, New Zealand, Canada, and the United States. At its peak (1881–1910), emigration was equivalent to 20 percent of the increase in Europe's population.[19] Between 1846 and 1932, emigration from Great Britain actually took care of nearly 45 percent of natural population growth. Similar conditions prevailed in Italy, Portugal, and Spain. The Irish population even shrank as a result of the high rate of emigration, though this was influenced by the great famine of 150 years ago.

The immigrants were very welcome workers and settlers in the countries to which they had travelled. In Europe today, by contrast, the addition of even a few ten thousand refugees driven by want or political prosecution can lead to substantial domestic political problems. Immigrants now seem to be welcome only when they bring money (as the Hong Kong Chinese do to Canada, for example) or have special skills that are of value to the economy of their new homeland. For those fleeing poverty, this is rarely the case.[20]

In view of the degraded conditions in many parts of developing countries and the tempting living standards in wealthy countries—as reflected, for instance, in advertising for western consumer products—people's desires and hopes to change their fortunes through emigration are entirely understandable.[21] As long as the disparity between rich and poor in the world remains as blatant as it is now, there will be refugees from poverty. And as long as mass misery in the feudal societies of developing countries fuels armed social conflicts and civil wars erupt from ethnic and tribal disputes, there will also be "genuine" refugees in great numbers.

Current debates in wealthy countries over whether "we" can or cannot tolerate immigrants from the so-called Third World politically and economically—and, if so, how many—need to be put into the proper context: industrial countries take only a minor part of the worldwide stream of refugees. Other countries in the developing world (which in comparison with all industrial countries are much poorer) take in more than three-quarters of the refugees of the world.[22] (See Table V-1.) The financial resources to pro-

Table V-1

Number of Refugees, by Region

Region	Refugee Population as of December 31, 1991	Refugee Population as of December 31, 1992
Africa	5,067,932	5,130,515
Asia and Oceania	835,093	1,092,931
Europe	1,202,568	4,407,461
The Americas	1,903,374	1,926,763
Southwest Asia, North Africa, and Middle East	1,998,516	6,441,107
Total	17,007,483	18,998,777

Source: United Nations High Commissioner for Refugees, October 1993.

vide a decent living for these people, together with the resources that industrial countries need to prevent mass immigration of destitute people from poor countries, could reach levels comparable to the resources now being spent on development cooperation. The domestic political price of consistently applied countermeasures would certainly be disproportionately higher.

For that reason, appropriate development cooperation with countries where refugee problems arise is surely a better long-term way of dealing with crass disparities in standards of living than the attempt to take in and absorb millions of people in industrial countries. Nor is a policy of taking only an educated elite from the developing world appropriate in support of economic and social progress in the countries of emigration. The departure of people with special skills and knowledge—the brain drain—is a serious obstacle to development.

Age and Frequency of Marriage

There are also significant differences between the traditional societies of Europe and those of the present-day developing world with respect to age at marriage and frequency of marriage, two important indicators in questions of population growth. In Europe, strict social norms ensured that the age of marriage remained relatively high,[23] for the most part substantially higher than in traditional societies of today's developing countries. In the Germany of the seventeenth and eighteenth centuries as well as in Belgium, England, France, and Scandinavia, the average age at marriage was approximately 25 years.[24] The World Fertility Survey showed completely different conditions in a number of developing countries regarding age at marriage and at the birth of the first child.[25] (See Table V-2.)

Table V-2

Average Age of Women at First Marriage and First Birth in Selected
Countries, Late Seventies

Country	Average Age at First Marriage		Average Age at Birth of First Child	
	Women Presently Age 40 to 44	Women Presently Age 25 to 29	Women Presently Age 40 to 44	Women Presently Age 25 to 29
Kenya	17.7	18.0	19.5	18.9
Senegal	15.7	16.3	18.0	18.6
Sudan (North)	15.9	17.0	20.1	19.4
Bangladesh	12.4	13.1	17.0	16.5
Nepal	15.6	15.2	20.9	19.8
Pakistan	14.8	16.5	18.3	19.9
Indonesia	15.5	16.1	19.5	19.4
Venezuela	18.9	19.9	20.4	21.2
Dominican Republic	18.0	17.9	19.8	19.8
Jamaica	19.4	17.8	20.7	19.2

Source: J. Cleland and J. Hobcraft (eds.): Reproductive Change in Developing Countries. Oxford
University Press, Oxford 1985, p. 69.

The fact that up to 30 percent of women in Europe at that time remained
unmarried compared with a figure today of 5 percent or less in many developing countries[26] is also a consequence of social norms.[27] In present-day
Bangladesh, for example, only 0.1 percent of women remain unmarried.[28]
Pressure to meet the requirement that all adults must be married can go as far
as the imposition of fines.[29]

Course and Persistence of Decline in Mortality Rates

The general decline in mortality rates in Europe followed a different course
than in most developing countries. The gradual rise in the standard of living
and the related improvements in sanitation and hygiene, along with better food
supply and a general rise in educational standards, resulted over some 150
years in a steady reduction of death rates for all age groups. At the beginning
of the nineteenth century, infant mortality in many European communities
stood at 200 per thousand live births; in Sweden, it was around 250 and in
Germany, more than 300 per thousand.[30]

Developing countries today, more or less independently of the modernization process in their societies, are in a position to import drugs (antibiotics, for
example), remedies against disease-carrying insects (DDT, for instance), and
vaccines (against measles, whooping cough, tetanus, and diphtheria) and to

make widespread use of them with the help of international development organizations. This has allowed a significant reduction of mortality rates within a matter of a few years in most developing countries—but in many of them it was not a steady progress.

Mortality has tended to rise again and again as a result of political unrest and inappropriate budgetary priorities on the part of governments. In recent years, a number of countries have responded to externally imposed debt reduction plans by cutting back on public social services and investments for the improvement of the drinking water supply, sewage and waste disposal, and basic health services. Among the lower classes, who in any case suffer the biggest burden of sickness and mortality, this has led—at least in the short term—to an increase in child and infant mortality.[31]

Availability of Modern Contraceptives

Modern contraceptives such as hormonal preparations or pessaries did not exist in premodern Europe. Frank Notestein attributes the lowered birth rate in the last phase of the demographic transition there to traditional contraceptive methods known at the time (such as coitus interruptus) that were used deliberately as a result of changed social circumstances.[32] Paul Demeny sees the same development in Austria-Hungary. He concludes that the traditional methods of birth control came into more frequent use when, around 1880, the social circumstances of people began to improve.[33]

All birth rates, those of premodern Europe as well as of traditional societies today, are significantly lower than the biologically feasible maximum—an interesting fact that demonstrates that knowledge of means and methods of birth control existed and continues to exist in premodern societies. Modern contraceptives can now be found in most developing countries but they are by no means readily accessible everywhere. The importance of accessibility of contraceptives is underlined by various studies of knowledge, attitudes, and practice of birth control that show a big gap between the "desired" number of offspring and the "actual" number.[34]

Religious and Cultural Differences

Difficulties in transferring European and North American historical experience can also stem from the fact that in religious and cultural respects, many developing countries have a completely different organization. So the same social changes, when applied to them, would not necessarily lead to the same changes in thought and behavior.

Given that religious and cultural norms such as those described in Part III highly influence reproductive behavior, it is impossible to make global predictions about a uniform effect on childbearing and adoption of family planning from such variables as income, education, and other factors often associated with economic development and modernization.

Social and Demographic Similarities Between Premodern Europe and the Contemporary Developing World

Mortality Rates Drop When the Quality of Life Improves

The tendency of death rates to decline as life gets better, which is most important for development policy and for humanitarian reasons, is true for all societies and at all times. In societies that enjoy peace and where the basic needs of the people are effectively met,[35] the infant mortality rate drops first. This is the most sensitive indicator of the quality of life of people.

In industrial countries, death rates dropped more and more during 200 years because the conditions regarding health, food supply, and education as well as the general quality of life improved steadily. In developing countries that pursued a basic-needs-oriented development strategy and thereby enabled people of the lower social classes to improve their quality of life, death rates dropped at least 50 percent within a relatively short period of time—25 years, for example, in Costa Rica and Sri Lanka.

Many other developing countries were also able to cut their mortality, but not to the same extent. There, the general living conditions continue to foster disease, the fatal consequences of which can only be limited by antibiotics and vaccines available from industrial countries[36] and by development programs that provide health and education on sanitary conditions.

Birth Rates Go Down More Slowly Than Mortality Rates

Birth rates remain high in developing countries today for the same reasons they did in traditional societies of old Europe. Because of traditional patterns of thought and behavior, moral and religious codes, and a series of other factors that vary from one culture to another, birth rates in developing countries also go down considerably more slowly than mortality rates. This is clearly demonstrated by a comparison of crude birth and death rates. (See Table V-3.)

The result of this gap between changes in birth and death rates has been, as the fathers of the theory of demographic transition predicted, high population growth, which dates approximately from the end of World War II. Since then, population policy has concentrated on trying to bring the birth rate down—in other words, on getting the third phase of demographic transition under way.

Many population policy experts thought at first that rapid and effective provision of contraceptives should have top priority, and they called on industrial countries to provide financial and logistic support for this purpose. Today,

Table V-3

Relative Changes in Birth and Death Rates

	Death Rate per 1000 Inhabitants			Birth Rate per 1000 Inhabitants		
	1960	1991	Change (percent)	1960	1991	Change (percent)
Low-Income Countries	26	10	−61.5	48	30	−37.5
Mali	30	19	−36.7	50	50	0
Uganda	21	19	−9.5	49	52	+6.1
India	22	10	−54.5	40	30	−25.0
China	14	7	−50.0	40	22	−45.0
Middle-Income Countries	17	8	−53.0	45	25	−44.4
United States	9	9	0	24	16	−33.3

Sources: World Bank: World Development Reports 1978, 1982, and 1991. Oxford University Press, New York.

however, there is general agreement that the mere availability of contraceptive devices and methods is not enough to bring about a lasting reduction of birth rates. What is needed first is a change in patterns of thought and behavior; otherwise, only a small part of population growth can be controlled—that resulting from unwanted pregnancies.

As long as there continue to be unexpected deaths of children and infants in a person's own family (or clan, tribe, or village), it is reasonable from the standpoint of the affected parents to mistrust a new "trend" that may be statistically true for the country as a whole but that provides no guarantee for the family. This skepticism leads parents who view their children as the only source of support in their old age, or who expect other economic or social advantages from them, to withhold support from any deliberate curtailment of the birth rate.

Thus the essential question continues to be what forms and priorities for social change in traditional societies would lead to a reduction in the number of desired children.

Conclusion

Generally it is still considered valid that "in traditional societies, fertility and mortality are high. In modern societies, fertility and mortality are low. In between there is the demographic transition."[37] But this transition from a society with high birth and death rates to one with low rates is much more complicated than the two demographic measures "fertility" and "mortality" reveal. These are mere indicators of comprehensive social change and of the economic and structural changes accompanying it in a given society.[38]

The historical demographic transition in Europe took place under remarkably varied social, economic, and demographic conditions.[39] Hence it is clear that attempts to explain it in terms of a single cause—the notion, for example, that a drop in birth rates resulted from one factor alone—are bound to fall short.[40] A simple lowering of the infant mortality rate is not likely to bring about a concomitant lowering of the birth rate within a reasonable period of time from the standpoint of population policy. Developing countries, due to the local and global ecological problems described earlier in this volume and their consequences for the quality of life, cannot afford to take 150–200 years to pass through the demographic transition, as Europe did.

Also disproved is the view formerly held by some population experts that high birth rates were merely the result of insufficient knowledge about basic biological relationships[41] and that better education was therefore the most important precondition for lowering them.[42] It is worth remembering that birth control has never been unknown in any culture. Since time immemorial, people have tried to delay pregnancy through long periods of breast-feeding and the use of medicinal herbs. Unfortunately, cruel practices like infanticide have also, whether deliberately or unconsciously, been used as methods of birth control.[43]

Our development concept has changed fundamentally since the demographic transition theory was first formulated and discussed. In the fifties and sixties, "industrialization" and "modernization" were synonyms for "development." The modernization process in the "developed" countries was the ideal to be followed by the developing ones. The "developed" countries were the western industrial nations; the "underdeveloped" ones, the agricultural societies of the "Third World." This doctrine was not only ethnocentric, it also overlooked—for lack of relevant data—the fact that the western path of development had involved such extensive exploitation of nonrenewable resources and so much environmental pollution that it was unsustainable.

Toward the end of the sixties, the priority in development policy shifted to satisfying basic needs, participation by the people concerned, and rural development with appropriate technologies—a policy emphasis that has grown in the years since then. In view of the increasingly clear global limits to ecological tolerance, the concept of "catch up" development and, along with it, the notion of modern industrial society as a model for the "Third World" has dwindled in importance. For ecological reasons alone it is no longer feasible

Figure V-2

Demographic Transition in Sri Lanka 1935–1989

Number per 1000 persons

Birth rate

Death rate

Source: Ministry of Health: Annual Health Bulletin, Sri Lanka 1989.

for all people on this earth to follow a path of industrial development comparable to that of the western industrial countries in the past.

The traditional version of the demographic transition put too much emphasis on the potential of "modernization" toward an industrial and urbanized society to alter behavior. If modernization, urbanization, and industrialization were the only requirements for a reduction of birth rates, that would be bad news for population policy.[44] It would mean that societies in which, for whatever reasons, such changes were not possible or desired and where as a consequence the traditional kind of agrarian social organization was maintained have little hope of slowing their population growth. Today, there are many indications that urbanization and industrialization are neither necessary nor sufficient conditions for the demographic transition but that, at best, they ease the way.[45] Agrarian societies in which birth rates went down existed in premodern Europe, just as they exist in the contemporary developing world.

Figure V-3

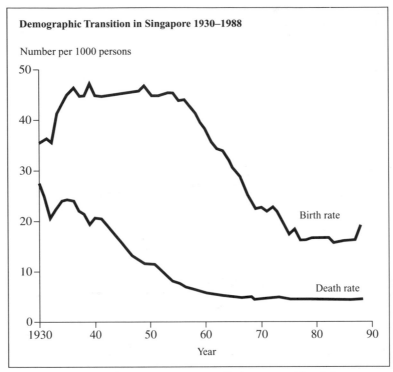

Source: K. Davis and M.S. Bernstam: Resources, Environment and Population.
Present Knowledge, Future Options. A Supplement to the Population and
Development Review, Vol. 16, 1990, p. 14.

    The birth rate of a society is still regarded as a figure that "depends" on economic, social, and political conditions. Procreative behavior is determined by reasonable decisions based on calculations of advantage and can be influenced by population policy.[46] There are developing countries that have gone through a demographic transition comparable to the European type in a relatively short time. Examples that might be mentioned here are Sri Lanka (see Figure V-2), Singapore (see Figue V-3), South Korea, Hong Kong, Costa Rica, and Taiwan.

    Hence, there appear to be a series of factors that, independently of the modernization of economic structures, favor a transition from the extended to the core family[47] and from a "multiple-child family" to one with only a few.[48] We need to identify these. In doing so, we must not, as Frank Notestein has already warned, be limited to the most obvious variables—those that offer themselves as an explanation—while neglecting less obvious ones.[49]

In view of the large and manifold differences between Europe of the eighteenth and nineteenth centuries and today's developing world, clearly it would be naive to believe that certain population changes will necessarily occur as a part of a given course of economic development. There was no clearly defined or quantifiable "ceiling" of an economic or social kind in premodern Europe,[50] nor is there such in the contemporary "Third World." The World Fertility Survey has been unable to identify a degree of social modernization beyond which the birth rate would inevitably sink.[51] The historical model of the demographic transition provides no basis for predicting the future of the so-called Third World, with its enormous cultural, social, and religious variety. It is too crude, simple, mechanical, and abstract for that purpose.

Almost 50 years ago, Notestein feared that the populations of societies in which no direct population policy measures were applied would continue to grow until they had exhausted their agricultural productive potential, and that thereafter Malthusian "checks" such as famines and epidemics, and perhaps chaotic political conditions as well, would ensure a rise in mortality.[52] Despite reductions in the birth rate in most countries, this danger has not disappeared. For many countries, such as in the Sahel zone of Africa, the danger remains highly acute.

If population policy is to be successful in the next 25 years—a period of decisive importance, we believe—it will have to be an active and internationally supported policy that attacks the problem at many levels with a variety of methods of economic and social control. But we must warn against any expectations of quick success. Technical solutions such as the general availability of contraceptives will only begin to acquire importance after there has been extensive social change involving growing social modernization and, along with it, a reduced role for traditional cultural and religious norms in influencing the childbearing decisions of parents.

Either excess population will lead to ecological collapse, poverty-related struggles over scarce resources, epidemics, and famines—producing a rise in mortality that will prevent further population growth or even result in an absolute reduction of population—or the international community will, on a large scale, put into practice its knowledge that social change is generally needed to reduce birth rates.

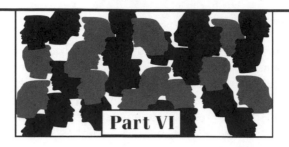

Part VI

Requirements for an Ethically Acceptable Population Policy

Population policy affects the most intimate area of human activity: procreative behavior. Depending on the content and structure of the policy, it involves in varying degrees an intrusion into the right of parents to decide responsibly and in an informed way how many children they will have. Although rapid population growth cannot be an intrinsic objective of a human development policy—especially when accompanied by an increase in absolute poverty—state intervention in the right to create new life must be ethically legitimized in both social and individual terms. This is true not only because of a general need to protect people, especially women, against state intervention and social pressure, but also because human values are at stake and—at least when abortion is one of the methods used to control births—human life as well. A discussion conducted purely in demographic terms cannot, therefore, do justice to the requirements of a humane population policy. After all, the goal of population policy is not to stabilize the population at a certain level or to reduce the birth rate for its own sake but to improve the quality of life for people.

Our species would not have been able to survive, let alone develop, without the continual supply of new human beings. For that reason, fertility has been highly valued since biblical times. But excessive population growth puts at risk both the prosperity or chances for prosperity of societies and the ecological system—and, thus, the future of humans as a species with a claim to individual freedom. These dangers are serious enough to call into question the traditional value of unlimited reproduction and a growing population. The relentless insistence of industrial countries that fast-growing developing countries must control their fertility in the absence of any simultaneous recognition that industrial nations must change their consumption and pollution patterns is, however, a serious danger as well.

If the unlimited right of parents to create new life is denied or if curtailment of this right by society (or the state) is being considered, what are the underlying values on which this should be based? What are the criteria for such curtailments, and who should undertake them? Should material criteria be applied, say, along the lines of "the rich may have as many children as they want but the poor must limit themselves"? Should there be ethnic guidelines, according to skin color—the darker the skin, the fewer children allowed? Or might we even consider applying the criteria of power politics on the grounds that those who have missiles or ABC weapons (atomic, biological, or chemical) at their disposal are able to get their way in the community of nations? Should we go back to a distinction between life that is worthwhile and that which is not? Hardly.

Reproduction is such a fundamental human activity, with such far-reaching personal and social consequences, that any control of it raises a number of ethical questions. What morally legitimate social and political processes exist for seeking possible alternatives to the right of unlimited reproduction? Against what values should such alternatives be measured? And what are the conditions under which actions might be taken?

Moral Issues in Population Policy

On the one hand, human values are put at risk by rapid population growth because its consequences interfere with sustainable development. As a result, measures to prevent or mitigate damage to humans and the environment are sometimes necessary. On the other hand, state intervention in the right of parents to make free and responsible choices about how many children they will have also represents a danger to human values. In this ethical dilemma, there is no unproblematic or easy solution open to us. The search for an appropriate course of action is a search for the "lesser evil."

Still, decisions have to be made because inaction also entails human suffering. The task of an ethically responsible policy is to balance the pros and cons in such a way that the following questions[1] can be answered:

- What human goods and values do we wish to strive for or maintain—that is, what is our goal?
- What methods and actions are consistent with these goals and what are their consequences—in other words, what means would be adequate?

- What procedure and rationale will help to bring about our decision on goals and means and on their relationship to one another in specific situations—in other words, what ethical criteria will support a decision?

The goals of a specific population policy must first be defined, for unless we know the nature of the objective, the appropriateness of means and methods cannot be determined. In order to avoid arbitrary decisions about the desired goals and the appropriate measures, we must seek a broadly based discussion of the ethical criteria to be applied to decisionmaking. Thus the tendency of population planners to consult only male-dominated agencies at crucial stages in decisionmaking and planning is not appropriate. Even conservative institutions have realized that the reduction of the birth rates is only possible if women are empowered to organize their own lives and control their fertility. Yet population programs of governments and multilateral agencies have been treating women as mere instruments for either reducing or raising birth rates. Moreover, fertility control has almost completely been centered on women, releasing men of their responsibility for contraception.

An adequate population policy recognizes the long struggle women have waged for some degree of procreative choice against patriarchal and state-imperial culture and institutions. There has been an objective gain in the quality of women's lives for those fortunate enough to have control over their procreative choices. But millions of women do not possess even the rudimentary conditions for such a choice. The moral goal should be to struggle against those real barriers—oppression and poverty—that prevent authentic choice from being a reality for all women.

Goals of Population Policy

A population policy aimed at lowering birth rates is nowadays justified in terms of an eventual improvement of the general level of prosperity and, at the very least, in terms of preventing the negative social, economic, and ecological consequences (in the short, medium, and long term) of rapid population growth, as discussed earlier. Among the objectives that are definitely not consistent with an ethically acceptable population policy are the protection of vested rights or material assets of the industrial countries, the political or economic predominance of a specific social or national group that historically determined patterns of resource use,[2] or the promotion or interference with human life according to certain criteria of "quality."

"Ethically acceptable" or "good and just" action in the field of population policy is defined here as action imbued with a spirit of humanity, informed by the mutual recognition that all human beings are of equal value, and driven by a constant determination to diminish human suffering and injustice and to promote freedom and justice. Paramount importance is attached to making sure that basic needs are satisfied and that people's social requirements are met under conditions of dignity and freedom. Such a population policy is guided by reverence for life in the spirit of Albert Schweitzer and aims therefore to "maintain life, promote life and raise life to its highest potential."[3] Reverence for life comprehends the life of future generations. In short, the goal of population policy is to provide for human existence in peace, freedom, and justice while preserving the Creation.

Appropriateness of Measures

Ethically acceptable governmental action in population policy is primarily aimed at creating the economic and social conditions that motivate parents, acting freely and on their own—that is, bearing in mind, among other things, the welfare of the whole society—to limit their children to a number consistent with sustainable development. All measures designed to reduce the birth rate of a country by appropriate social and development policies are preferable to government-ordered limits on procreation, especially those that use coercion. The acceptance of ethical principles in family planning not only gives the concept ethical legitimacy, it is also a prerequisite for willing participation by those affected.

Ethical Criteria for Decisionmaking

A discussion of whether—and, if so, how—external intervention in the family can be allowed poses significant interdisciplinary problems. The whole issue of creating new human life, like all questions involving human life, cannot be viewed solely in biological, psychological, demographic, sociological, theological, or legal terms. "It is the whole man and the whole mission to which he is called that must be considered." This statement from the Encyclical *Humanae Vitae* (II.7) is in our view generally valid, quite independent of the religious affiliation of those involved in a discussion on population policy. It makes clear that a simplistic rejection of the Encyclical—despite all the legitimate controversy about the narrow view of human sexuality laid down in it—does not do justice to the breadth of the statements it contains.

Even if one does not agree with the inseparability of loving union and propagation (HV II.12) and the listing of "unlawful birth control methods" (HV II.14), we believe, for example, that it is possible to base a rational population policy on the assertion that "responsible parenthood is exercised by those who prudently and generously decide to have more children, and by those who, *for serious reasons,* and with *due respect to moral precepts,* decide not to have additional children for either a certain or an indefinite period of time. . . . the exercise of responsible parenthood requires that *husband and wife,* keeping a right order of priorities, recognize their own *duties toward* God, themselves, *their families and human society."* (HV II.10, emphasis added). In addition, the Encyclicals *Populorum Progressio* and *Gaudium et Spes* affirm the idea of family planning within the context of responsible parenthood.

Respect for human life must underlie any ethically justified public policy on population. The mere striving for certain economic or demographic objectives does not legitimize state intervention in procreative behavior. The inviolable dignity of human life and the equal right to life do not depend on psychic, physical, or intellectual achievements and certainly not on sex or race. Human life—in all its stages—is an end in itself and not determined by external decrees or purposes.

The right to give life, like the right to life itself, is a human right—that is, all human beings enjoy it, inviolably and inalienably, on the basis of their individual dignity.[4] Everyone has a right to insist on the observation of his or her human rights, independent of social position, religion, or any other criteria used to distinguish between people, simply by virtue of the fact that he or she was born a human being.

In 1948, the United Nations issued a declaration of "equal and inalienable rights of all members of the human family" that, in addition to the "right to life" and the "right to found a family," included the following that are relevant to a discussion of population policy:

- right to liberty and security of one's person;
- equality before the law;
- protection from arbitrary interference with his privacy and family;
- motherhood and childhood are entitled to special care and assistance;
- freedom of thought, conscience, and religion; and
- right to social security and the free development of personality.[5]

In many countries, the UN's Declaration of Human Rights was made part of the constitution, generally called "basic rights." The interpretation and realization of human rights depend, however, on local political, ideological, and cultural circumstances. Thus a culture with an individualistic view of humankind (such as the United States or Germany) interprets the "right to life" differently than does a culture with a collectivist view (such as China)—with corresponding consequences for what individual sets of parents can expect from or be subjected to by population policy. Historical experience shows that totalitarian states have a different relationship to human rights and their realization than democratic states do.

Interventions by the state in the private spheres of people should generally be viewed with suspicion. Whenever the freedom of individuals to decide how many children to have is limited or abrogated by political means or other forms of coercion, more than a mere intervention is involved. It is a violation of their human rights. Such a policy has little chance of sustained success when it is not supported by a majority of the people. An ethically acceptable population policy is based on the enlightened agreement of everyone involved as to the measures to be taken and the individual's freedom of choice regarding the form of contraception.

For this reason, state intervention should not be resorted to until all other development policy measures have been taken to improve the quality of life of the target population, thus creating social conditions in which parents can decide freely, responsibly, and in an informed manner on a number of children that is consistent with the long-term development possibilities of their society.

Even a limitation on the right of procreation, should it turn out in the final analysis to be unavoidable, must be directed toward the goal of humane development and optimal self-realization of human beings, along with their individual and social concerns, in dignity and freedom. If there is a conflict of objectives, the actions taken should aim at ensuring that any curtailment of freedom of choice is a temporary exception representing the lesser evil.

Daniel Callahan puts it this way: "Those choices of action that ought to be preferred are those that accord primacy to freedom of choice; if conditions appear to require a limitation of freedom, this should be done in such a way that the direct and indirect harmful consequences are minimized and the chosen means of limitation are just—the less harm, the higher the ranking."[6]

Ethical Dilemmas

Ethical dilemmas are predicaments in which a decision must be made between two or more alternative courses of action, each of which involves some measure of wrong because it neglects moral requirements. Such dilemmas are characteristic of situations in which a concrete choice—in population policy, for example—between ethically imperative action and ethically prohibited behavior does not exist but in which the choice is between two or more evils. It is very important to note here that inaction or toleration of a problematic situation can also be ethically impermissible.

As a matter of principle, ethical values and norms cannot be subject to negotiation. Nor can unethical action be transformed into something "relatively" ethical by virtue of its perceived utility. Although a concerned individual can reject unethical alternatives, governments—which must act for others—are obliged when there are conflicting claims to weigh the alternatives in order to find optimal solutions. Consequently, ethical dilemmas represent an unsatisfying search for the least possible wrong. Quandaries of this kind are present everywhere in human life.

An example of the way in which ethical dilemmas arise in connection with population policy is the current tendency to justify family-size limitations recommended to people or even imposed on them in terms of the quality of life for future generations. In evaluating Chinese population policy, which has been criticized for its politically coercive character,[7] one should bear in mind that the present "third baby boom" in China will have resulted by the year 2050 in a population of 1.6–2 billion.[8] That number, according to today's estimates, can at best be maintained at a very low level in terms of the satisfaction of basic needs and can be expected to lead to unimaginable ecological consequences. As of today, China finds itself with only a third of the world average of arable land per capita.

How much leeway is left for individual decisions about the desired number of offspring when the size of the population exceeds the carrying capacity of the ecological, economic, and social systems to support it? When people cannot survive physically, there is no possibility of freedom—either to give life to a future generation or of any other kind. How should we proceed when there is a direct conflict between upholding human dignity and providing for full development of personality in the present generation and doing the same for future generations? Which has priority? Leaving theological considerations aside, is there an ethical justification for demanding sacrifices of our contemporaries so that in 100 years people who do not yet exist will be better off? There are controversial moral questions being discussed in this connection, such as who or what is to be regarded as a person or as the subject of moral reflection.[9]

Questions of this kind cannot be answered by the arguments of population policy alone and without reference to moral philosophy. It continues, of course, to be true that all measures of a less intrusive kind should be exhausted before the state intervenes in people's private lives. Once these measures have failed, however, we have no recourse—short of appealing to a theological interpretation of humankind[10]—but to use the argument of solidarity between generations in order to persuade our contemporaries to make sacrifices for future generations. There is still a lot of educational work to be done in this area, however.

Our definition of "morality" affects our answers to certain ethical questions. Indeed, it determines what questions we regard as ethical and, therefore, of concern to us. For example, a narrow view of morals, which looks only at human sexuality from a moral and ethical standpoint, would omit questions of social justice and behavior vis-à-vis the environment. Many people's sense of responsibility and justice tells them that securing tolerable conditions of life for their own children's generation has priority over a senseless dissipation of nonrenewable resources by today's affluent societies. A call for equal or priority rights for future generations in the developing countries would, however, presumably be rejected by most people in industrial countries at the present. Given the attitude many people display toward asylum-seekers and refugees, sensitivity toward the difficulties of others is clearly in considerable need of development. Only a minority of people in industrial societies see that the future well-being of our own children and grandchildren cannot be separated from the well-being of the majority of the population on this planet.

As already stated, children contribute to the happiness of people; they give love and receive it and they also, at least in the short and medium term, make a significant contribution to the maintenance and social security of the family. Parents' adherence to certain cultural and religious norms can represent an additional strong obligation to support a high birth rate. There is thus a conflict, at least in embryonic form and for the short term, between individual welfare, which arises from self-determination and the pursuit of private interests, and the general welfare of present and future generations—in economic terms, between internal and external costs or benefits of childbearing.

"Externalities to childbearing"[11] are costs and benefits of children that do not accrue directly to the parents but instead are passed on to society at large. If there were no such externalities, then individually optimal fertility decisions would also be socially optimal. With his classic paper on "The Tragedy of the Commons," Garrett Hardin gave an example of the dilemma between individual and social welfare:

> The tragedy of the commons develops in this way. Picture a pasture open to all. It is to be expected that each herdsman will try to keep as many cattle as possible on the commons. Such an arrangement may work reasonably satisfactorily for centuries because tribal wars, poaching, and disease keep the numbers of both man and beast well below the carrying capacity of the land. Finally, however, comes the day of reckoning, that is, the day when the long-desired goal of social stability becomes reality. At this point, the inherent logic of the commons remorselessly generates tragedy. As a rational being, each herdsman seeks to maximize his gain. Explicitly or implicitly, more or less consciously, he asks, "What is the utility *to me* of adding one more animal to my herd?" This utility has one negative and one positive component.
>
> 1) The positive component is a function of the increment of one animal. Since the herdsman receives all the proceeds from the sale of the additional animal, the positive utility is nearly +1.
>
> 2) The negative component is a function of the additional overgrazing created by one more animal. Since, however, the effects of overgrazing are shared

by all the herdsmen, the negative utility for any particular decision-making herdsman is only a fraction of −1.

Adding together the component partial utilities, the rational herdsman concludes that the only sensible course for him to pursue is to add another animal to his herd. And another; and another. . . . But this is the conclusion reached by each and every rational herdsman sharing the commons. Therein is the tragedy. Each man is locked into a system that compels him to increase his herd without limit—in a world that is limited. Ruin is the destination toward which all men rush, each pursuing his own best interest in a society that believes in the freedom of the commons. Freedom in a commons brings ruin to all.[12]

The problematic behavior involved when individuals or societies externalize costs, which we have already discussed in connection with the environment, is highly relevant to population problems as well. It is of great importance for population policy to know, in specific cases, whether the externalization of the social costs of a large number of children in a family represents conscious behavior, action taken on the basis of inadequate information, or action in which the consequences are simply repressed. Or, as Hardin would put it: "Natural selection favors the forces of psychological denial. The individual benefits as an individual from his ability to deny the truth even though society as a whole, of which he is part, suffers. Education can counteract the natural tendency to do the wrong thing, but the inexorable succession of generations requires that the basis for this knowledge be constantly refreshed."[13]

In any event, education is vital because it is the only way of making clear the social and ecological consequences of a large number of children per family and of demonstrating the necessity of limitations. The argument that constraints on procreative freedom are the only way to ensure other and more valuable forms of freedom for the long term may seem very abstract to a family of nomads in the Sahel zone. But if one points at the same time to the ever scarcer local environmental resources, it ought to be easier to reach a consensus on family planning.

Appeals to conscience or to a sense of common responsibility—however it may be defined—are just as ineffective in achieving a fundamental change in procreative behavior as in behavior toward the environment. As long as individual actions contrary to the general welfare continue to be (or are felt to be) advantageous, such appeals could even result in an undesired selection.[14] Those whose insight or sense of responsibility impelled them to accept limits could in the end turn out to be a minority whose correct behavior was unable to avert a catastrophe. For both population and environment policy, the solution lies in an overall package of measures of a social, political, and economic nature, as will be discussed here.

Intervention in the rights of individuals is not automatically illegitimate in seeking solutions to conflicts between individual and general welfare, but the priority of general welfare is a matter on which there is substantial international consensus, although in varying degree from one country or society to another. Thus one can argue, in the context of population policy too, that the right to free development of the personality always finds its limits when the fundamental rights of other people are affected.

The subordination of the rights of the individual to those of an overarching collective has in the past been used again and again by totalitarian states to repress their citizens, or certain portions of the citizenry. For that reason, legitimate intervention by the state in the freedom of individuals calls for specific political and legal arrangements—at a minimum, the existence of a democratically legitimated state based on law—that in cooperative fashion seek and promote the welfare of all.

The only imaginable justification for a violation of freedom of choice would be to avert a greater evil for society as a whole—whether ecological catastrophes, insufficient means for an existence worthy of human beings, mass poverty, or military struggles over the distribution of dwindling resources. It should be noted, however, that wherever coercive measures have been used by the state (in India in the seventies, for example), they have done significant long-term damage to the cause of family planning.

An Evaluation of Various Programs for Controlling Population Growth

Programs That Go "Beyond Family Planning"

Among the programs that go "beyond family planning"[15]—in other words, that apply coercive measures—are ones that respond to a failure to hold to a prescribed number of children by withdrawing public services (such as places in kindergartens or training opportunities) or by imposing progressively higher taxes. As far as we know, China and India are the only countries so far that have used this kind of state pressure on a large scale.

State interventions of this kind are hard to understand from the vantage point of our value system which, to be sure, has been influenced by completely different and substantially more pleasant conditions of life during the last 40 years. Considering the dimensions of the problems the Chinese people will have to face in the next millennium, and recalling the state-ordered mass murders that were committed in the twentieth century in the heart of Europe, arrogance in judgment and superior ethical claims are hardly likely to move the discussion forward. However, there is still no definitive proof that state pressure is the only way to bring about the desired reduction of the birth rate.[16]

Moreover, coercive population policies may have psychological and social consequences that indeed cannot be reconciled with the claimed goal of human quality of life: While the one-child policy of China may well have had some positive effects on women (such as more time and energy in production and better health conditions), according to a Chinese study it has also brought out the problems of wife beatings, unfair punishment, and the reprivatizing and confining women in the household—apart from forced abortions and sterilizations. The study's author concluded that the one-child policy tends to reinforce gender inequality both within and outside the family.[17] Again, with the focus on the "control" of a woman's fertility, women are especially victimized and this tendency goes so far as to result in the almost exclusive preference for male children and the abortion of female fetuses.

Our view is that the suspension of the human right to life and the giving of life would be ethically defensible only as a last resort after all the following measures have been exhausted:

- a development policy oriented toward the satisfaction of basic needs;
- political and social reforms to create equality of opportunity and a just distribution of wealth;
- worldwide solidarity actions to ensure a development policy commensurate with individual national requirements and to effect the necessary reforms for this purpose; and
- changes in the ecologically destructive behavior of the affluent minority of this world with respect to consumption, production, and waste disposal.

Only if it would turn out that these measures would not bring about a demographic transition quickly enough to prevent serious social, economic, and ecological problems from arising can state-imposed limitations of the freedom to procreate be considered. However, the ethical claim remains that such serious interventions should be limited to the shortest possible time and symmetrically distributed among all members of affected societies.

Incentive Programs

To achieve certain goals of population policy (such as the one-child family), incentive programs offer benefits in return for sterilization or for holding to specified time intervals between births. These programs do not employ coercion; indeed, incentive programs sometimes give rise to options that would otherwise not exist. The problem with such programs lies in their socially selective effects: rich families can have as many children as they want while poor families have markedly limited freedom of choice. Under conditions of absolute poverty, it is not clear when incentives develop into economic pressure or coercion. An additional problem is the avoidance of coercion through corruption—again, a method that only those with the necessary means can afford.

Whenever the long-term survival of a society under conditions worthy of human beings is at risk, incentive programs—despite all their social asymmetries—are a lesser evil than disincentive programs or coercive measures of the state. If incentive programs that call for a maximum of, say, one or two children were combined with measures to provide for parents in their old age or with favorable credits and inputs for agricultural production, this would represent a first step toward internalizing the social costs of a large number of children, because families with many children would by definition be denied these advantages. Let us point out, however, that a policy of this kind poses requirements of quality and fairness in execution that are currently the exception rather than the rule in developing countries.[18]

Disincentive programs, such as withdrawal of guardianship rights over children beyond a certain number or withdrawal of motherhood benefits, are directly coercive because they impose punishments. Here again, the poor are hurt more than the rich and the prosperity gap is widened. Moreover, such programs are undesirable in another respect: they endanger the health and welfare of mothers, families, and children. The loss of social benefits generally hurts children more than their parents. In practice, it can lead to poorer education, clothing, housing, and nourishment. The consequences of the parents' procreative behavior would be unjustly shifted onto their children.

Population policy measures that in varying degrees pressure parents can only be justified if voluntary methods have been properly and adequately tried and have nevertheless failed or are bound to fail in the future—something that, until now at least, has not been proved. Daniel Callahan would find a state-imposed limitation on the procreative freedom of individuals acceptable only if a number of prior conditions have been met:

- the government has proved the absolute necessity of limiting people's freedom, whereby the burden of proof is exclusively on the government (this burden may be discharged by a demonstration that continued unrestricted liberty poses a direct threat to distributive justice or security-survival);
- all members of the society are able to participate in the political process and the decision is a collective one;
- the proposed short-term limitation of freedom will, over the long term, create more opportunities to exercise freedom;

- the limitation of freedom is regulated by law and the burden falls equally on everyone; and
- the methods chosen to lower the birth rate are consistent with human dignity, which will here be defined as respecting those rights specified in the U.N. Universal Declaration of Human Rights.[19]

The end—even security and survival—does not justify the means when the means violate human dignity and logically contradict the end.

Callahan's rule of thumb is "the more coercive the proposed plan, the more stringent should be the conditions necessary to justify and regulate the coercion." "In addition," he believes,

> one must take account of the possible social consequences of different programs, consequences over and above their impact on freedom, justice, and security-survival. Thus if it appears that some degree of coercion is required, that policy or program should be chosen which (i) entails the least amount of coercion, (ii) limits the coercion to the fewest possible cases, (iii) is most problem-specific, (iv) allows the most room for dissent of conscience, (v) limits the coercion to the narrowest possible range of human rights, (vi) threatens human dignity least, (vii) establishes the fewest precedents for other forms of coercion, and (viii) is most quickly reversible if conditions change. While it is true to say that social, cultural, and political life requires, and has always required, some degree of limitation of individual liberty—and thus some coercion—that precedent does not, in itself, automatically justify the introduction of new limitations. Every proposal for a new limitation must be justified in its own terms—the specific form of the proposed limitations must be specifically justified. It must be proved that it represents the least possible coercion, that it minimizes injustice to the greatest extent possible, that it gives the greatest promise of enhancing security-survival, and that it has the fewest possible harmful consequences (both short- and long-term.)[20]

Today there are many convincing indications that people can be persuaded, through their own free and responsible decisions, to accept family planning when offered and to use appropriate means and methods of contraception. Unsatisfactory results in the past can usually be explained by inadequate social preparation, bad organization, or insufficient funding of family planning programs rather than any fundamental impossibility of reducing birth rates without state coercion.

Family Planning

In 1968, the International Conference on Human Rights included in the revised Charter of Human Rights the statement that "parents have the fundamental human right to decide freely and responsibly on the number of their children and the intervals between births." Many of the 157 countries that signed the Charter of Human Rights added to this statement the phrase "and have the right to receive the information and the means which will enable them to do this."

Family planning is often still viewed critically from the vantage point of protection of human life. If abortion is excluded as a means of family planning, that is not justified. If means and methods to prevent conception are used as a part of family planning, then family planning can only have the effect of saving life. As we have already noted, births that are too narrowly spaced can have critically dangerous consequences for mothers and children. Preventing pregnancy in women who are too young or too old and in those who have not had at least two years free of pregnancy could save the lives of millions of children and tens of thousands of mothers each year.[21]

The Concept

Family planning is more than the availability and use of contraceptives. It signifies a rational approach to life in which parents think seriously about the size of their family. Family planning presupposes appropriate social and political conditions as well as the availability of information and the technical means for birth control. Finally, family planning requires of men an attitude that not only accepts contraception but views it as a comprehensive responsibility of both partners.

The use of contraceptive means and methods plays a central role in the overall concept of family planning. To expand their use, individuals must go through the following stages:

- awareness: discovery of the existence of an idea or practice;
- information: accumulation of basic information concerning the new practice;
- evaluation: weighing the alternatives of use or nonuse, ending in a decision to try the new practice;
- trial: first use of the idea or practice; and
- acceptance: full-scale use, which becomes habitual and an integral part of behavior.[22]

A variety of measures and incentives for various user groups are required in order to accelerate these stages.

In the process, "user groups" should not be defined in terms of the family status "married,"[23] much less in terms of "women of reproductive age," but also in terms of "men of reproductive age." It is regrettable that few studies look at the attitude of men toward contraception and their willingness to use contraceptive means and methods themselves. Nor are there any studies of men's desire to have children. For that reason we must rely on data relating to women. This sex-specific bias is not wise, however, because family planning programs could work much more efficiently if they took account of the influence of men on birth rates. It is nowadays conventional wisdom that in patriarchal societies men more often than women decide how many children are to be produced, and it is also widely known that son-preference due to prevailing female discrimination in many spheres of life doubles the necessary number of children. Thus, population policy would be well advised to be oriented much more toward male-centered attitudes and societal power structures than just toward "fertility control"—in other words, the female uterus.

Social marketing and studies on people's knowledge of, attitutes toward, and practice of contraception could help recognize the characteristics of target groups and take appropriate account of them in family planning campaigns.[24] Regular evaluation and supervision are of the utmost importance for lasting success. They make it possible to correct mistakes and ensure permanent contact with the customers so that their needs can be met. Proximity to customers can improve the quality of work substantially.[25] Thus it is possible, for example, to find out whether there are gaps in information or problems of acceptance relating to specific contraceptive means and methods.

Current Prevalence and Success of Family Planning

According to information from the U.N. Population Fund, approximately 381 million people in developing countries used contraceptives in 1991.[26] (See Table VI-1.) Significant regional differences are found in the prevalence of contraceptive means. Africa south of the Sahara has been substantially less successful than Asia and Latin America.[27] In Asia, especially, the success of family planning was so great that a substantial reduction of birth rates was realized.[28] In general, the state plays the largest role, but it varies from region to region.

Whether active inclusion of the private sector would entail significant advantages is a question that has not yet been adequately answered. Preliminary experience provides some reason for optimism, however.[29]

Overall, there has been a sharp increase in the use of contraceptives in developing countries in the last 30 years. In the sixties, only 10 percent of couples (probably mainly women, to be more exact) used contraceptives, whereas today the figure is about 51 percent.[30]

The demand for family planning services is much greater today than it was a generation ago. A recent study cited by the U.N. Population Fund on the "desired" number of children in a family showed that in every one of 48 population groups studied, the parents had more children than they wanted. In some cases the discrepancy was striking. Overall, the share of undesired births

Table VI-1

Use of Contraceptive Means and Methods

Region	Number of Users in Thousands	Number of Devices Provided by State (Thousands)	(Percent)
Sub-Saharan Africa	10,521	1,732	16.5
North Africa & Middle East	15,634	2,312	14.8
East Asia	216,865	199,379	91.9
South Asia	93,791	66,252	70.6
Central America	13,081	6,260	47.9
South America	30,952	7,255	23.4
Total	380,844	283,190	74.4

Source: W.P. Mauldin and J.A. Ross: Contraceptive Use and Commodity Costs in Developing Countries, 1990–2000. International Family Planning Perspectives, Vol. 18, No. 1, 1992, p. 9.

was 22 percent. In Kenya, half of all married women said they did not want any more children. Another 26 percent said that they would like to wait at least two years before having another child. Only 27 percent of the women in Kenya used contraceptives.[31]

The use of family planning is as yet far from satisfactory in view of the pressing economic, social, and ecological problems caused by rapid population growth. A World Bank study concluded that at least 10 percent and perhaps as many as 40 percent of married women in the subject countries used no contraceptives, even though they did not want any more children.[32] In Africa, fewer than a quarter of the women who do not want more children use contraceptives; in Asia, the figure is 43 percent and in Latin America, 57 percent.

If all women would—or could—realize their need for longer intervals between births and for fewer children, and if they had the support of their husbands or enjoyed the blessings of the extended family in this, the number using contraceptives would be 100 million higher. If all women who say they do not want more children really did not have any more, the number of births in Africa would be reduced by 27 percent, in Asia by 33 percent, and in Latin America by 35 percent. The mortality rate in childbirth could be halved.[33]

The number of women of childbearing age will rise by 28 percent in the nineties, from about 757 million to 970 million. This growth alone calls for substantial family planning efforts[34] from both women and men. If the population estimates presented by the United Nations are to prove correct, world population during the nineties cannot increase by more than 969 million. W. Parker Mauldin and J.A. Ross calculated that this would require an 8-percent increase in the use of contraceptives (from 51 to 59 percent) by the year 2000.[35]

Based on the current pattern of contraceptive use, this would in turn mean huge expenditures for the services of existing family planning institutions. During the nineties, they would have to carry out 150 million sterilizations, distribute 8.8 billion monthly packages of oral contraceptives, give 663 million contraceptive injections, install 310 million intrauterine devices, and give out 44 billion condoms.[36] The related costs would be top $5 billion.

It is difficult to say how serious a problem an inadequate supply of contraceptives is for the further expansion of family planning. However, it is probable that the current supply is inadequate. The World Fertility Survey, carried out between 1972 and 1984 in 41 developing countries, revealed a surprisingly large unsatisfied need for contraceptives and family planning programs. John Bongaarts calculates that there was a "substantial" inadequacy of supply for 17 percent of married women[37] (and their husbands).

As to conditions that might lead to greater availability and use—price, channels of distribution (commercial or governmental), and other relevant conditions—no general statements are possible. The particular local conditions have to be taken into account. Studies by the Population Crisis Committee indicate that people are willing to pay about 1 percent of their monthly income for family planning.[38] Data from the World Fertility Survey show that the pill is the most widespread method of contraception in many countries, as it is in most industrial ones, although there are important countries (India, for example) where it is very rare.[39] The use of intrauterine devices is in second place in many nations.

Sterilization is also very widespread. Toward the end of the seventies it was the chief method of family planning in China and India.[40] As one would expect, the sterilization of women, even though it is the more expensive and dangerous operation, was considerably more frequent than the sterilization of men.[41] No doubt one factor contributing to the relatively low reliance on vasectomy for family planning is a lack of understanding regarding the procedure. In many cultures, and no doubt for some men in all cultures, any surgery in the scrotal area is automatically ethically equated with castration.[42]

Abortion, whether legal or clandestine, is also used as a method of family planning in many countries. All empirical studies show that women prefer contraception to abortion and are willing to terminate a pregnancy only as a last resort.[43] Naturally, it is difficult, for many varied reasons, to get dependable data on abortions. Although unwanted pregnancies are terminated all over the world by women of every social level,[44] the subject is—for legal, religious, and cultural reasons—practically never discussed openly and without reservations. The quality of statistics reflects this fact. Available data indicate, however, that China leads all developing countries, at least in legal terminations of pregnancy. Other nations, such as India, have far fewer abortions, although the numbers are clearly rising.[45] The annual number of abortions worldwide is unknown. Estimates from the seventies range from 14 million to as high as 30–55 million abortions a year.[46] Today's estimates of 26–31 million legal and 10–12 million illegal abortions are in approximately the same range.[47] In the worst case,[48] this would mean about one abortion for every two births.

It is not possible to make a general judgment about the moral or health-related advantages and disadvantages of the various means and methods of contraception in use today.[49] But this much can be said: from the standpoint of our own values, the means and methods to be given preference should entail the least possible risk to health, not violate human dignity, be easiest to use, have the lowest production costs and—where this is necessary for cultural reasons or because of age—hold open the possibility of reversal.

No Alternatives to Contraception

There can be no substantial lessening of birth rates by ethically acceptable means without a reduction of the desired number of children per family. The provision of contraceptives,[50] however, is no substitute for policies leading to favorable social conditions. But they are of great importance for attaining the objectives of population policy. Their influence in reducing births is substantial[51] and indispensable.[52] In the 48 countries that John Bongaarts studied, simply avoiding undesired births (which in various countries still account for 35 percent of births)[53] would have reduced birth rates on average by 22 percent.[54] New data from the World Bank show that between two-thirds and three-quarters of the decrease in birth rates in Indonesia, India, Bangladesh, Brazil, Colombia, Mexico, Kenya, and Senegal can be attributed to increased use of modern means and methods of contraception.[55]

The significance of family planning for the size of the world's population can be seen clearly from two figures: without the successes of family planning programs there would have been 412 million more people in developing countries in 1990; and if all couples were in a position to plan the size of their families precisely, it is estimated that this could mean 2.2 billion fewer people in developing countries by the year 2100. The difference between effective family planning programs and no programs at all could amount to 4.6 billion people by 2100, corresponding to the entire population of the earth in the early eighties.[56]

In many countries (for example, China,[57] Colombia, the Republic of Korea, Indonesia, Thailand, Sri Lanka, and parts of India like Kerala), the availability

Table VI-2

Regional Averages (Unweighted) for Modern Contraceptive Innovation
Stage by Age

	Percentage of Age Groups			
Innovation Stage	Age 15–19	Age 20–24	Age 25–29	Total
Awareness				
Asia	74	82	85	82
Latin America	91	95	95	94
Africa	59	67	69	66
Evaluation				
Asia	48	54	58	47
Latin America	50	62	65	68
Africa	22	24	26	22
Trial				
Asia	13	26	36	31
Latin America	28	46	54	46
Africa	4	7	11	9
Adoption				
Asia	8	15	21	21
Latin America	18	31	38	34
Africa	2	3	6	5

Source: World Fertility Survey, in A. Ong Tsui: The Rise of Modern Contraception. In J. Cleland and
J. Hobcraft (eds.): Reproductive Change in Developing Countries. Oxford University Press,
Oxford 1985, p. 122.

of effective family planning programs has had a substantial influence on
population growth. A few countries had positively sensational successes in a
very short time. In Thailand, for example, the average number of children per
woman was reduced within eight years from 6.5 to 3.5.[58] The success rate was
particularly high when family planning programs were combined with training
programs especially developed for women.[59] Unfortunately, men are still not
included on an equal basis in such programs.

National experience has been quite varied. (See Table VI-2.) It is interesting to note that family planning approaches that have worked in small projects
are not necessarily transferable to country-wide programs. In Bangladesh, for
example, they have only had positive experiences when the programs were
small as well as well controlled and supervised.[60] Whenever they were spread
over larger areas and other program activities were included, the results were
worse. They were frequently well planned but in the final analysis incompatible with the local realities of rural Bangladesh. Local interest groups, power-

ful landowners, and politically influential families were easily able to undermine well-meant government programs or to prevent important services from reaching the poorest groups in the population.

The Role of the State

The state's role in family planning efforts is controversial, as noted earlier. On the one hand, the state is supposed to offer services in order to create a broadly based consensus in favor of family planning and to help couples attain their family planning objectives.[61] On the other hand, it is not supposed to interfere with pressure or coercion in the right to procreate.

The state's responsibility for supplying information is unquestioned, however. Accurate information for parents and potential parents plays a significant role. The fact that infant and child mortality have declined may be statistically easy to prove and still not "known" in the sense that all parents are aware of this important change. The health advantages of family planning—especially the relationship between the health of the child, the spacing and the frequency of pregnancies, and the age of the mother—may be familiar to specially trained personnel even in the remotest areas. But it will not result in changed behavior unless this knowledge is indelibly impressed on parents.

Information programs on means and methods of contraception are of great value. It is equally important to make the appropriate contraceptives regularly available. Most contraceptives can only work successfully for long periods of time if both partners have agreed on their use. For this reason and also because the condom, for example, not only prevents pregnancies but can help to avoid disease while interfering only minimally with intimate relations between the partners, it is vital that men be drawn more fully into the work of education and persuasion.

The creation of a broad network of family planning institutions is an indispensable element of a successful program. In addition to buildings, equipment, and the means of contraception, this means training personnel. Wherever possible, traditional birth attendants should be included in the establishment of family planning services because they have considerable knowledge, enjoy the confidence of the women, and belong to the same culture.

P.N. Hess demonstrates that there is a close correlation between the establishment of effective family planning programs and steady economic growth.[62] This could be interpreted in two ways: the growth in family planning could be attributed to the progressive modernization of thought and behavior that can be observed in connection with urban-industrial development, or it could mean that in many cases there already exists a demand for family planning services that cannot be satisfied until steady economic growth makes the necessary resources available. In the latter case, family planning should receive fuller support as a part of international development assistance so that scarcity of local resources does not destroy the work already done to motivate people toward using it.

But the state must do more than just provide information and affordable contraceptives. As long as people continue to depend on large numbers of their own children for support in their old age, they cannot be expected to adjust their procreative behavior to the interests of an anonymous entity called the "state" or of future generations. In the internal cost calculations of families, possible costs to the society as a whole or to future generations (external costs) play no role. In Africa south of the Sahara, for example, the large number of children in each family continues to influence the availability of tillable land or pasture. If all families go on acting in the same way for a long time, however, the shortages will become noticeable. In such a case the state must strike a balance between private and social interest; it must act as trustee for the society and for future generations.

Even information on the existence of external costs can, with time, lead to a questioning of traditional expectations. In view of high unemployment or underemployment in most developing countries, it ought to be possible to make clear to many parents that their own child's chances of getting a good education and a decently paying job are lessened if all parents in the country also have many children.

Still, it is not enough for the state simply to appeal to a sense of responsibility on the part of the whole society. Success can only be expected when the state has convinced its citizens that it is a credible, responsible, and constructive actor rather than an arbitrary, repressive, and exploitative evil. Institutionalization of care for the aged—thus relieving children of this responsibility—can only develop where people have sufficient confidence in the state. Hence one can say unequivocally that upholding human rights, security under the law, democratic structures, and a disciplined bureaucracy—in other words, good governance[63]—are necessary conditions for a population policy that enjoys social acceptance and is, therefore, successful.

These social, ethical, and performance requirements on the state lead us to a discussion of the social, economic, and political conditions that underlie decreasing birth rates. Only after that will a discussion of the "technical" means of contraception have relevance.

Social Change

Removing Patriarchy

The term "patriarchy"—the "rule of the father"—was originally used to describe a male-dominated family. It has been extended to mean the power structure of a society, by which values, norms, and behavior patterns governing social organization are being imposed, shaped, controlled, and represented by men, generally older men. Grounded in the authoritative power of men and their control over material resources, patriarchy is supported by elements of kinship as well as by political and religious systems.

In many parts of the world, households and family life have changed and given women greater opportunities. But due to the prevailing socialization, women almost everywhere retain the primary responsibility for household work. This has resulted in a more complex and sometimes more difficult struggle to balance family, household, and economic responsibilities.

The status of women increasingly depends on their roles in the public sector, and the family institution loses its centrality in society. This does not, however, mean that there is a decline of patriarchy. It just shifts its locus from the domestic to the public realm. The assumption that increased female labor force participation and nearly equal formal education have substantially and generally promoted equality is false: domestic activities continue to reduce women's opportunities for market work participation. To have an advantage in selling labor, lifelong availability is important; women are thus disadvantaged, especially those who already have children.

A quasitraditional division of labor emphasising women's fertility cycles and men's careers as "breadwinners" promoted a segmentation of the labor market, so that women mainly occupy positions that are "typically" female and subordinate to men; very few women have access to high-status, high-paying positions. This must be seen as an implicit value judgment rather than a structural necessity. Even where women have moved into occupations dominated by men, their income often remains lower.[64]

Thus there is still enough evidence that "modern" societies have not yet broken with the tradition of patriarchy even if this is not reflected in high fertility rates or overt oppression of women. In most developing countries, however, patriarchy is much more pronounced and pervasive throughout a female's life. This is particularly shortsighted, "a luxury" that poor countries in the red on the balance sheet of human development cannot afford; each and every person who is healthy, educated, and able to work and be a participating citizen should be welcomed as an essential value added to the national economy.

The domination of self-centered male interests increasingly threatens the survival of large parts of the populations in developing countries, with women constituting the most vulnerable groups. Being completely denied or having severely restricted access to education and economic resources, not to speak of political participation, women remain dependent on men. At the same time, men unload onto them the most toilsome and time-consuming work, which moreover carries so little prestige that it justifies meager compensation or none at all.[65]

Women in the lower strata of developing countries, especially in rural areas, live at the edge of absolute poverty in a mud-walled thatch, along with their husbands, several children, and other dependants. Although theoretically poverty has the same implications for both sexes, women in poor regions of the developing world are more affected in terms of health, nutrition, and education. Among the various and sometimes quite subtle discriminations against females, the distribution within the family of basic supplies such as food and health care, which favors the old and the male, is probably a major factor in raising female mortality.[66]

Estimates suggest that, as of the mid-eighties, 500 million women were severely anaemic, almost 500 million were stunted as the result of childhood protein-energy malnutrition, about 250 million suffered a range of consequences of severe iodine deficiency, and some 2 million were blind due to Vitamin A deficiency. Human welfare losses associated with women's malnutrition include reduced quality of life, increased child mortality, and diminished capacity for domestic and income-generating work.

Because women also have to care for children and the household, they are the ones who feel most directly the deficiencies in their living conditions and the quality of the environment—deficiencies that, once again, have to be compensated for by work that is not only time-consuming but enjoys little "social prestige."

The vicious circle of patriarchy and poverty becomes a deterring factor for the symmetry of social development and is thus detrimental to society as a whole.

Almost everywhere the stereotype of the productive male breadwinner prevails even where male unemployment or underemployment is high and where women's productive work actually provides the primary income. The fact that the wife has the responsibility of the subsistence of the household is likely to be ignored, whereas the majority of men's work is valued, either directly through cash remuneration or indirectly through status and political power. Under normal conditions, women are generally not in a position to assume a leadership role in the family due to traditional prejudices and power structures that favor men.

There are, however, an increasing number of female-headed households. Caroline Moser has identified two main types:

> First, there are *de jure* women-headed households, in which the male partner is permanently absent due to separation or death, and the woman is legally single, divorced or widowed; second, *de facto* women-headed households in which the male partner is temporarily absent, due for instance to long-term work migration, or refugee status. Here the woman is not legally the head of household, and

is often perceived as a dependent despite the fact that she may, for the majority of her adult life, have primary if not total responsibility for the financial as well as the organizational aspects of the household.[67]

Such households tend to be among the poorest because women, many of them with numerous children to raise as well as older relatives to care for, face a labor market highly restricted in terms of distance, function, quality, and quantity of job opportunities. The dilemma of these women and their households is that the same patriarchal structures that restrict their mobility and deny them access to productive labor have a self-destructive effect: national economies unnecessarily suffer in terms of forgone production, diminished social welfare, and rapid population growth.

Although it is evident that women's agricultural production activities will become increasingly important with the rising needs of growing populations, there is still a conspicuous lack of policy response in the mainstream development agenda. Agricultural extension services tend to ignore women's many problems in agriculture because of a focus on exports. This kind of discrimination has particularly undesirable effects in Africa, where today up to 70 percent of the farms are run by women.[68] Moreover, women benefit from technological progress (such as labor-saving or more productive technologies for the production, processing, and preparation of food, or stoves that use less firewood) only rarely.

This discrimination is not only unjust, it is senseless in terms of development policy because wherever women are given the necessary leeway they are as successful as men. Women are represented in growing numbers in grassroots movements and nongovernmental organizations, in no small part as a protest against institutional restrictions. They organize themselves independently and informally (for example, for environmental protection, the Green Belt Movement in Kenya or the Chipko Andolan Movement in India) and on a self-help basis do concrete and very successful work (such as training children and young people, but also production and sales cooperatives).[69] These successes nourish confidence in a person's own powers of accomplishment—and also, on occasion, create the potential for conflict between the sexes.

The insecurity that patriarchy imposes on women in Bangladesh has been analyzed in detail by Mead Cain, Syeda Rokeya Khanam, and Shamsun Nahar.[70] To the interesting question of why patriarchy is perpetuated in the face of the poverty in the lower economic classes, the authors note:

> That men benefit materially from the power that they exercise over women is clear. First, they are provided with services and amenities that they would otherwise have to provide for themselves or do without entirely. Second, there is at least qualitative evidence that the distribution of food and consumer goods within the household favors males in general and adult males the most. Less tangible but probably no less important benefits include satisfaction gained from

exclusive access to various aspects of social life and a feeling of importance. . . .

Potential agents of change and sources of resistance to the current system of patriarchy are undermined by the interaction of age, sex, and class hierarchies. Among women, solidarity and resistance to patriarchy are undermined by an age hierarchy that allies older women with patriarchal interests and by class differences between women. Moreover, the institution of purdah [seclusion] confers social status upon women, while at the same time serving as an instrument of repression. Similarly, among poor men, for whom the material benefits of patriarchy are less than for the relatively rich, and whose well-being might improve if their wives could find more employment, potential resistance is blunted by their position of dependence in the class hierarchy.[71]

Discrimination against women has consequences for population policy, for whenever their position in society is weak, their list of responsibilities long, and their rights few, birth rates remain high. But this should not be the first reason for supporting human rights for women. It is mainly the women (and the children) who bear the burden of underdevelopment while enjoying few of the fruits of progress. Because of women's family obligations, from which they cannot withdraw, social and economic crises hit them harder and more directly. They suffer from open and concealed violence, both sexual and political, as well as from poverty. When there are shortages, they have to try to overcome them by even greater diligence in productive activities and by a constant search for paying jobs.

On balance, developments have been bitter for the majority of women in developing countries. Article 60 of the United Nations Charter, which calls for "the realization of human rights and fundamental freedoms for all, without regard . . . to sex," still has not had practical results. On the contrary, women suffer discrimination in most developing countries, and in some Asian countries with fatal consequences, whether through neglect of nutrition and medical care for girls[72] or through the aborting of female fetuses.[73]

In patriarchal societies, agreements on human rights are no guarantee that women actually enjoy those rights. In contrast to the discrimination of ethnic minorities in South Africa, the discrimination of women is not perceived as a problem of violation against human rights. It is true that the "status of women" is explained differently in Western and non-Western cultures—male domination, however, which reduces women nearly to a commodity, should not simply be put into the straightjacket of cultural ambivalence. There is no doubt that many specific cultural elements are important for social development and stability. The right to cultural identity must not, however, be misused to justify denying women elementary human rights. Cultural identity and authenticity lie not only in the past, but also in the future.

The issue of family size is closely related to patriarchy. Generally, men gain in power and respect if they have many children, as it provides an archaic demonstration of manliness. Women are regarded merely as biological aids for this purpose.[74] At the same time, in many African countries, family legislation and custom give men all rights over wives and children but little responsibility for economic support of either.[75] The phenomenon of externalizing costs described earlier, or the "free-rider phenomenon," as Harvey Leibenstein calls it,[76] arises thus also within the family itself. Where the responsibility for the consequences of many children falls more heavily on the wife than on the husband, a high fertility rate may reflect the husband's opportunity for free-riding—so his incentive for birth control is weak.

Forms of marriage such as polygyny (having many wives) and related spatial patterns of marital living arrangements that yield a household with numerous focal points provide further opportunities for free-riding.[77] Polygyny helps a husband minimize his financial contribution to child-support expenses while increasing his opportunities to satisfy his reproductive goals. To reduce the financial contribution per child, it is convenient to have a number of wives who provide the remainder. A Nigerian study explains this with the "proportionality effect":

> Consider the financial advantages of a polygynist, who, claiming equality of treatment, gives his two wives the same amount of annual financial support per child. However, his senior wife has an expensive secondary school-aged child, while the junior wife is the mother of a primary school child. As a result, the husband's proportional burden is lessened as the financial cost of the older child is passed on substantially to the senior wife.[78]

A polygynist's free-riding opportunity is further facilitated if the age range of each wife's children is wide enough to enable older children to finance their younger siblings' education.

Policies aimed at making fathers more accountable for the economic support of their children and raising the status of women would no doubt promote male interest in family planning. However, potential polygyny is a constant threat with economic consequences for financially dependent wives, since an additional marriage often leads a husband to reduce his contribution to child-support expenses. To prevent this, a wife may have more children than she desires in order to satisfy her husband's reproductive goals. Therefore, changing family legislation so that marital insecurity is eliminated for women seems highly desirable.

Outside Africa, providing economic support for the family is mainly the obligation of the father, whereas the mother is primarily or exclusively occupied with domestic chores. Take the example of Bangladesh. Certainly men there are also free-riders, as the countless household activities, especially in poor rural settings, require a large amount of labor they are not expected and are not willing to contribute. But the primary incentive for high fertility rates in Bangladesh is tied to the high risk of loss of economic and social status that patriarchy generates for women. Women often face a high probability of widowhood as a consequence of a large age difference between the male and female at marriage. A widow's potential for self-support will have been weakened because custom and religion condemn her to confinement in the homestead and to lifelong dependence on men; in addition, the Muslim law of inheritance disproportionately favors male heirs, and there is social proscription against remarriage of widows. So a woman needs at least one son as early as possible if she wants to avoid becoming a vagrant beggar.[79]

If the state exerts pressure in this situation to lower the birth rate, it is women who generally suffer. A population policy based on voluntary action does not have much prospect of success in this social context because the women usually have no choice but to try to improve their lot by having many children.

When state support and broadly based public education combine to seek a relationship of equality and partnership between husband and wife, the social and economic opportunities for women to shape and develop their lives will grow, both at the family level and in society as a whole. In this context it is important, once again, to recall the political obligation of leaders in developing nations to create equal social conditions, including political and institutional reforms. Appeals by the North about the ethical responsibility of political leaders in the South on this issue could legitimately be tied to a preferential allotment of development assistance. In today's world, however, "gender conditionality" has not yet been seriously considered.

Other important considerations relating to an ethically desirable social framework for population policy concern individuals and have to do with sexual ethics. The discussion of these issues is, in particular, of central importance in church documents.[80] At the heart of these arguments is a relationship between man and wife that is characterized by an absence of sexual egoism and aggression. If sexual behavior and family decisionmaking are characterized by loving consideration for the needs of a lifetime partner and joint responsibility for decisions on the number of children, this automatically creates favorable conditions for diminishing birth rates.

The point here is not to create a moralistic and unrealistic ideal of human beings and their relationships within the family, nor is it to administer reproaches[81] or even condemnations founded in moral theology or natural law. At issue is the question of human dignity, which is also the foundation of the U.N. Declaration of Human Rights. Thus the call for upholding human dignity as a part of responsible parenthood is no clerical imposition on a secularized society; rather, it identifies conditions fundamental to an acceptable population policy. It does not signify repression or disregard for human sexuality, but it does rule out excesses like the degradation of women to being mere objects of men's sexual or reproductive desires.[82]

Improving Educational and Training Opportunities for Women

The right to education and to acquisition of knowledge is a human right of central importance. This is still denied to most women in the developing world, thus limiting their opportunity to find alternatives to the role of mother and wife. The widespread view is that education for girls is unnecessary because it is of no value in their later lives: girls will leave home at some point, and going to school is useless for their future role as wife and mother.

Quite apart from population policy considerations, appropriate general education and professional training are a central requirement of development policy and, indeed, of human rights. Education and training are among the fundamental conditions for development of a person, for social security, and for equal participation in the economic, political, and cultural life of a society. Without a suitable education it is impossible for people to reflect on their own lives and, hence, to work for more justice, freedom, and tolerance. Discrimination against women is inconsistent with the goal of broadly based social and human development.

Improvements in the education and training of all members of a society are also desirable from the standpoint of population policy. Empirical studies from many countries show a clear relationship between the quality of education (measured in school years) and reductions in the birth rate.[83] When the level of education and training goes up in a society, many other social and economic conditions change as well.

In principle, a population problem arises because the interests underlying the various individual decisions about the size of a family do not add up to an overall interest that serves the long-term general welfare. Only the appropriate kind of education and training will permit parents to see their personal procreative activity within the framework of society as a whole, to see the consequences of various behavioral options, and to sharpen their individual and social awareness of responsibility.

A general improvement of education and training, however, does not have anywhere near as clear a relationship to sinking birth rates as raising the level of education and training of women in particular does.[84] Various empirical studies have shown that improved education for women lowers birth rates up to three times as much as educational improvements for men do.[85] Moreover, the level of women's education has a significant influence of its own on reducing infant and child mortality, the most important factor influencing the birth rate.[86]

A comparison of 98 developing countries shows that secondary education for women is one—if not *the*—key factor influencing the level of the birth rate.[87] Other studies have come to similar conclusions.[88] The data of the World Fertility Survey also point to the extraordinary significance of women's education, although with variations from one culture to another. (See Table VI-3.)

Improved education for women has a significant influence on their age at marriage. Susan Cochrane regards this as the most important effect that a rising level of education for women has on birth rates.[89] Other studies show that better-educated women, owing to their higher status within the family, have a clear desire for fewer children and are in a better position to get their way than those with a poorer education.[90]

There is a big deficit in developing countries with regard to support of education and training for women, as there is clear discrimination against them. According to *The World's Women*, which the United Nations presented for the first time in 1991:

Table VI-3

Average Number of Children of Married Women in Selected Countries According to Level of Education and Type of Residential Area

Country	City Residents Categorized by Years of Schooling				Rural Residents Categorized by Years of Schooling			
	0	1–3	4–6	7+	0	1–3	4–6	7+
Colombia	5.27	3.58	2.92	2.09	4.76	4.43	3.99	—
Jordan	5.60	5.45	5.29	3.50	5.35	—	5.42	—
South Korea	3.11	3.19	2.76	2.13	3.83	3.51	3.04	2.25
Mexico	5.15	4.52	3.54	2.25	5.08	4.58	4.26	2.59
Peru	4.68	4.47	3.78	2.58	4.48	4.49	4.15	—
Philippines	—	4.31	3.59	2.70	3.45	4.35	4.11	3.21
Indonesia	3.49	3.72	3.59	3.02	3.34	3.46	3.63	3.38
Kenya	3.86	—	4.19	4.06	4.54	4.78	4.76	4.47

Source: World Fertility Survey, in S. Singh and J. Casterline: The Socio-Economic Determinants of Fertility. In J. Cleland and J. Hobcraft (eds.): Reproductive Change in Developing Countries. Oxford University Press, Oxford 1985, p. 205.

Table VI-4

Variations in Education in Selected Countries According to Sex,
1985–1987

Country	Percentage of Illiterates	
	Women	Men
Cameroon	40.9	20.4
Central African Republic	82.0	46.0
Egypt	61.9	37.0
Mozambique	74.7	36.0
Bolivia	24.2	8.5
Peru	10.2	3.5
Afghanistan	88.9	54.2
Bangladesh	72.8	55.4
China	17.9	4.8

Source: United Nations: The World's Women 1970–90. New York 1991.

- women in the so-called Third World go to school only half as long as men;
- worldwide, the number of illiterate women increased by 50 million during the last 20 years (even today, half the women in developing countries cannot read or write); and
- the same wretched conditions exist in the areas of informal education and training: although women everywhere make significant contributions to economic development, they get only a fraction of the available educational opportunities.[91]

In many countries, the education gap between men and women is very large. (See Table VI-4.)

Eliminating Political, Professional, and Economic Discrimination

Although women enjoy the right to vote almost everywhere in the world, including developing countries, and constitute more than 50 percent of the voters, they are under-represented in parliaments and hold few public positions of leadership. (See Table VI-5.) Consequently, they also have fewer opportunities to participate in the formation of national and local policies that would improve, or assist in improving, their lot.

Even in industrial countries, women only occupy about 12–14 percent of

Table VI-5

Female Participation in Public Life in Selected Countries, 1987

Country	Women's Share of		
	Seats in Parliaments (percent)	Leadership Positions in Governments (percent)	Ministerial Positions (number)
Switzerland	14.0	2.9	0
Federal Republic of Germany (former)	5.8	4.9	2
German Democratic Republic (former)	31.8	4.1	4
United States	5.3	11.5	1
Cameroon	14.2	3.1	2
Egypt	3.9	0	0
Kenya	1.7	0	0
Brazil	5.3	5.0	1
Mexico	10.8	0	0
Venezuela	3.9	4.5	0
People's Republic of China	21.1	1.4	0
Iran	1.5	0	0
Thailand	3.5	3.8	0

Source: United Nations: The World's Women 1970–90. New York 1991.

the top public positions, and then only those that carry a "female" tag such as education, culture, or women's and children's affairs.[92] Men continue to monopolize the more influential departments of trade, finance, and defense.

In developing countries, the situation is even more precarious. There, women occupy only 6–9 percent of public leadership positions.[93] In the bureaucracy and in private firms they hold mostly subordinate jobs. Their numbers diminish toward the top of the hierarchy, where the better-paying and more influential jobs are to be found.

The segregation of the labor market on sexual lines that exists in industrial countries has established itself in much more rigid form in many developing countries. Many women are predominantly condemned, in the formal labor market, to work in unskilled jobs without promotion opportunities and at low pay.[94] Most women continue to work in the "informal sector" under unprotected conditions. The gainful employment of women depends not only on the social structures that determine their access to the labor market, to education and training, and to property ownership, but also on the weight women carry within the family and, hence, their authority to make decisions. For that reason, there is here—as with all other correlations—at best a weak causal relationship between the gainful employment of women and the number of their children. According to Machiko Osawa, the correlation between women's increased labor force participation and the fertility decline that has been observed in industrial nations is weaker in developing countries, and appears to break down completely in the case of post-World War II Japan.[95] The author contends that the time-cost hypothesis (which associates women's employment with increased time-cost, resulting in lower fertility) is valid, but only for women employed outside the home in the formal sector. Those who are unpaid family workers or self-employed in the home have the same fertility rates as wives who do not work. Thus, the time-cost hypothesis may not be relevant for developing countries and economies where women's labor force participation is likely to be in informal-sector activities that do not increase the cost of raising children.

Areas where women enjoy a higher social position, according to the U.N. Population Fund, show higher economic growth and more rapid improvement of the quality of life; the opposite is true of areas where women are disadvantaged.[96] Moreover, there is much evidence that "women's income" has highly beneficial effects on the family because women use their income more sensibly than men do. They use their pay first and foremost for the children, the household, and improvements in the family diet, while men in many cases seem to succumb to the temptations of superficial consumption (such as radios, watches, mopeds, and alcohol).[97]

Changing the Direction of Wealth Flows Within Families

John Caldwell maintains that "fertility behavior in both pretransitional and posttransitional societies is economically rational within the context of socially determined economic goals and within bounds largely set by biological and psychological factors." He distinguishes two types of society: "one of stable high fertility, where there would be no net economic gain accruing to the family (or to those dominant within it) from lower fertility levels, and the other in which economic rationality alone would dictate zero reproduction. The former is characterized by 'net wealth flows' from younger to older generations, and the latter by flows in the opposite direction. These flows are defined to embrace all economic benefits both present and anticipated over a lifetime" (including goods and money, labor and services, protection and guarantees, and social and political support).[98]

Caldwell argues that the traditional theory of demographic transition puts too much emphasis on "modernization," "industrialization," and "economic growth" as factors leading to a reduction of birth rates.[99] He suggests that the conditions of stable high fertility and of subsequent destabilization lie largely in the nature of economic relations within the family, whereby "family" is not just those living under one roof—husband, wife, children, and additional relatives. The "family" here encompasses groups of close relatives living in close proximity who share land, economic interests, and mutual obligations. This larger and demographically more significant entity is described as "extended family."[100]

Extended families are often organized on strictly patriarchal lines. As a rule, these structures are closely tied to traditional rural ways of life and work habits; learning these and passing them on is made possible, or at least easier, by the counsel of old men. The larger the family is, under these circumstances, the easier it is to develop a division of labor within it and the less reliance there must be on the paid work of outsiders, even for the most difficult and unpleasant tasks.

In such societies, the network of family relationships enhances the social security of the individual and, under certain circumstances, makes for greater political influence (in the village, tribe, and so on). For the most part this has positive economic consequences.[101] Enlarging this network of relationships, which is equivalent to gaining more political and economic influence, is possible in only two ways: either through a high birth rate in one's own family or through strategically favorable marriages of one's children. Such conditions help explain the results of a survey taken among the Yoruba in Western Nigeria (who live in a traditional society): 80 percent of the respondents said that children are to be preferred to material wealth or are identical with it. Only 6 percent thought that children detracted from wealth.[102] The social system of the extended family makes it possible to divide up the cost involved in children and their care. From the moment they cease to be babies, children are enlisted to help in the field and the household and thereby contribute to their own maintenance.

The economic roles and productive contributions of children are an important motivation for high fertility rates in Bangladesh as well. Mead Cain looked at child labor inputs and relative consumption in a village and found that boys become net producers at least by age 12, compensate for their cumulative consumption by age 15, and compensate for their own and one sister's cumulative consumption by age 22 if the sister marries and leaves the household at age 15.[103] Due to the rigid division of labor by sex, the related inequality in productive work opportunities, and the restricted mobility for females, girls are less engaged in directly productive activities that would require them to leave the homestead area.

Caldwell suggests there is a "net flow" of wealth from the generation of the children to that of the parents in all traditional societies. In his view, high birth rates will drop only when social conditions have changed so that the factors that make the extended family socially, economically, and emotionally attractive no longer operate, resulting in advantages for small families. He argues that when ɯere is a concentration of concern and expenditure on children instead of the expectation of benefit and utility from them, family size will be considerably smaller.[104]

Caldwell cites the import of a different culture ("westernization") and its widespread diffusion through mass media and mass education as causing families to close together emotionally into a nuclear family unit. He suggests that these ideological influences precede, and probably induce, other social and economic changes associated with modernization.[105] The mechanisms through which education affects the attractiveness of having many children include:

- a reduction of the child's potential for work around the home;
- increased cost of children;
- delaying the child's capacity as an economic producer, which increases dependence on families and society;
- cultural changes, which are hastened by schooling; and
- dissemination of Western middle-class values in schools in developing countries.[106]

Caldwell's wealth-flow theory grows out of strong evidence from West African cultures and has become a mainstream position.

This hypothesis might, however, be weakened when applied to the entire developing world. It is important therefore to consider objections and alternative hypotheses that have been put forward.

With regard to the proposition that net wealth in traditional societies flows from younger to older generations, Paul Turke, for example, maintains that resources are "recycled" back to children.[107] Based on his own research and citing other authors, he argues that offspring (presumably sons) traditionally gain from receiving inheritances, that mothers in Trinidad provide assistance that measurably helps their reproductive-age daughters to reproduce, that elderly women of a tribe in Tanzania work extremely hard so that the products of their labor benefit their children and grandchildren, and so on.

Turke furthermore doubts that reproduction always is based on a conscious decision: children often just "happen" to their parents rather than being the result of their economic calculus. Yet when confronted with a structured interview on this issue, people might give the desired economic answer or provide a reason that makes some sense to themselves or to a Western interviewer.[108]

According to Harvey Leibenstein, "family size may be determined by a lack of calculation of considerations, or by extremely gross calculation, or by a lack of appreciation (or caring) of the connection between current behavior and future consequences."[109] External changes that would affect the cost of children would have no impact on the many households affected by traditional small group norms that support high fertility rates. It is assumed that fertility behavior is unlikely to change unless there are significant external changes such as economic development, increases in education, changes in location, new job opportunities, as well as sufficiently large subsidies or other means of attraction to family planning programs in order to overcome the inertia of many people in the targeted population.

Moreover, the effects of kin solidarity on fertility are not so obvious. While access to kin support is used to explain high fertility in West African countries, the lack of it is said to contribute to delayed fertility decline in Bangladesh. If the kin support system were to disappear, the parents could depend even on their own adult children. Kinship systems could just as well facilitate fertility decline in that they prevent children from becoming the focal point of parental concerns for security.[110]

As noted earlier, Caldwell identifies the spread of the ideology of the modern family through mass media and mass education as critical to promoting a value change that involves emotional and economic nucleation. Veena Thadani instead holds social and structural conditions responsible for such shifts in the family's allocation of material and emotional resources. She rightly notes that institutional and structural factors might either act as a constraint to the process of change or facilitate it, such as the access to or lack of institutional forms of security. There may well be an attitudinal predisposition to accept an idea, Thadani notes, but it must not necessarily translate into behavioral support, because "the opportunity and incentive for economic nucleation is open only to those who have the economic resources to be independent of extended kin support. The evidence of nucleation that Caldwell cites is provided by cases among the elite, those who clearly have the economic resources to secure a financial independence."[111]

According to Mead Cain, the erosion of joint households and the increase in the number of nuclear households in rural Bangladesh reflects the increase in the impoverishment of the population and is a symptom of the strain that poverty places on the bonds between kin. Joint households in rural Bangladesh are those of relatively large landowners; among the poor and the landless, there is too little land or too little space to house more than the members of the nuclear household.[112] Given the high fertility rates in Bangladesh, household nucleation does not seem to be a sufficient precondition to smaller family size.

These examples of diverging viewpoints show that the conditions that provide an argument for unconstrained fertility or an incentive to the adoption of birth control methods in one country or context do not necessarily do so in another. Likewise, the extent to which a given social event or innovation—be it mass education or economic self-sufficiency of the nuclear family—involves a society in other important social changes varies considerably from context to context.

Changing the Modes of Production

Although patriarchal institutions have prevailed in most human societies and therefore cannot be attributed to any particular mode of production, the interdependence between patriarchy and the property structure of feudal modes of production is an important determinant of the fertility rate. Caldwell distinguishes two fundamentally different kinds of production:

- "familial modes of production," which take place primarily in the family and by its members; and
- "non-familial based capitalist production," which is characterized by the fact that individuals produce goods or offer services and sell them outside their homes.[113]

Production organized so that essential economic activities take place within the family and are carried out by its members creates favorable conditions for a high birth rate.

As long as families form the productive center of a society—and that is largely the case in traditional rural societies—the relations between workers are family relationships. These are by their very nature unequal and tend to favor older people and men. The larger a family is, the more obvious the hierarchy and differentiation of rights and duties.

In family-centered production structures, family decisions cannot be separated from economic ones, and the decision-making power in economic matters is a dominant influence in all other areas of family life. Whenever economic dependence or, as the case may be, economic power is so closely bound up with the power of decision in the family, the older generation is able to exercize substantial influence on the most intimate intrafamily decisions, such as how many children to have. The old men or the family elders decide whether someone will get married, to whom, and when. Depending on the degree of influence the elders have on younger family members, they will also have a say in whether or not means and methods of family planning are used—all in accordance with economic criteria.[114] The patriarch's unquestioned power of decision in economic matters is less obvious and direct when it comes to decisions about pregnancy, but it is effective nonetheless because his economic power gives him significant influence over the behavior of the family members subordinated to him.

Why do the adult offspring, primarily the sons, abide by these decisions?

The reasons are, once again, mainly economic—the possibility of profiting from submission and/or the fear of losing something as a result of rebellious-ness. Still, immaterial incentives such as reputation also have a powerful influence: loose talk, rumors (for example, about a man's possible impotence if pregnancy does not follow soon after marriage), or a demonstration of the patriarch's disapproval in the course of everyday decisions if his orders are violated or his desires not taken into account. Disregard of the patriarch's instructions could, as a result of talk about his supposed weakness and in-ability to get his way, endanger his social position, and the sanctions are accordingly severe.

Under such circumstances there are often tragic cases in which involuntary infertility (as a result of sickness, for example) can have serious negative consequences for a woman. Infertility is regarded in patriarchal societies as such a terrible personal failure that it leads to contemptuous treatment and even divorce or polygamous behavior.[115]

Even assuming that basic needs are being met, that infant and child mor-tality have been reduced, and that women's social status has been strength-ened, a decisive demographic transformation will not begin, according to Caldwell, until the system of production has been transformed in such a way that those holding economic power either derive no advantage from high birth rates or are not in a position to influence them.[116]

Economic Prerequisites

Sustained Economic Growth

The principle that child and infant mortality drop wherever everyone in a population enjoys relative prosperity holds true all over the world. In a compu-ter analysis of per capita income in a variety of countries plus number of births and life expectancy at birth, the following trends emerge clearly:

- the higher the per capita income of a country, the lower its birth rate (see Figure VI-1); and
- the higher the per capita income of a country, the higher the life expec-tancy at birth (see Figure VI-2).

These statements also hold true within individual countries for various population groups. In Colombia and Malaysia during the seventies, for exam-ple, the 20 percent of the population with the lowest incomes had three times as many children as the richest 20 percent did.[117]

If it were not for important exceptions to these correlations, along with a

Figure VI-1   Fertility in Relation to Income in Developing Countries, 1972 and 1982

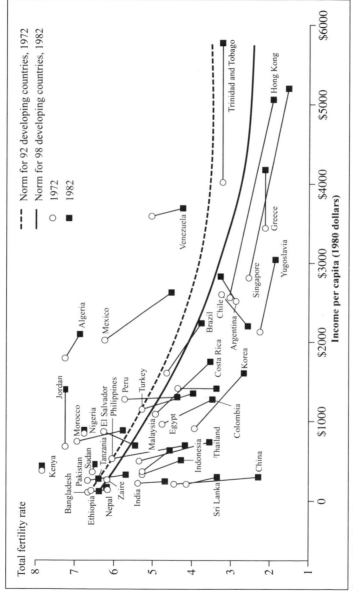

Source: World Bank: World Development Report 1984. Washington, D.C. 1984, p. 70.

Figure VI-2   Life Expectancy in Relation to Income in Developing Countries, 1972 and 1982

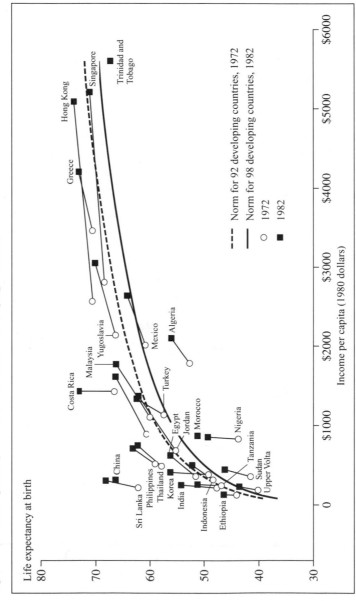

Source: World Bank: World Development Report 1984. Washington, D.C. 1984, p. 80.

certain time pressure for lowering birth rates, the strategy for internatonal development could be limited to promoting stable economic growth in various countries, simply waiting for birth rates to begin to go down.

But looking at the relationship between per capita income growth and birth rates in Figure VI-1, it is clear that some countries with relatively low per capita income have succeeded in making substantial progress in lowering their birth rate. Countries such as China, Sri Lanka, Thailand, Indonesia, and Costa Rica have much lower birth rates than the "norm" for all developing countries under investigation would lead us to expect.[118] Conversely, countries like Kenya, Jordan, Algeria, and Nigeria are far from having reached the level of birth rates they should have on the basis of their per capita income. The explanation for these deviations, extremely important for population policy, lies primarily in the quality of social policy. This will be dealt with in detail later.

Improvements in Income Distribution

Different population groups benefit in varying degrees from economic development. In most cases, those who profit more and earlier from economic development are the ones who enjoy initial advantages stemming from their social status, their greater wealth (through landownership, for example), or their higher level of education. For this reason, the infant and child mortality rates also drop more quickly for these groups. More than 100 years ago, this was true of Germany as well. There, real incomes rose substantially between the middle of the nineteenth century and the beginning of World War I. And there, too, it was the upper classes who benefited first, with the middle and lower classes following after and with corresponding consequences for infant and child mortality: "Between 1877/79 and 1912/13 infant mortality went down by more than 50 percent in the families of public officials and employees while for servants and the families of unskilled workers the rates were 24 and 16 percent respectively."[119]

Many studies have suggested that inequality may be an important macrosocial influence on fertility: the more unequal the distribution of income, the higher the birth rate.[120] The incomes of the lower 60 percent of earners correlate much more closely to death and birth rates than does the average income of an entire society.

Other authors examining the hypothesis that income redistribution would reduce fertility in developing countries found, however, that inequality has little or no apparent direct influence.[121] Part of the explanation may be that reliable data on personal or household income inequality are lacking or are incomplete for many countries,[122] that the definition of income is too narrow (for example, when it is broadened to include nonmarket sources, relative income increases),[123] or that income inequality influences fertility only indirectly. Also, most studies have given insufficient attention to the specific role of gender inequality, especially with regard to the intrahousehold distribution of income. The relative status of women appears to exert a statistically and substantively significant influence on fertility.[124]

Land reform is often advocated as a solution to problems of inequality in developing countries.[125] A re-examination of the relationship between land tenure distribution and fertility, drawing on 1952–1978 survey data from Nepal, India, the Philippines, Bangladesh, Thailand, Egypt, Iran, Mexico, and Brazil, evaluated two hypotheses:

- the land-labor demand hypothesis, which proposes that the greater the size of landholdings, the more valuable children's labor will be, thus increasing the level of fertility; and
- the land security hypothesis, which proposes that landownership negatively affects fertility because land is substituted for children as a security asset.

It has been concluded that the evidence does not support either hypothesis, but that fundamental structures of economic inequality and social injustice must be altered to achieve sustained fertility decline.[126]

But systems of land reform characteristically work against matrilineal systems and systems of co-ownership (where they exist), even though these may be more favorable to meeting human needs than the landownership by individual men that is favored by development projects. This has been illustrated in a case study of the Lilongwe Land Development Program in Malawi, which failed through its disregard of the traditional rights of women. Similar problems exist in many other poor countries.[127]

In sum, overall economic growth is undoubtedly necessary for improving the conditions of life of people in the developing world. But this point of agreement with conventional development theory calls for an important amplification. The benefits of economic development must reach the lower classes, and within those especially women, within an appropriate period of time, either directly through a noticeable improvement of their income or indirectly through government social services financed by growing tax revenues (or by development assistance).

Social Market Economy

At the beginning of this book we pointed out the advantages of the social market economy for development policy. Long before the political and social opening of Eastern Europe, the African Development Bank had recommended to its members that they should "ease the way for private initiative, eliminate unrealistic and productivity-dampening prices and subsidies, and get a grip on wasteful spending and mismanagement by the state." In addition, it was recommended that members "decentralize decision-making power, i.e. shift it from central authorities to individual producers and firms."[128] Nevertheless, the state remains one of the most dominant economic factors in many countries of the developing world.

Since the book *El Otro Sendero* (The Other Path) appeared in Peru a few years ago,[129] the subject of "less government" has come to play a significant role in development policy. Hernando de Soto and his colleagues investigated how the state-dominated Peruvian economy, with its wildly proliferating flood of laws, decrees, regulations, and instructions, actually worked. This was done not just theoretically but by using concrete examples.

De Soto asked a "typical Peruvian small businessman" to apply for an operating permit for a tailor shop. All the legal requirements were to be fulfilled. To get the permit, 11 different ministerial or governmental departments had to be dealt with. Ten of eleven officials were willing to carry out their responsibility only in return for an additional financial incentive. Two of them threatened to "bury" the file if they were not paid. Ultimately, 289 days were spent and in actual costs and lost time $1,231 went down the Urubamba—an amount equivalent to 32 times the Peruvian minimum wage at the time.

Another experiment had a comparable result. A permit to sell fruit and vegetables at roadside took 43 days to get and cost $590. This took place in a poor country without any developed social security net, a country that should value highly every additional bit of economic activity and job-creating opportunity.

The lack of clear title or of property rights altogether is a particularly strong brake on development because without them there is little incentive to invest in maintenance and improvement of land and real estate. Without property there can be no mortgage and, without mortgage collateral, no credit.

Because unemployment is a luxury that poor people in the developing world cannot afford, they have to find some kind of gainful employment simply for physical survival. For that reason, many look for opportunities in the "informal sector" or "shadow economy." They avoid the state and produce, sell, and offer services on the black market, without regard to official rules and requirements. In many developing countries—and also, according to rumors, in industrial countries such as Spain or Italy—the informal sector accounts for up to 40 percent of gross domestic product and employs about half the work force.

As a general rule, the more inefficient the government is and the more "powerful" its bureaucracy, the larger the informal sector. De Soto and his team demonstrated that Peru's "shadow economy" works, not only for plumbers, painters, and street vendors but broadly throughout the economy. In Lima alone it involves about 500,000 people. About 80 percent of the markets in Lima are black markets. Furniture, television sets, clothing, refrigerators, shoes, cement—all these things can be obtained more cheaply and dependably on the shadow market than on the official one. In construction and public transportation, the informal workers actually are dominant.

The poor people of Lima and other large Latin American cities established the informal "shadow economy" because they were unable to survive the "official" way, which entails too much government and bureaucracy, involves too many requirements, permits, and decrees, and serves mainly the personal interests of the bureaucrats while creating opportunities for corruption.

Contrary to stereotypical notions, it is not the big people but the little ones who are hurt by "too much government." Big firms can hire specialists to deal with bureaucratic obstacles and obscure rules. They also have the financial resources to "oil" the administrative machinery (if they choose to do so). Small firms do not have these resources; they are helpless and at the mercy of arbitrariness and corruption. They have to try to survive in an illegal framework, constantly at risk of prosecution or having to pay "protection" to a public servant.

The militant left-wing extremists of Peru, whose radicalism recalls the Khmer Rouge and who call themselves Sendero Luminoso (Shining Path), regard armed revolution and a complete reorganization of society as the only course. De Soto and his colleagues recommend "the other path" for Peru and for most developing countries: a market economy and entrepreneurial freedom, embedded in law and social order.

Where this approach has been followed, it has invariably led to more vitality and creativity than a planned economy and a centrally administered bureaucracy have. Shortage of natural resources (raw materials), inadequate education, and lack of financial means are not the only things that hamper the economic and social development of a country; unfavorable political conditions and the lack of a market economy (which does, however, need to be socially and ecologically compatible) can also obstruct development to a significant extent.

Political will is not all that is needed to create the social conditions for a consistent population policy. Appropriate economic growth is also needed to finance it. In the countries of the developing world, as elsewhere, this is more easily accomplished under a market economy.

Government Budget Priorities to Promote Development

The traditional explanation for human suffering in developing countries is that these governments are simply too poor to pay for a minimum of infrastructure and services to meet the basic needs of the poorer classes. In June 1991 the U.N. Development Programme (UNDP), in its *Human Development Report 1991,* presented an equally relevant conclusion: "The lack of political commitment, not of financial resources, is often the real cause for human neglect." The authors conclude that much current spending is misdirected and inefficiently used. If the priorities are set right, more money will be available for accelerated human progress.[130]

Here we have an official United Nations statement that says bluntly what development experts have been complaining about for years: the failure of politicians in many if not most developing countries is a fundamental obstacle to development. There are too many wrong priorities, too much wastage of resources, expenditures for military purposes that are too high (and sometimes rising), too many inefficient public enterprises, too many prestige projects, too much capital flight, and proliferating corruption. The "trilogy of imperfection," as it was once called by Commonwealth General Secretary Shridath Ramphal[131]—namely, rampant concentration of political power and/or dismantling of democratic structures, excessive military expenditures, and chronic corruption—weakens any sensible development strategy in its earliest stages and makes lasting economic and social improvements impossible.

If priorities were set properly and corresponding budgetary changes made, it would be possible within a short period of time and without a single extra dollar of development assistance to make $50 billion available for the fight against human misery—for elementary education, for example, and basic health services, rural water supplies, family planning, food programs, and social security. Even politically conservative institutions like the World Bank have now acknowledged the substantial and lasting success of development strategies oriented toward basic needs—so we are not engaging in speculation.[132]

The largest share of already existing resources would be freed by reducing the size of the military apparatus, which in most cases far exceeds legitimate defense needs. Wherever military expenditures have high priority, human misery is widespread. In Ethiopia, there are roughly 500 soldiers for every teacher; in Somalia, the figure is 525; in Vietnam, 309; in Iraq, 428. Iran spends 3.8 times as much for military purposes as for health and education combined; in Zaire, the figure is 2.5; in Chad, 2.3; in bitterly poor Uganda, 3.2; in Iraq, 7.[133] Although the trends have changed in many countries during the last two to three years, the problem remains: where more is spent on the military than on health and education together, it is no wonder that there is not enough medicine in the country and far too few people who can read and write.

Along with many experts, UNDP is now demanding that we draw the obvious conclusion: development assistance to individual countries should be tied to conditions such as a reduction of military expenditures and/or the introduction of concrete economic and social reforms.

Before the opening of Eastern Europe, the merest hint at such conditions on cooperation in international development would have triggered extremely loud protests from developing countries against "interference in internal affairs" or "neo-imperialism." Protests of this kind, as a distraction from their own real problems, worked quite well for decades, not least because despots found it easy, against the background of a smouldering East-West conflict, to play one superpower against the other. Since the end of the so-called cold war, which in the developing world was often enough a hot war by proxy, that is no longer possible. And the despotic regimes are already beginning to collapse, whether in Ethiopia, Angola, or elsewhere.

Of course, many developing countries will continue in the future to need financial and technical support from rich countries. Many of them, and hence a large part of the world's population, are too deeply mired in poverty and— even after the requisite housecleaning in terms of development policy—have too few resources to enter onto an appropriate path of human development. In the future, however, the best argument for making more development assistance available to a country will be the rational expenditure pattern of its own already available resources.

When the European Bank for Reconstruction and Development was founded in 1990 to accelerate the economic reconstruction of Eastern Europe, observation of human rights and democratic forms of government were made the main criteria for the granting of credits. Why should our development assistance organizations not offer to the people of the developing world the same protections against irresponsible holders of power? The results of polls on the subject of "development assistance" tend to support such a procedure because, almost everywhere, most people favor solidarity with the poor and needy.[134] Upholding benefices and despotic power for the dominant elite at the expense of the poor majority of a society—and this with tax money or donated money from industrial countries—is neither sensible nor legitimate.

Suitable national budget priorities and appropriate international development cooperation will produce different project concepts and programs from one country to another. But in the poorest countries, strategies oriented toward basic needs, including family planning programs, will be in the forefront, along with support for rural infrastructure, strengthening the role of women, and ecologically acceptable programs for modernizing agriculture.

"Sustainable Development"

By "sustainable development" we mean development so organized by the present generation that future generations will continue to be able to live at a standard worthy of human beings. But there is still disagreement over what that means in detail for various societies because the definition is too broad to permit concrete conclusions about the required steps.[135] The question as to how possible clashes between the objectives of North and South or between present and future prosperity are to be solved remains for the time being unanswered.

Certain fundamental requirements for all societies are uncontested. The rate of use of renewable resources should not, for example, exceed the capacity to restore them (such as firewood or water) and the depletion of nonrenewable resources should not proceed more rapidly than alternative renewable resources are made available (use of fossil fuels, for example, versus development of solar energy). Nor should emissions of harmful pollutants exceed the absorptive capacity of the environment.[136]

Long-term sustainability does not mean "zero economic growth"—not for the highly industrialized countries of today and certainly not for poor countries, which are still for the most part agrarian. For industrial countries, however, moving their societies in the direction of sustainable development does mean a shift from quantitative expansion to qualitative development; for developing countries, it means quantitative development at a qualitatively rising level. Based on our present knowledge and assuming social and institutional reforms, greater economic efficiency through technological innovation will permit the developing world to achieve significant and durable improvements in its quality of life. We have already pointed to the need for international solidarity, humanization of thought and action, preservation rather than consumption, and a clearer understanding of the common interests of present and future generations.

These requirements turn all countries into "developing" ones, albeit with varying priorities. For poor countries, development policy has acquired a new dimension—environmental compatibility. Development policy is no longer conceivable independently of environmental policy. Indeed, the point can hardly be overstressed: environmental policy is not everything, but without environmental policy there will be nothing.

The U.N. Conference on Environment and Development in Rio de Janeiro in 1992 pulled together, in its 800-page *Agenda 21,* data that demonstrate the necessity of changing our ecological course. The new information contained in this document and the immense international learning process related to it mark a tidal change in our thinking about development policy.

Prerequisites of Social Policy

After three decades of impressive and rapid progress in lowering infant and child mortality, the pace began to slacken in the mid-seventies in many parts of the developing world; in some countries there was even a reversal of the trend at times.[137] Similar developments can be seen with respect to school attendance rates and other basic needs.

During the eighties, many countries that export raw materials faced sharp reductions in their export earnings[138] and as a consequence slipped into deep domestic recession with shrinking government revenues. Once again the people in Africa south of the Sahara were particularly hard hit. In many countries, more and more people fell below the poverty line.[139] The "terms of trade"— the measure of how much a country can receive in imports for a unit of its export goods[140]—began sinking for the countries of Africa south of the Sahara in 1985.

At the same time there was a stagnation of development assistance and all other capital transfers to poor countries. Repayment obligations on old loans meant that during this period there was even occasionally a net capital transfer of several hundred million dollars a year from developing countries to industrial ones.

When, as a result of shrinking export earnings—or for whatever reason[141]—countries became more indebted and international rescheduling became necessary, the reduction of government deficits often resulted in a dismantling of social services such as food subsidies and nutrition programs.[142] In some cases there were also cuts in health and education.[143] Only very rarely were military expenditures reduced.

Those who suffered most were, as one would expect, the most vulnerable members of society: poor families. Especially imperilled by cuts in basic health services were children under five and their mothers, as well as pregnant women from the lower classes, a group for whom free or heavily subsidized government services often represent the only chance for any form of health care. A UNICEF study in 1988 found that, as a result of the recession and the related cuts in social services, child mortality and malnourishment increased and the quality of education deteriorated in a number of countries.[144]

The wealthier classes in developing countries were also affected by the recession, but it was not life-threatening for them as their purchasing power allowed them to escape into the private sector.

There is a vital need for debt-reduction agreements and for national and international efforts to reduce debt in such a way that debtor governments' expenditures, at least over the medium and long term, are keyed to their revenues. But this scenario should not be played out on the backs of the lower classes and their children. Alternative adjustment programs have been proposed by UNICEF[145]—but rarely put into practice.

Whenever recession and programs of structural adaptation lead to cuts in government social services and basic health programs, child and infant mortality rises. Not only does this cause avoidable human suffering, it promotes patterns of thought and action undesirable in terms of population policy: for security reasons, people aim to have more children.

Satisfaction of Basic Needs as a Top Priority

"Satisfaction of basic needs" can be defined in various ways. Along with the notable speech of World Bank President Robert McNamara in 1973,[146] the International Labour Organization contributed a breakthrough on this concept:

> Basic needs are defined as the minimum standard of living which a society should set for the poorest groups of its people. The satisfaction of basic needs means meeting the minimum requirements of a family for personal consumption: food, shelter, clothing; it implies access to essential services, such as safe drinking-water, sanitation, transport, health and education; it implies that each person available for and willing to work should have an adequately remunerated job. It should further imply the satisfaction of needs of a more qualitative nature: a healthy, humane, and satisfying environment, and popular participation in the making of decisions that affect the lives and livelihood of the people and individual freedoms.[147]

The positive deviations from the norm that "economic growth lowers birth rates" demonstrate the great influence that development strategies oriented toward basic needs can have on birth rates. The result of such a policy, in the first instance, is to lower infant and child mortality and raise the standard of education. But there is more to it than that: development policies that set the highest priority on meeting basic needs reach the lowest social strata of a society—those who, because of the conditions in which they live, accept high mortality rates and try to insure themselves against this with high birth rates.[148]

Development strategies oriented toward basic needs reduce mortality and birth rates within a relatively short time, independent of the overall level of the economy (as measured by per capita national product).

The Human Development Index introduced by UNDP shows clearly how dramatically the quality of life of people in some countries can improve, despite a relatively low per capita income. (See Table VI-6.)

The idea for the Human Development Index and the calculations related to it are based on the realization that average per capita income alone is not an adequate indicator of the quality of life. For that reason, three further

Table VI-6

GNP, Quality of Life, and Birth Rates

Country	Per Capita GNP (U.S. dollars), 1989	Human Development Index, 1992	Child Mortality,[a] 1990	Birth Rates,[b] 1992
China	350	0.612	42	20
Sri Lanka	430	0.651	35	21
Colombia	1,200	0.758	50	26
Costa Rica	1,780	0.842	22	27
Cuba	2,000	0.732	14	18
Sierra Leone	220	0.062	257	48
Guinea	430	0.052	237	47
Mauretania	500	0.141	214	46
Angola	610	0.169	292	47
Cameroon	1,000	0.313	148	47
Gabon	2,960	0.545	164	41

Source: UNDP: Human Development Report 1992. Oxford University Press, New York 1992, p. 127
    ff; Population Reference Bureau: 1992 World Population Data Sheet. Washington, D.C. 1992
    (for birth rates).
[a]Children under five per 1000 live births.
[b]Per 1000 inhabitants, not adjusted.

indicators—providing information on health, likelihood of survival, and possibilities for human development—were added to per capita income to create a two-part indicator:

- life expectancy at birth (including presence or absence of any special health problems or other risk factors), and
- the level of education in a society, approximated in terms of the level of literacy (hence, the professional and personal development opportunities of the people).[149]

Countries that geared their development policy to satisfying basic needs scored consistently better than the ones with comparable or higher per capita gross national product but without a development policy oriented toward basic needs.

Health Services

There is a relationship of mutual dependence between "health" and "development." Although it does not necessarily hold true that economic growth will improve the health of the poorest groups in a society, it is clear that these are the people whose health is most jeopardized by a decline of economic strength. Health, however, is not only an end in itself; it is also an essential prerequisite for attaining social and economic goals.

A vicious circle arises here: The less social and economic development a country has had, the poorer its people are. The poorer the people, the less they are able to satisfy their basic needs. That means that they cannot obtain enough food of adequate quality or find housing to satisfy the most basic hygienic requirements and protect them from the weather. These deficiencies create a heightened susceptibility to disease. Bad health impairs productivity and leads to income loss, which makes it impossible for them to break out of this pattern: "Men and women were sick because they were poor, they became poorer because they were sick, and sicker because they were poorer."[150] It is obvious that "sickness" is a factor that cannot be eliminated without at the same time attacking all the other problems that make for "underdevelopment." Along with the political will and the necessary resources to make changes, this undertaking will above all require one thing: time.

Still, hundreds of millions of people in the "Third World" are sick right now, as evidenced by high infant and child mortality rates, high mortality among mothers, invalidity, and low life expectancy. No one can expect these people to wait for long-term improvements. As already noted, high infant and child mortality have particularly serious and cumulative consequences.

Even though life expectancy and infant mortality have generally and substantially improved in the last 20 years, this remains an area where the North-South gap can be observed with special clarity. (See Table VI-7.)

In the *World Development Report 1993,* the World Bank drew attention to the positive trends of the last 40 years, as well as to the remaining problems:

> Over the past forty years life expectancy has improved more than during the entire previous span of human history. In 1950 life expectancy in developing countries was forty years; by 1990 it had increased to sixty-three years. In 1950 twenty-eight of every 1000 children died before their fifth birthday; by 1990 the number had fallen to ten. Smallpox, which killed more than 5 million annually in the early 1950s, has been eradicated entirely. Vaccines have drastically reduced the occurrence of measles and polio. Not only do these improvements translate into direct and significant gains in well-being, but they also reduce the economic burden imposed by unhealthy workers and sick or absent schoolchildren. These successes have come about in part because of growing incomes and increasing education around the globe and in part because of governments' efforts to expand health services, which, moreover, have been enriched by technological progress.
>
> Despite these remarkable improvements, enormous health problems remain. Absolute levels of mortality in developing countries remain unacceptably high: child mortality rates are about ten times higher than those in the established market economies. If death rates among children in poor countries were reduced

Table VI-7

Health Indicators for Selected Countries

Country	Life-Expectancy (in years), 1991	Infant Mortality (per 1,000 live births), 1991
Sierra Leone	42	145
Ethiopia	48	130
Afghanistan	42	171
Guinea-Bissau	39	148
Mali	48	161
Mozambique	47	149
Federal Republic of Germany (former)	*76*	*7*
Switzerland	*78*	*7*
Japan	*79*	*5*
United States	*76*	*9*

Source: World Bank: World Development Report 1993. Oxford University Press, New York 1993, p. 238 ff.

to those prevailing in the rich countries, 11 million fewer children would die each year. Almost half of these preventable deaths are a result of diarrheal and respiratory illness, exacerbated by malnutrition. In addition, every year 7 million adults die of conditions that could be inexpensively prevented or cured; tuberculosis alone causes 2 million of these deaths. About 400,000 women die from the direct complications of pregnancy and childbirth. Maternal mortality ratios are, on average, thirty times as high in developing countries as in high-income countries.[151]

The burden of disease (see Table VI-8) amounted to 1.35 billion disability-adjusted life years in 1991—the equivalent of 42 million deaths of newborns or of 80 million deaths at age 50.[152]

Pattern of Sickness in Developing Countries

The pattern of sickness in developing countries is completely different than in industrial nations. The social system of poverty, with its undernutrition and malnutrition, lack of hygiene, lack of clean drinking water, and so on, particularly favors infectious and parasitic diseases. A World Bank model shows the differences. (See Table VI-9.)

It is hard to get dependable data on the prevalence of individual diseases. This is partly because of inadequate diagnostic skills and partly a "poverty undercount." In the remote land areas where the problems of poverty and

Table VI-8

Burden of Disease by Sex, Cause, and Type of Loss, 1990 (millions of DALYs)

Sex and Outcome	Disease Category		
	Communicable[a]	Noncommunicable	Injuries
Male			
Premature Death	259	152	70
Disability	47	146	39
Female			
Premature Death	244	135	33
Disability	74	142	20

Source: World Bank: World Development Report 1993. Oxford University Press, New York 193,
    p. 25.
[a]Includes maternal and perinatal causes.

Table VI-9

Pattern of Sickness in Industrial and Developing Countries

	Industrial Countries (percent)	Developing Countries (percent)
Infectious, parasitic, and respiratory diseases	10.8	43.7
Cancer	15.2	3.7
Circulatory diseases	32.2	14.8
Accidents	6.8	3.5
Other diseases	35.0	34.3
Total	100.0	100.0

Source: World Bank, 1981.

health are greatest, medically trained personnel rarely if ever come to collect dependable statistics, particularly during the rainy season.[153] Consequently, the figures fluctuate, even for illnesses the World Health Organization (WHO) would most like to concentrate on: tropical diseases. (See Table VI-10.)

Contrary to the popular view that tropical diseases are the only ones poor countries need to deal with, diseases that are widespread in industrial countries (circulatory diseases, rheumatism, and cancer, for example) are also a growing problem. These occur for the most part in population groups that must be regarded as atypical of the majority in terms of their social and economic positions as well as life-style and purchasing power. They are special cases,

Table VI-10

Tropical Diseases

	Number of People in Millions	
	Already Sick	At Risk of Infection
Leprosy; Trypanosomiasis	11–12	1,600
Chagas' Disease	20	70
Filariasis	300	600
Leishmaniasis	unknown	unknown
Bilharziasis	200	600
Malaria	150	600

Source: WHO, 1983, 1986.

too, in the sense that solutions for their problems can be found outside the public health system.

Even though their health problems are huge, people in the developing world have little money, few doctors, and few hospital beds at their disposal. (See Table VI-11.) For cultural, geographic, and financial reasons, the vast majority of the rural population scarcely has access to trained medical professionals.

Even though health programs are of great economic and social value, they still have a shockingly low priority for most governments in developing countries:

- Basic health services, where they exist at all, are poorly developed and lack an adequate infrastructure.
- Medical personnel are given little support and their training is often inadequate to the challenges of local health problems.
- The personnel structure is too heavily "loaded" with doctors, even though "barefoot doctors" could often handle a large part of the job.[154]
- Seventy-five percent of humanity lives in developing countries and receives less than 20 percent of the medicine produced throughout the world. And those living in poor rural areas, who after all are in the majority in the so-called Third World, get the smallest share.
- Those who are poorest, most vulnerable, and most threatened by disease and death are hardly reached at all.
- The conditions causing disease and death are not being eliminated.

Health policy is often pursued on an ad hoc basis only and in isolated cases. Rarely is the effectiveness of health measures and administrative arrangements reviewed in terms of goals. Too few governments acknowledge in their

Table VI-11

Health Infrastructure and Services

Demographic Region	Doctors per 1,000 Population, 1988–92	Nurse-to-Doctor Ratio, 1988–92	Hospital Beds per 1,000 Population, 1985–90	Percentage of Children Immunized (age less than 1 year), 1990–91	
				Third Dose of DPT	Measles
Sub-Saharan Africa	0.12	5.1	1.4	52	52
Mozambique	0.02	13.1	0.9	19	23
Tanzania	0.03	7.3	1.1	79	75
Ethiopia	0.03	2.4	0.3	44	37
Uganda	0.04	8.4	0.8	77	74
Burundi	0.06	4.3	1.3	83	75
Chad	0.03	0.9	—	18	28
Madagascar	0.12	3.5	0.9	46	33
Sierra Leone	0.07	5.0	1.0	75	74
Malawi	0.02	2.8	1.6	81	78
India	0.41	1.1	0.7	83	77
China	1.37	0.5	2.6	95	96
Latin America and the Caribbean	1.25	0.5	2.7	71	75
Established Market Economies (EME)	2.52	2.1	8.3	80	77
United States	2.38	2.8	5.3	67	80
Japan	1.64	1.8	15.9	87	66
Switzerland	1.59	2.6	11.0	90	90

Source: World Bank: World Development Report 1993. Oxford University Press, New York 1993, p. 208 f.

practical policies that development also depends on an efficient health infrastructure.

Health Policy Under Conditions of Poverty: Primary Health Care[155]

A national health policy that aims to deal fairly with all groups within a
population while providing both short-term curative and long-term preventive
services entails immense requirements. Since improving everyone's physical
and mental well-being is the real goal, a health policy operating under conditions of poverty has to follow the principle that it is better to have less for all
than a great deal for a few and nothing for the rest. The objective of basic
health services is to establish the first contact between individuals and communities and the national health system and to provide health services where
the people live and work.

Priorities must be established to have the greatest effect in lowering the
incidence of sickness as well as invalidity and mortality rates. The most
serious health problems and the highest mortality rates occur in infants, small
children, and their mothers from the poorest sections of the population. For
that reason, a national health policy must as a matter of priority be oriented to
these segments of society.

Even the best basic care will not have more than a temporary influence on
people's health, however, if there are no preventive measures calling for their
active participation. Nor will it help much if groups who are in a position to
pay for their treatment insist on using government-subsidized health services.
Hence it is good policy to distinguish between the private and public sectors.

Many people in developing countries enjoy relatively high prosperity
despite the great poverty prevailing elsewhere in their societies. Their living
conditions, style of consumption, and professional circumstances are comparable to those of most people in industrial nations. As noted earlier, their health
problems are entirely different in character from others in their country who
live under conditions of dire poverty. These individuals live for the most part
in cities, have a regular (fairly high) income, and are often covered by insurance. This lets them choose different health care arrangements and pay at least
the costs of the services. In such cases, the public sector should not offer
subsidies that, in the final analysis, would only worsen the health service
bottlenecks for the majority of poor people in the country.

Lowering Infant and Child Mortality

The foremost desire of parents everywhere in the world is not just to "give
birth to babies" but to have surviving children. This means that a visible,
dependable, and durable lowering of infant and child mortality rates is an
indispensable condition for lower birth rates.[156] Wherever the mortality rates

Figure VI-3

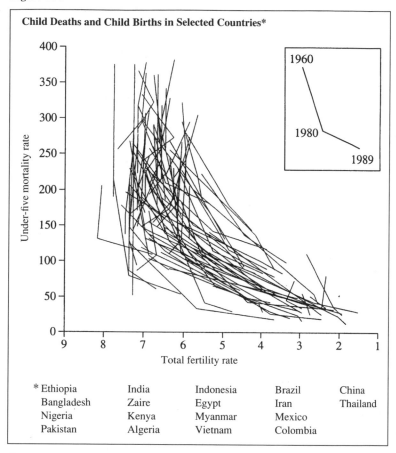

Child Deaths and Child Births in Selected Countries*

* Ethiopia   India   Indonesia   Brazil   China
  Bangladesh Zaire   Egypt   Iran   Thailand
  Nigeria   Kenya   Myanmar   Mexico
  Pakistan   Algeria   Vietnam   Colombia

Source: UNICEF 1992 with statistics from the Population Department of
the United Nations.

of newborns, infants, and children remain high, so do birth rates. Wherever mortality rates are lowered, birth rates also go down. (See Figure VI-3.)

Deaths in children under five are principally related to diseases tied to bad hygienic and sanitary conditions, malnutrition, poor education, and a lack of essential health arrangements. (See Table VI-12.)

According to WHO, 27.4 percent of these deaths could have been avoided by vaccination and another 25.2 percent—the ones resulting from diarrhea alone or in combination with other diseases—could have been avoided by the simplest means, such as oral rehydration salts.[157]

For the reasons already described, parents tend to insure themselves against

Table VI-12

Selected Causes of Death in Children under Five in the Third World, 1990

Cause of Death	Death Rates (Numbers)	in (Percent)
Acute Infections of Respiratory Passages (including Pneumonia)	3,560,000	27.6
Diarrhea	3,000,000	23.3
Cessation of Breathing at Birth (Asphyxiation)	860,000	6.7
Malaria	800,000	6.2
Lockjaw (Tetanus) in Newborns	560,000	4.2
Infections of Respiratory Tract and Measles	480,000	3.7
Measles (Alone)	220,000	1.7
Premature Births	430,000	3.3
Blood Poisoning and Meningitis in Newborns	300,000	2.3
Other Causes	2,690,000	21.0
Total	12,900,000	100.0

Source: WHO, Program Manager, MCH/FP: Private communication, January 21, 1992.

high risks of infant mortality by having many children. Only when they can count on better survival chances for their children does the size of the family begin, with time, to diminish.[158] As noted in Part V, this was also largely true of the demographic transition in premodern Europe. Some researchers talk about the "audio-visual evidence" of surviving children.[159]

But the opposite experience also affects the rationality of parents' behavior. When children die in one's own family or in a neighbor's, the desire to have many children continues to exist and there is little willingness to accept family planning measures. There is a tendency to "replace" children who have died with newborns.[160] Many field studies show that this replacement effect over-compensates for the actual deaths. This kind of behavior occurs more frequently at the lower social levels, and the more strongly the number of children is influenced by cultural and institutional factors, the more pronounced it is.[161] If after many years it turns out that the parents significantly "overinsured" themselves against the death risk to their children and thus had more children than they had planned on, this is generally accepted as the much lesser evil in comparison with the unexpected dying off of the next generation.[162]

Along with the factors already discussed in connection with the demographic transition, a conscious perception of the changed circumstances is significant for explaining the often considerable time lapse between the statistically measurable reduction of mortality in a society and a correspond-ing lessening of the birth rate. D. Heer and D.O. Smith have observed that the birth rate goes down faster than the death rate when the survival of a son has been secured in most families of the society and people perceive that to be the case.[163] Appropriate communication and training programs are therefore of great value. Knowledge of the fact that mortality in their societies had been substantially reduced played an important role in the speedy demographic transition of Japan and Taiwan.[164]

Finally, there is also a biological explanation for the statistically demon-strable relationship between mortality and frequency of births, at least in traditional societies. Other things being equal, breast-feeding lengthens the time between two pregnancies. Hormonal processes triggered by breast-feeding delay ovulation and, hence, menstruation.[165]

GOBI-FF

For about the last 10 years, GOBI-FF has stood for an idea, and the mea-sures derived from it, developed by UNICEF to bring about a significant reduction of infant and child mortality at a reasonable cost. It saves the lives of millions of children every year and helps maintain the health as well as the physical and mental growth of an even larger number while reducing popula-tion growth. GOBI-FF stands for:

G Growth Monitoring—weight and growth checks to ensure early detection of malnutrition and to prevent its consequences;

O Oral Rehydration—replacing the hydration and mineral losses that diarrhea causes in a child's body with a mixture of glucose, salt, and minerals dissolved in drinking water;

B Breast-Feeding—encouraging mothers to nurse their children for at least six months and, if possible, longer;

I Immunization—multiple inoculations against avoidable diseases such as neonatal tetanus, measles, polio, tuberculosis, whooping cough, and diphtheria;

F Female Education—elevating the level of women's education, par-ticularly that of mothers; and

F Family Spacing—lengthening the interval between births.

The essential elements of GOBI-FF are products and services at a reasonable cost, such as education in preventive measures to promote the health of mother and child. And until recently, the package included a seventh component of food supplements for pregnant women and newborns who were severely malnourished.

Growth Monitoring.   Regular weight gain is the most important single indicator of the healthy growth of a small child. But neither the doctor nor the mother can see this with the naked eye. Only serious clinical malnutrition is obvious to the unschooled eye. It occurs, thank God, in only about 1 percent of children.[166]

Even so, more than a quarter of the children in the developing world are undernourished or malnourished. A detailed study of this problem by the Harvard Institute for International Development came to the following conclusion:

> The average moderately undernourished child aged 6–24 months looks per-fectly normal. It is just a little too small for its age, has reduced resistance to infectious disease and therefore gets sick frequently. A child which is getting only sixty percent of what it needs in calories will not necessarily show any outward signs of hunger apart from a frequent desire to nurse. A Philippine study reports that 58 percent of the mothers of children suffering from under-nourishment of the second and third degree thought that their children would develop normally.[167]

The use of simple and easily understandable weight and growth checks to make undernourishment and/or wrong nourishment "visible" is therefore one of the most important measures for protecting the health and ensuring the future of young children. The diagrams for weight and growth checks (see Figure VI-4), which have been developed by David Morley, cost less than 20¢. Regular weighing and entry of the weight in the appropriate diagram tells the mother whether her child is developing normally. Not only do the diagrams prevent "creeping" undernourishment, they give the mother an important basis for future action. She can see progress or relapse and can see the favorable outcome when she acts correctly.

Today, Morley diagrams are being used within the framework of GOBI-FF and other programs to carry out regular checks on millions of small children. The result is not only that unnecessary deaths are being avoided but that millions of mothers discover that they hold the health and life of their children in their own hands.

The way food is distributed within the family in households that are gener-ally well provided for can, however, also conceal undernourishment, particu-larly in the case of girls in families with many children. The superiority that the patriarch and other men in the family claim for themselves is strongly reflected in the intrafamilial distribution of food. Mere concentration on the supply of modern medical services may bring limited returns unless they are reinforced by appropriate social changes—in particular, those affecting the social status of women and the female child.

To increase child survival, it is necessary to identify the social factors that trigger child morbidity and mortality. Future work could benefit from assessing how women's roles in different economic sectors (subsistence versus cash cropping in the farm sector, formal versus informal markets in the nonfarm sector) structure the amount and stability of income and determine women's ability to retain control of their earnings.[168]

Oral Rehydration. There are two particularly acute risks for children at the weaning age (6–8 months). Either the child gets solid (adult) food in addition to the milk, or it does not get solid food at all and the mother's milk remains the only source of nutrition for the child. In either case, the child enters into one of the most critical phases of life.

After five or six months, mother's milk alone is no longer sufficient to meet the food requirements of a small child. If there is no supplementary nutrition, growth will falter, weight will stagnate, and the body's defenses against disease will be weakened. Nevertheless, in many countries—India and Bangladesh, for example[169]—a third of the children receive only mother's milk until after the first year. This leads to creeping undernourishment, generally invisible to the layperson.

Yet if, as reasonable and necessary, the child receives a supplementary diet, then there is a greater risk of infection. Suddenly the child comes into contact with an environment that is characterized by dirty drinking water, unclean food, and a lack of sanitary facilities. Diarrhea is one of the consequences. About 500 million children in the developing world suffer attacks of diarrhea three or four times a year. It is so widespread that it is almost regarded as a "normal feature" of a young child's life.[170] In any case, it is not something that particularly worries parents. Yet diarrheal disease is still the greatest single killer of children in the developing world.

According to a study by WHO and UNICEF, about 5 million children in the developing world—10 children per minute—died in 1980 before the age of five from the consequences of diarrhea.[171] During the eighties, about 1.2 million children under five died each year in Africa south of the Sahara alone.[172] This generally occurred as a result of excessive loss of liquid (dehydration).

It is considerably more difficult to prevent the spread of diarrhea than it is to avoid its fatal consequences. The bacteria, viruses, and parasites that cause diarrhea are excreted with the stool and retain their active potency for varying lengths of time, depending on environmental circumstances. Transmission of diarrheal diseases does not decrease until fecal matter is disposed of at a safe distance from the drinking water and people come to understand what bodily hygiene means.

Thus more is needed to protect a child against diarrhea than simply the

Figure VI-4
Weight and Growth Checks by Diagram

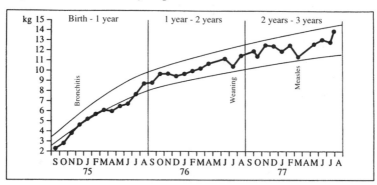

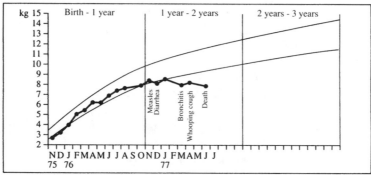

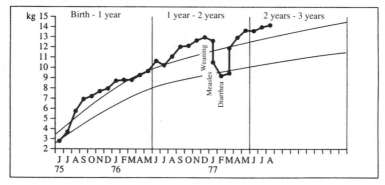

Diagram 1

The progress of the child whose weight growth is shown in this diagram is normal. After weaning and during a bout with measles the weight drops temporarily, but not under the critical limit.

Diagram 2

This child developed almost normally; then fell victim, in rapid succession, to measles, bronchitis, and whooping cough. Without time for recovery between the different diseases, the child finally died. The cause of death was diagnosed as "whooping cough," but actually it was a combination of mutually reinforcing undernourishment and infectious diseases.

Diagram 3

This child also developed normally at first, but encountered problems after weaning. He lost more than one-quarter of his body weight, partly through dehydration caused by diarrhea. The diagram helped disclose this weight loss and indicated the need to introduce additional nutrition, with good results.

good will of the mother. The sources of infection that cause it in the first place must be eliminated, and that calls for comprehensive efforts in development policy. But even when the political will exists, infrastructural improvements of this kind take time. Immediate steps are called for, because waiting for development to take its course would exact a high price in human lives.

One out of 20 children born in developing countries dies from diarrhea-related dehydration or from kidney failure resulting from extensive liquid loss—and there are simple steps that can be taken to prevent this. A mixture of glucose, salt, and minerals dissolved in water can stabilize the liquids in a small child's body. This preparation can easily be manufactured locally at a reasonable cost. There are even training programs that encourage the use of cheap, locally available raw materials (ordinary salt, plain sugar, and potash in the form of bananas or papaya). Since a common reaction of parents is to withhold food and fluids during a diarrheal attack, an additional important lesson is that the child should continue to be nourished in the normal way and the rehydration therapy should be continued despite ongoing diarrhea.

It is much more difficult and expensive, however, to correct dehydration after it has progressed. Until the early eighties, the only effective treatment—intravenous feeding—was expensive and unavailable to most mothers because it could only be administered by qualified medical personnel. Now, in 90–95 percent of the cases, oral rehydration salts can be used. Intravenous therapy is limited to the most difficult cases (when the patient is unconscious, for example).

The ways in which men affect family and environmental health should, however, receive more attention, as the World Bank recently noted: "It is self-defeating for health education programs to target women without equally targeting men. If men and boys continue to defecate in the open and to use traditional water sources for bathing, while women and girls use sanitary latrines and tubewell water, little will be accomplished for environmental or family health."[173]

Increasing Mothers' Willingness to Breast-Feed.   Mother's milk is the ideal infant food, and breast-feeding is the healthiest form of nourishment for every child during the first six months. Mother's milk not only has more nutritional value and is more hygienic than any imaginable substitute, it also gives the child greater resistance to communicable diseases.[174] No other infant food does this. Moreover, mother's milk is always and everywhere available to the infant. It does not have to be transported over unreliable distribution networks or thinned or prepared with water that may be unclean.

Studies from India, Chile, Yemen, the Philippines, and many other countries show that breast-fed children have one-third the incidence of diarrhea and respiratory illnesses as other children.[175] The fact that breast-fed children are healthier than those who, for whatever reason, receive substitute nourishment, was also demonstrably true in Germany at the end of the nineteenth and beginning of the twentieth centuries. The mortality rate of "bottle babies" there was four to six times higher than for breast-fed infants—and in summer, as much as ten times higher.[176]

Educational programs on the advantages of breast-feeding are very important. Every mother who can be persuaded to breast-feed for an adequate period of time almost certainly spares her child life-threatening infectious diseases. This alone would justify programs to encourage the practice. From the standpoint of population policy, however, there is another important result: breast-feeding has a significant contraceptive effect that contributes in an important way to longer intervals between births.[177] It stimulates production of the hormone prolactin, which prevents ovulation. This effect has been confirmed unambiguously by World Fertility Survey data from all countries studied.[178] According to recent studies, the contraceptive effect of the nonoccurrence of menstruation as a result of breast-feeding is comparable in its dependability—at 98 percent—to modern contraceptive methods.[179]

W.B. Arthur and G. McNicoll report in their Bangladesh study on periods of infertility resulting from breast-feeding (lactational amenorrhea) of up to 19 months. A reduction of the breast-feeding period to only 11 months—other factors remaining equal—would have resulted in a 25-percent rise in the birth rate.[180] Kathleen Newland has noted that in Bangladesh there were variations, determined by breast-feeding, of up to 13 months in the interval between two successive births.[181] Similar results have been shown for Africa south of the Sahara.[182]

Generally speaking, breast-feeding is still widespread in most developing countries. According to B. Ferry and D.B. Smith, the vast majority of children in most countries involved in the World Fertility Survey were still being breast-fed at the beginning of the eighties.[183] Sociological and behavioral factors can, however, influence a woman's decision to initiate or terminate breast-feeding. The effects of urbanization and the socioeconomic status of breast-feeding women and their work load are commonly ignored by those concerned with the medical aspects of breast-feeding. Women in developing countries increasingly face social conditions that do not allow them to breast-feed. To encourage the practice, it is necessary to create structures to support women in their multiple roles, such as support groups for lactating women as well as child care facilities near employment centers.[184]

Immunization Programs. For as little as $5, a child can be fully immunized against six of the most common and dangerous childhood diseases—measles, tetanus, whooping cough, diphtheria, polio, and tuberculosis. Still, every six seconds a child dies of a disease that could have been avoided by immunization. During the same interval, another child suffers lasting physical damage for the identical reason. This does not have to happen.

Where immunization has been introduced, the results have been impressive: in Bangladesh, the immunization part of the GOBI-FF program alone led to a reduction in mortality of from 23 to 47 percent.[185] Moreover, tens of thousands of children were spared illnesses that would have resulted in severe physical impairment (polio, for example).

To save the lives of 5 million children a year and prevent physical impairment in another 5 million—assuming that about 100 million children are born each year in the developing world—$500 million is needed annually. That is, admittedly, a lot of money. But there is one thing we can point out: even though East-West tensions have been reduced and we have recognized that peaceful ways of settling conflicts must be found, more than $950 billion was spent in 1990 for military purposes.[186] That is more than $500 million a day. So the financial means are available. This ratio has remained unchanged for many years: one day's military expenditures would more than suffice to immunize all of the world's children against the most frequent childhood diseases.[187] (See Table VI-13.)

Immunization programs are substantially more complicated than the use of oral rehydration salts or educational campaigns to promote breast-feeding. They entail a number of administrative and logistical requirements that in practice are rarely available in poor countries. Well-trained, reliable, and safe personnel are needed. Some serums and vaccines have to be refrigerated all the time, from the moment of their manufacture until they reach the child who is to be vaccinated. Some diseases call for several inoculations. This can lead to problems in identifying and controlling the patients. To prevent tetanus in newborns, for example, the mothers must be immunized during pregnancy.

The poor transportation infrastructure and the lack of adequate conveyances make it hard enough to provide people with the goods to meet their ordinary daily needs, let alone with serums and vaccines that have to be kept refrigerated and transported with special care. Under the conditions that prevail in underdeveloped rural areas, adequate leadership and control of these programs (including their evaluation) is very expensive.[188] Finally, the multiple use of needles without adequate sterilization can become a problem, particularly in connection with the spread of AIDS.

Immunization programs call for more than just serums and vaccines. They require political will, from the top levels of the government down to the village; regular provision of the necessary equipment; and good management.[189] Still, those programs help directly to save the life and health of at least 10 million children every year—a level of success that justifies an enormous effort.

Table VI-13

Social Welfare or Military Procurement? A Cost Comparison

Required Health Investments	Annual Cost in Billions of U.S. Dollars	Military Goods of Same Cost
Supply of clean drinking water and sanitary facilities for half the world's population	12.0	9 TRIDENT submarines
Maternal health care and training for pregnant women to prevent millions of cases of maternal mortality	6.0	2 Aircraft Carriers of the NIMITZ Class
Supplementary feeding programs for small children to prevent malnutrition	3.0	4 Destroyers of the ARLEIGH BURKE Class
Immunization of all children, thus saving one million lives a year	1.0	2 STEALTH Bombers

Source: Dr. Saadet Deger, International Peace Research Institute (SIPRI), Stockholm: Private communication, September 1992.

The number of children saved might be twice as high if—to return yet again to this issue—the female child were "worth" the same as the male child. Just one example: records of 1,000 Indian children who received vaccinations at the immunization clinic of the general hospital in Udaipur, Rajasthan, were analyzed for sex, age at first vaccination, nutritional status, parents' socioeconomic status, and maternal literacy. Girls were brought for first immunization at a significantly later age than boys, and were observed to have poor nutritional status.[190] In view of the importance of immunization to present and future generations, program planners should emphasize the optimum age for first immunizations and overcome the bias against girls.

Despite all these obstacles and difficulties, immunization programs are the success story of the eighties in health policy.[191] Fifteen years ago, fewer than 5 percent of children in the developing world were immunized against avoidable diseases. The price: 4.5 million children's lives each year. By 1993, more than 80 percent of the children in developing countries are immunized against diphtheria, polio, and tetanus (DPT three-way vaccination) and almost as many against measles.[192] This success saves 3.2 million children's lives, year for year. And yet there are still 1.7 million avoidable deaths, with neonatal tetanus being the biggest of the preventable problems.[193]

Establishing a permanent and universal system of immunization is not only vitally important in the fight against avoidable childhood diseases; it is also a prerequisite for victory against fatal diseases like AIDS and malaria, should we one day develop vaccines against them.

Female Education.   Development agencies responding to the problem of infant mortality and population growth identified women, in their reproductive role, as the most significant family health care provider and as primarily responsible for limiting the number of births. It has been recognized that female education affects the health of children and fertility patterns as more children survive. It is true that children's chances of survival and of enjoying good health increase in proportion with the level of the mother's formal and informal education. The step from "no school education" to "four years of school education" is the most important. In Pakistan and Indonesia, children of mothers with four years of school registered 50 percent lower infant mortality rates than those of illiterate mothers.[194]

However, the underlying dogma that motherhood is the most important role for women remains, and this casts a shadow over the entire concept of "female education," which intrinsically includes overt and covert role expectations. Female education programs are so popular because they are politically safe: they do not challenge the traditionally accepted sexual division of labor or gender ideologies.[195] Paths to development cannot, therefore, be the same for women and men. "Female" education tends to exclude women from mainstream development programs[196] and to maintain their dependence rather than to help them become more independent.

Paulo Freire's philosophy of education for liberation is highly applicable to the situation of women in developing countries.[197] Using his approach to education could promote a critical consciousness among women and promote vital social change and economic growth. The more that women from all levels of society get equal (as distinct from female) education, the more literate citizens there will be who can be integrated into the civic culture. Equal educational opportunities for both sexes would promote economic modernization and the social mobility of households—and social justice. Unless women have equal career opportunities in the wage labor market, their dependence on men will continue and their bargaining power within the family will be limited—also in terms of the number of children they will bear.

This objection is not meant to downplay or negate the importance of courses in hygiene and sanitation, child care, nutrition, and home economics. These are and remain vital for family health and the survival of children. Putting the solution to family welfare and smaller families solely in female hands, however, is not enough. It would be reasonable and desirable to train boys and young men as well, since they are or intend to become fathers and since their behavior significantly influences family health and family size. Women already now face many demands on their time, so a shared responsibility for childrearing and caring would enhance an overall improvement in family health. And family welfare also depends on men's ability to understand that their contribution to hygiene and sanitation is vital, along with reasonable food distribution according to the physical needs of all members of the family.

Family Spacing. As noted earlier, too short an interval between births is bad for the health of both mother and child.[198] For this reason, the family planning part of the GOBI-FF package focuses on child spacing. According to the current view, there should be at least two years between births.

A large and growing number of field studies demonstrate the enormous significance of the techniques and procedures of family planning for the health of mother and child—whether aimed at holding to the desired period of time free of pregnancy, avoiding pregnancy in women who are either too young or too old, or limiting children to the desired number.[199]

Child spacing is known and practiced in many traditional societies.[200] For this reason, little effort is needed to gain acceptance for it. Sexual abstinence on the part of the parents for a limited period of time after the birth of a child (postpartum abstinence) has significant consequences for population size, especially where the period of abstinence is long.[201]

As a result of modernization, postpartum abstinence is now becoming rarer throughout developing countries.[202] It is mainly younger, urban-dwelling, better educated women and their husbands who are promoting this change. A revival of postpartum abstinence or even slowing down its decline is hardly consistent with social modernization. Here, the wheel cannot even be held still, let alone turned back. What can be done, however, is to rescue the underlying principle of preventing pregnancy for a certain period of time to give the mother a chance to regain her strength and to spare the children an unhealthy competition for mother's milk, care, and attention (for example, for growth and weight checks).

As a substitute for postpartum abstinence, a period of at least 18 months of postpartum contraception could be introduced. This would be a way of upholding in modern societies the goal inherent in traditional behavior of maintaining a certain interval between births. The wish to ensure better health for a child is quite consistent with the patterns of thought and behavior in traditional societies. Once the methods of family planning have been accepted as a way to maintain the desired interval between births, it will be easier to make their use more widespread.

Right after delivery is a promising time to give out information on family planning. The fact that limiting births is not only an important part of population policy but also contributes to better health for mother and child should be in the forefront of the argument, particularly where there is cultural and religious resistance to contraceptive methods. The successes of the "Post-Partum Program" are well documented.[203] Counselling on the advantages of maintaining an appropriate interval between births, information on (modern)

means and methods of contraception,[204] and the ready availability of these in
health centers for mother and child are things that could be built into existing
health programs for mothers and children without significantly greater outlays
in money or personnel.

Promoting Food Supplements.   The GOBI-FF package used to include an
additional component—"food supplements" for pregnant women and newborns in critical condition from malnutrition—as noted earlier. A balanced
diet remains probably the most vital requirement for the welfare of mother and
child since the 10–15 percent of children who are born underweight (less than
2,500 grams) account for 30–40 percent of infant mortality.[205] They have a
significantly diminished resistance to infectious diseases.

But the problem lies not just in the children. Malnourishment of the mother
has a decisive influence on birth weight and on her ability to nurse. It is true
that low birth weight occurs more frequently when there has been less than
two years since the last birth and when the mother is younger than 16. But the
decisive factor for birth weight is the mother's nutritional status. If she is
undernourished or suffers from wasting diseases (malaria, tuberculosis, worm
infections, and so on), the fetus will not get enough nourishment. In industrial
countries, mothers gain approximately 26.4 pounds during pregnancy; in
developing countries, the figure is often only 13 pounds or less.[206] Babies who
weigh too little at birth have a difficult time from the beginning. The vicious
circle of undernourishment and infectious disease kills 4 million babies every
year, accounting for about one-third of infant mortality in the developing
world.

A balanced diet of high quality for expectant and nursing mothers helps
both mother and child avoid the most severe health problems. After the age of
four to six months, food supplements are of the greatest importance for the
children themselves. Even though they are still being (or should be) breast-fed,
the children need locally available supplementary foods that are rich in vitamins and protein, such as vegetables, peas, beans, grain, fruit, peanuts,
yogurt, and milk.

We have now come to realize that artificial food supplements such as
vitamins, proteins, or mineral preparations can generally be avoided if
mothers are appropriately counselled about the great importance of a balanced
diet both for themselves and their children. A balanced diet can usually be
achieved with locally available foods; for this reason, appropriate counselling
is now generally favored over the distribution of enriched food supplements.

One final important point in connection with a balanced diet for mothers
and children is the distribution of food within the family. A series of studies
has shown that social custom requires men and boys to eat separately, and it is
generally agreed that this means they receive more and better food than

women—even pregnant or nursing women.[207] Thus, a World Bank study in Gambia, for example, showed that pregnant and nursing women got up to 40 percent fewer calories than did the men in the same village and that their food contained much less protein—just when they needed it most.[208] Since, as already pointed out, the work load of women generally is substantially greater than that of men, it is clear that this way of thinking and behaving results directly in more sickness for women and their children.

GOBI-FF's Targets. In all parts of the GOBI-FF package, measures aimed specifically at the most vulnerable members of society are of the greatest importance. It is above all the social and economic inequalities between social classes and, within these classes, between the sexes that determine the level of mortality and illness as well as access to the health care infrastructure. These inequalities must be attacked at the same time. This is not only feasible in practice; it is an absolute requirement for the development of a humane society.

The Role of Birth Control Techniques and Technology

A population policy that aims to reduce birth rates makes use of various means and methods of contraception. A basic distinction can be made between "natural" methods (making use of the woman's naturally infertile phases) and those that use mechanical (such as condoms or intrauterine pessaries), chemical (spermicide salves or foam), or hormonal (oral contaceptives) means, as well as operations.

Since official population policy and the measures it relies on are legitimized by the goal of "protecting human life," the means and methods used to reach this goal cannot be chosen arbitrarily but must be measured against the ethical nature of the goal.

Natural Regulation of Birth

Contrary to an often repeated opinion, the Catholic Church supports family planning and calls for "responsible parenthood."[209] But it imposes narrow limits on the means and methods—too narrow for most people in Western society. The church's statements in *Humanae Vitae,* which are valid for the area over which the Catholic Church holds sway,[210] note that the only legitimate method of family planning is to "take advantage of the natural cycles immanent in the reproductive system and engage in marital intercourse only during those times that are infertile, thus controlling births in a way which does not in the least offend the moral principles."[211]

Even though the understanding of love and partnership between man and wife that underlies this encyclical arouses sympathy and represents a worthy ideal,[212] this method of birth control is in practice rarely used. Whenever family planning is practiced nowadays, it is done predominantly with modern contraceptive methods. It would appear, therefore, that the knowledge of biological relationships so important for the rhythm method is largely lacking and that the calculations it calls for overtax the insight, scrupulousness, and discipline of most people.

Calculating the infertile days becomes even more difficult under conditions of poverty because inadequate nutrition leads to serious disturbances of the menstrual cycle (lengthening, shortening, or occasionally causing it to stop altogether) and because irregularity of menstruation often occurs as an "economy measure" when the body is weakened by illness.

The weak social position of women can also help to explain lack of cultural acceptance of the rhythm method, as sometimes women want to practice periodic abstinence with their husbands but are unable to get their way. In view of these facts, greater dependability in regulating births can only be achieved if other means and methods of family planning are made available for responsible use.

Artificial Means and Methods of Contraception

Simplicity and safety, along with cost, must play a primary role in any discussion of the ethical acceptability of the various means and methods of birth control suited to the special conditions of developing countries. Reversibility of infertility is also important, however, as is the degree of encroachment on the human organism and the maintenance of human dignity. Birth control methods that minimize encroachment on humans, are readily reversible, and are consistent with human dignity (as well as a sense of modesty) will reduce the potential for ethical conflict. Applying these criteria would, for example, mean that condoms, pessaries, and intrauterine devices (IUDs) are preferable to surgical sterilization of either women or men.

A clear line has to be drawn between contraception and abortion. Any form of contraception is always preferable to an abortion. Although abortion is used in many countries, both legally and illegally, as a way of limiting births, it cannot from an ethical point of view be proposed as an instrument of population policy or a regular method of birth control. That is why, first, all safe means and methods of contraception must be available and why, in addition, we must fight against the social and economic obstacles that force women into abortion.

The requirement for legal and social conditions that permit a woman to carry a pregnancy to term without being permanently impaired in her opportunities for self-determination or at a disadvantage compared with men in the society is needed not only in developing countries but also, albeit somewhat less urgently, in industrial ones. The fact that this will, among other things, call for a change in discriminatory forms of male thought and behavior is also something not unique to the developing world.

We must continue to maintain a heightened sense of responsibility for unborn life. The often discussed issue of how far along in a pregnancy abortion should be allowed is a moral question to which even the most competent biologists, doctors, and lawyers can give no relevant answer based on their fields of speciality—simply because there is no possible answer that is exclusively of a biological, medical, or legal character. The inadequacy of a merely biological conception of human life is demonstrated by the significance that death holds for our life. It represents, of course, the end of certain biological functions—but it is precisely death that gives life its unique and irrecoverable value, and it does this independently of any assumptions about the immortality of the soul or about reincarnation.

That many hundreds of thousands of women die each year from improperly performed abortions is a sorrowful and scandalous evil that gets too little attention because society represses it.[213] Abortions are not only a demonstration of social deformation but also an indication of the large unsatisfied demand for contraceptives. It is quite reasonable to argue, in this connection, that—other things being equal—the availability of contraceptives saves lives. This is true in relation not only to abortion but also to maternal mortality. A Pakistani study seems to show that the avoidance of all undesired births would reduce maternal mortality by 40 percent.[214]

For the same reasons, the usefulness of the recently developed alternative to early surgical abortion—RU 486—should be reconsidered. Despite the fact that it could significantly contribute to a reduction in female mortality as a consequence of induced or clandestine abortions, it is so far available only in France (since 1988) and Great Britain (since 1991).[215] According to Caroline Woodroffe, the manufacturer (Roussel Uclaf) is reluctant to launch the product in other countries not for legal reasons, since 75 percent of women live in countries where abortion is allowed, or for medical reasons, the method having been tested in clinical trials in 20 countries and used by 70,000 women in France. Rather, she reports, the company faces threats from pressure groups, particularly in the United States. Such groups have succeeded in lobbying the U.S. government to withdraw funds from overseas abortion aid even in countries where abortion is legal, effectively denying women in developing countries the choice available to women in the United States.[216]

Shared Contraceptive Responsibilities of Both Partners

Family planning and, hence, contraception is a responsibility of both men and women. This obvious fact requires special mention, however, because in practice most men delegate the responsibility to women, even though the use of a condom, for example, would be a substantially less intrusive act than the taking of hormone preparations. Common complaints—that condoms interfere with "spontaneity" or with "intimacy," or that they are "unmanly" or even a deceitful "imperialistic plot against sexual pleasure"—say more about the lack of emancipation and the excess of sexual egoism on the part of the men than they do about any genuinely insuperable obstacles to the use of condoms.[217]

Women as Agents of Change

The third decade of development has been marked by a tremendous deterioration of the global economic and ecological situation. Women in developing countries are the ones most affected by the subsequent impoverishment due to their structural disadvantage.[218] The "feminization of poverty," for which the matching development paradigm "feminization of development" has been created, has led to a broad mobilization of women in the name of "integrating women in development."

Conceptually, the so-called integration of women in development is ambiguous. On the one hand, it has helped uncover the previously invisible work of women. Women have also by and large gained more access to education and resources. On the other hand, however, it has also increased the work load of most women in poor developing nations without yielding a significant and broadly based improvement of their social and legal status, their participation in decision-making processes, or their control over economic resources.

There are no generally valid models for improving the situation of women in the developing world. Women's roles, their status, the social order, and economic and social conditions vary, not only from country to country and from one ethnic group to another but often within regions as well. A serious problem is often the fact that women continue to be divided by attitudes and practices of years of subordination; another is their lack of representation on decision-making bodies. There is potential for negative reaction and backlash when men feel threatened by the improved status of women. The need to socialize everybody, men and women, toward a changed order to meet the challenges of changing roles is a major task of our time.

In any project it is necessary to identify specific problems that could be obstacles to women taking part in development programs, such as education or income-generating projects, or to their use of health care services. Time allocation studies have shown that women in developing countries face severe time constraints due to their overwhelming work load. These may be a significant deterrent to mothers' use of child survival technologies, for example.[219] Thus projects should aim to lessen women's work load and provide time-saving technologies such as water tubewells near their homes or milling machines.

The mere use of women as instruments for development or population policy is not consistent with human development. A development policy that invests in women and ensures them equal access to property, credits, and jobs with fair compensation will give them more leeway for action and self-realization over and above their traditional roles, more economic and social independence, and, therefore, more freedom to attain their personal and political rights—not least in the area of procreation.

For the last two or three decades, new schools of thought and a different path to development have been promoted by women's organizations in the Third World. The most comprehensive and far-reaching concepts question the patriarchal value system and search for new paths that can be followed by both men and women. One of the most prominent organizations is DAWN (Development Alternatives with Women for A New Era), a network of women from Asia, Africa, and Latin America who have devised a vision of a society in which human rights and the rights of humanity become reality:

> We want a world where inequality based on class, gender, and race is absent from every country, and from the relationships among countries. We want a world where basic needs become basic rights and where poverty and all forms of violence are eliminated. Each person will have the opportunity to develop her or his full potential and creativity, and women's values of nurturance and solidarity will characterise human relationships. In such a world women's reproductive role will be redefined: Child care will be shared by men, women, and society as a whole. We want a world where the massive resources now used in the production of the means of destruction will be diverted to areas where they will help to relieve the oppression both inside and outside the home. This technological revolution will eliminate disease and hunger, and give women means for the safe control of their fertility. We want a world where institutions are open to participatory democratic processes where women share in determining priorities and making decisions.[220]

There is no better way we can think of to summarize what this chapter intended to say. Critics may say that this vision has no operational character. But it does not claim to be operational. It just wants to give a new basic orientation of development. We are convinced that many of our contemporaries who downplay the importance of gender issues in the context of overall development or object to rethinking and revising the path society has been following for too long will sooner or later recognize that there is no other option. They will see that this has become a mainstream position they will hastily join.

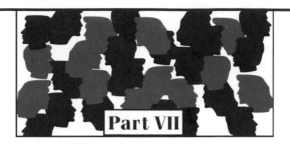

Part VII

Overview and Conclusions

The Facts

Never before in history has our planet been so densely populated—the total
now exceeds 5.6 billion. And never before have so many people been added to
the earth's population each year; in 1993, the total reached some 95 million.
That translates into more than 250,000 additional people a day, around 10,500
an hour, almost 3 a second. Nine out of ten children are born in the poor
countries of the world.[1] This will persist until the next millennium, even
though birth rates in most of the so-called Third World have dropped rapidly
since the eighties.

The Problems

Rapid population growth (more than 2 percent annually in Africa, much of
Asia, and many Latin American countries) has a great number of economic,
social, and environmental consequences. Taken together, these make human
development difficult and jeopardize the quality of life of future generations.
Rapid population growth threatens life directly in precisely those places where
great poverty already exists today. Although this is but one factor in the
complex mosaic of underdevelopment in any country, without a perceptible
reduction of the birth rates even the best development policy will not be able to
eliminate mass poverty in the Third World.

The absolute total of human deprivation has actually increased, and so
much additional investment is needed to raise the quantity of health, education, and other services to meet present and future needs that the quality of
these services suffers. "Racing to provide services to fast-growing populations

is like running up the down escalator," notes the head of the U.N. Population Fund. "You have to run very fast indeed to maintain upward motion."[2]

The Beam in Our Eye

A great deal of the responsibility for global environmental equilibrium rests with people in industrial countries, despite the statistics just given about where population is growing fastest. The rich minority of the world (800 million people, around 15 percent of the total) through its alarming ability to consume resources and create waste has contributed far more to the deplorable state of the global environment—the greenhouse effect, depletion of the ozone layer, and so on—than the poor majority in the developing world. A child born in a rich, industrial country, where the per capita consumption of energy and materials is high, places a much greater burden on the planet than a child born in a poor country does. And it is just this fact that makes ecologically motivated calls for a reduction of population growth rates in the developing world so politically explosive; they are indeed not legitimate unless they are accompanied by changes in our own life-styles and production methods.

Nevertheless, it is true that larger numbers of people consume more resources and produce more waste, independent from the level of their development. In developing countries, the combination of poverty and population growth is damaging the environment (though usually just on a local and regional basis) so that a number of communities and regions, such as the Sahel zone of Africa, have already crossed critical thresholds. Scant resources and soils are being overused and destroyed out of sheer necessity and lack of alternatives. The impoverishment of the environment furthers the impoverishment of the affected populations, and vice versa. If mass poverty and the rate of population growth that put such a heavy strain on local life-sustaining resource bases are not reduced significantly and soon, increased hunger and death—and political instability and conflicts—will be the inevitable result.

Population Policy with a Human Face

The basis for action on these problems is well known—it is possible to lower population growth with appropriate approaches to development policy and with international development cooperation. The satisfaction of basic needs and social and economic equality for women are the two most important single elements of such a policy.

Reduction of Child Mortality Through Satisfaction of Basic Needs

The world over, parents do not just want many births—they want surviving descendants. The motivation to have a smaller family thus arises only when development policy consistently succeeds in satisfying the basic needs of people in the lower strata of society so that their life expectancy increases. A drastic drop in mortality, particularly infant and child mortality, is the clearest evidence of a higher standard of living. All empirical experience shows that programs and projects that achieve this contribute to middle- and long-term reductions in population growth. For social or religious reasons, this process of adaptation may take longer in some regions of the world (such as sub-Saharan Africa) than in others (Southeast Asia, for example), but it does take place eventually nevertheless.

Equal Rights and Opportunities for Women

A second change is necessary, namly the elimination of the many forms of discrimination against and exploitation of women. If social and economic equality for women is not achieved, attempts to slow population growth will be in vain. It is vitally important to encourage women's sense of control over their personal destiny and the possibilty of choices beyond accepted tradition. Education is particularly significant, because it offers a view of sources of status beyond childbearing. The opening up of equal opportunities to economic and political participation for women has to be an integral part of development and population policies.

The End Does Not Justify the Means

Reducing population growth rates is not an end in itself. Its meaning lies in the general and long-term improvement of the quality of life of humanity in dignity, peace, freedom, and justice and in the preservation of the Creation. The means toward this end are not merely neutral, ethically indifferent tools. They are ingredients and should therefore be chosen with greatest care.

The most important ingredients are the social and economic conditions under which people are motivated to keep the number of their children voluntarily at a level compatible with sustainable development. Although people have radically different cultural interpretations of "development," some criteria are virtually universal: a long and healthy life, education, access to and sustainable use of the resources needed for a decent standard of living, political freedom, and guaranteed human rights. These means, which are in fact proximate ends, will open up perspectives of hope. Hope is a liberating motivation. It stimulates energy and inspires forward-looking action. People without hope—people taken up entirely with the constant, day-to-day struggle to survive and with no improvement in sight—are poor candidates indeed for family planning programs.

Cooperation is Indispensable

Even though the prime responsibility for creating the basic conditions for human development lies in the developing nations themselves, concerted and collective action by all members of the international community, and particularly by the economically powerful, is indispensable. The privileges associated with the material well-being, technical and scientific knowledge, and superior economic capacity of industrial countries carry with them the reciprocal moral obligation to provide rapid and sustained support to poor countries that have the courage and the vision to take steps toward their social, economic, and environmental recovery. Development cooperation is not only important from a humanitarian point of view; it is a matter of enlightened self-interest.

Our concern for global development, population, and environment issues must, however, also be reflected in the practical consequences we draw with regard to our own life-styles and our consumption and production patterns. A change of our current course is urgently needed, which will have considerable political, administrative, economic, technical, and behavioral consequences. As far as sustainable development for the whole planet is concerned, at least as much—and in the short term, certainly more—will be gained from a life-style change on the part of the rich minority than from a reduction in birth rates among the poor majority.

A change of course by the rich would significantly reduce environmental pollution worldwide. This could create the environmental latitude that developing countries need for their economic growth, with some inevitable environmental consequences, and thus for social development.

Of course, a change of course toward economic growth for industrial and developing countries that takes due account of the future will create all kinds of difficulties, and will also meet resistance from various social groups bent on defending their vested interests. Careful and calculable political and economic strategies based on social consensus therefore have the greatest chance of success. As the long-term survival of the human race is at stake, a common sense of responsibility is clearly needed.

It is to be hoped that the International Conference on Population and Development being held in Cairo in September 1994 will result in more than just another rhetorical proclamation that "something" must be done. There is an abundance of knowledge about population and its interactions with resources and the environment, but this wealth of knowledge has in the past been accompanied by a poverty of wisdom—and by a lack of political will to translate knowledge into practice. To go on like this against better judgment would be not only immoral, but also highly unwise. As the Club of Rome recently noted: "Time is running out. Some problems have already reached a magnitude which is beyond the point of successful attack and the costs of delay are monstrously high. Unless we wake up and act quickly it could be too late."[3]

Notes

1. "Address to the Board of Governors," World Bank, Washington, D.C., September 30, 1968.
2. World Bank, *World Development Report 1984* (New York: Oxford University Press, 1984).

Part I

1. This is supported by data of the World Fertility Survey analyzed in J. Cleland and J. Hobcraft (eds.), *Reproductive Change in Developing Countries: Insights from the World Fertility Survey* (Oxford: Oxford University Press, 1985).
2. G. Myrdal, *Asian Drama, An Inquiry Into the Poverty of Nations, Vol. I* (Harmondsworth, U.K.: Penguin, 1968), pp. 32, 49–128.
3. P. Ehrlich, *The Population Bomb* (New York: Ballantine, 1968); the reference to the "yellow threat" is from conservative German politicians during the Bundestag election of 1969.
4. Of course, many factors influence the availabiilty of investment capital, such as a country's economic and financial policy. See H. De Soto, *The Other Path* (New York: Harper & Row, 1989).
5. See U.N. Population Fund, *Population, Resources, and the Environment: The Critical Challenges* (New York: 1991).
6. See H. Birk, "Der Konflikt zwischen Space Ethics und Lifeboat Ethics und die Verantwortung der Bevölkerungstheorie für die Humanökologie," in Deutsche Gesellschaft für die Vereinten Nationen (ed.), *Dokumentationen, Informationen, Meinungen zur Diskussion gestellt.*, No. 40, Bonn, November 1991.
7. Not being unrealistic idealists, the authors expect that an internalization of environmental costs—which until now have been externalized for operating cost systems—will lead to rapid acceleration of a change in thought and behavior patterns. Humans do not always react to moral appeals but rather to economic incentives or fines. Therefore, it is obvious that the price of goods and services will have to speak the ecological truth—that is, that they will increasingly have to reflect the use of environmental goods. See S. Schmidheiny and the Business Council for Sustainable Development, *Changing Course: A Global Business Perspective on Development and the Environment* (Cambridge, Mass.: The MIT Press, 1992).
8. Independent Commission on International Development Issues, *North-South: A Programme for Survival* (London: Pan Books, 1980), p. 48.

9. See D. Goulet, "Development: Creator and Destroyer of Values," *World Development,* Vol. 20, No. 3, 1992, p. 469 ff.

10. Behrendt defines development very generally as "directed dynamic cultural change in a social entity (regardless of size), associated with a growing participation of an even greater number of the members of the social entity in the support and guidance of this change and in enjoying the benefits of this change." R.F. Behrendt, *Soziale Strategie für Entwicklungsländer* (Frankfurt am Main: 1965), p. 130.

11. See, for example, "Die protestantische Ethik und der Geist des Kapitalismus, Chapter II.2. Askese und kapitalistischer Geist," in J.C.B. Mohr, *Max Weber: Gesammelte Aufsätze zur Religionssoziologie, Vol. I* (Tübingen, 1988), especially p. 204.

12. See, for example, R. Grabowski, "Development as Displacement: A Critique and Alternative," *Journal of Developing Areas,* July 1989, pp. 505–518.

13. A. Inkeles, "Becoming Modern: Individual Change in Six Developing Countries," *Ethos,* Summer 1975, pp. 323–342; A. Inkeles et al., *Exploring Individual Modernity* (New York: Columbia University Press, 1983). See also J.S. Migdal, "Individual Change in the Midst of Social and Political Change," *The Social Science Journal,* April 1988, pp. 125–135.

14. Goulet, op. cit. note 9.

15. The Club of Rome used this section heading as the title of a chapter that points to the central question of whether traditional political, institutional, and administrative systems are in a position to solve the complex problems poised today on the national and global level. Title and quote from A. King and B. Schneider, *The First Global Revolution: A Report by the Council of the Club of Rome—The World Twenty Years After "The Limits to Growth"* (London: Simon & Schuster, 1991), p. 137.

16. World Bank, *Governance and Development* (Washington, D.C.: 1992), p. 9.

17. International Labour Organization, *Employment, Growth, and Basic Needs: A One-World Problem* (Geneva: 1976).

18. Ibid.

19. World Bank, *World Development Report 1990* (New York: Oxford University Press, 1990).

20. U.N. Development Programme (UNDP), *Human Development Report 1991* (New York: Oxford University Press, 1991), p. 1.

21. Der Bundesminister für Wirtschaft, *Wirtschaftsordnung, sozio-ökonomische Entwicklung und weltwirtschaftliche Integration in den Entwicklungsländern* (Bonn: 1982).

22. A. Müller-Armack, *Wirtschaftsordnung und Wirtschaftspolitik. Studien und Konzepte zur sozialen Marktwirtschaft und zur europäischen Integration* (Freiburg i.Br.: 1966), p. 243.

23. UNDP, *Human Development Report 1993* (New York: Oxford University Press, 1993).

24. P. Ehrlich in R.J. Hoage, *Animal Extinction: What Everyone Should Know* (Washington, D.C.: Smithsonian Institution Press, 1985), p. 163.

25. World Bank, *World Development Report 1991* (New York: Oxford University Press, 1991), p. 11.

26. World Commission on Environment and Development, *Our Common Future* (Oxford: Oxford University Press, 1987), pp. 8–9.

27. I. Kant, *Grundlegung zur Metaphysik der Sitten* (Hamburg: Felix Meiner Verlag, 1965), p. 42 (421).

28. UNDP, op. cit. note 23, p. 5.
29. Streeten Foreword in G. Myrdal, *Das Wertproblem in der Sozialwissenschaft* (Bonn-Bad Godesberg: Verlag Neue Gesellschaft, 2nd ed., 1975), p. 13.
30. King and Schneider, op. cit. note 15, p. 181.

Part II

1. United Nations, *The World Population Situation in 1970* (New York: 1971).
2. U.N. Population Fund (UNFPA), *Population, Resources, and the Environment: The Critical Challenges* (New York: 1991), p. 11.
3. To be more precise, the total fertility rate, which means the number of live births that a woman would have if she lives to the end of her childbearing years and gives birth to children in accordance with the predominating age-specific fertility rates.
4. The technical term for this is achieving a net reproduction rate of 1.
5. N. Keyfitz, "The Limits of Population Forecasting," in K. Davis, M.S. Bernstam, and H.M. Sellers (eds.), *Population and Resources in a Changing World: Current Readings* (Stanford, Calif.: Morrison Institute for Population and Resource Studies, Stanford University, 1989), p. 77.
6. UNFPA, *The State of World Population 1992* (New York: 1992), p. 3.
7. Ibid., pp. 1–2.
8. Ibid., p. i.
9. U.N. Population Division, *Population Bulletin*, No. 19/20, 1986, p. 36.
10. U.N. Population Division, *Long-Range Global Projections Based on Data as Assembled in 1978*, ESA/P/WP.75 (New York: 1981), p. 9.
11. Population Reference Bureau, *Population Today*, June 1992, p. 3.
12. For the value of population projections in general, see C. Haub, "Understanding Population Projections," *Population Bulletin*, December 1987, reprinted in Davis, op. cit. note 5, pp. 57–76. See also Keyfitz, op. cit. note 5, pp. 77–88.
13. World Bank, *World Development Report 1984* (New York: Oxford University Press, 1984), p. 86.
14. K.M. Leisinger and K. Schmitt (eds.), *Überleben im Sahel. Eine ökologische und entwicklungspolitische Herausforderung* (Basel/Berlin/Boston: Birkhäuser Verlag, 1992) (to be published in English as *Survival in the Sahel*).
15. R.D. Lee, "Long-Run Global Population Forecasts: A Critical Appraisal," in K. Davis and M.S. Bernstam, *Resources, Environment and Population: Present Knowledge, Future Options, Population and Development Review*, Vol. 16 (Supplement), 1990, pp. 44–71.
16. This led, for example, to a reduction of the projections for Uganda for 2025.
17. Haub, op. cit. note 12, p. 61.
18. H. Jonas, "Auf der Schwelle der Zukunft: Werte von gestern für eine Welt von morgen," in H. Jonas and D. Mieth, *Was für morgen lebenswichtig ist. Unentdeckte Zukunftswerte* (Freiburg i.B.: Herder, 1983), p. 22 ff.
19. Population Reference Bureau (PRB), *World Population Data Sheet 1994* (Washington, D.C.: 1994).
20. Ibid.
21. P. Demeny, "A Perspective on Long-term Population Growth," *Population and Development Review*, Vol. 10, No. 1, 1984, p. 122.

22. All data in this section are from World Bank, *Population and Human Resources: Europe, Middle East, and North Africa Region Population Projections* (Washington, D.C.: 1990–91 ed.), p. XIV ff.

23. S.H. Cochrane and S. M. Farid, "Fertility in Sub-Saharan Africa: Analysis and Explanation," World Bank Discussion Paper No. 43, Washington, D.C., 1989, Table 3.1, p. 81.

24. R.S. McNamara, "Africa's Development Crisis: Agricultural Stagnation, Population Explosion, and Environmental Degradation," Address to the African Leadership Forum, Ota, Nigeria, June 21, 1990.

25. E. van der Walle and A.D. Foster, "Fertility Decline in Africa: Assessment and Prospects," World Bank Technical Paper No. 125, Washington, D.C., 1990.

26. J.C. Caldwell and P. Caldwell, "High Fertility in Sub-Saharan Africa," *Scientific American,* May 1990, pp. 82–89.

27. UNFPA, *The State of World Population 1991* (New York: 1991), p. 3.

28. S.A. Moustafa, "Problematic Population Phenomena in Arab Countries," *Free Inquiry in Creative Sociology,* May 1988, p. 45 ff.

29. E.J. Cross, "Production Versus Reproduction: A Threat to China's Development Strategy," *World Development,* March 1981, pp. 85–97. See also Demeny, op. cit. note 21, p. 118.

30. The reference here is to the crude birth rate, which is the number of births per year per 1,000 population, without taking account of the population structure. Therefore it can increase, for example, because more couples are entering their reproductive years due to the population's young age structure. Age-specific fertility figures would be more meaningful. They relate the number of births for women of a specific year of birth to the mean number of women born that same year. For technical details, see J.A. Hauser, *Bevölkerungs- und Umweltprobleme der Dritten Welt,* Band 2 (Stuttgart/Bern: UTB/Haupt, 1991), Chapters 11–13. For details on China, see Z. Yi et al., "A Demographic Decomposition of the Recent Increase in Crude Birth Rates in China," *Population and Development Review,* Vol. 17, No. 3, 1991, pp. 435–458.

31. A.J. Coale, "Population Trends in China and India," *Proceedings of the National Academy of Sciences,* Vol. 80, 1983, pp. 1757–1763.

32. PRB, op. cit. note 19.

33. R.D. Retherford and J.R. Rele, "A Decomposition of Recent Fertility Changes in South Asia," *Population and Development Review,* Vol. 15, No. 4, 1989, pp. 739–747.

34. PRB, op. cit. note 19.

35. World Bank, *World Development Report 1993* (New York: Oxford University Press, 1993), p. 292, Table 28.

36. This is the so-called mean value—the age that divides the population into two groups of equal size: an older and a younger group. See World Health Organization, *World Health Statistics Quarterly,* Vol. 40, p. 12 ff.

37. PRB, op. cit. note 19. If China—which is more of an exception due to its strict population policy measures over the past 10 years—is included in the statistics, the figure is 36 percent.

38. World Bank, op. cit. note 13, p. 88.

39. UNFPA, *The State of World Population 1990* (New York: 1990), p. 1.

40. H.W. Richardson, "The Big, Bad City: Mega-City Myth?" *Third World Planning Review,* Vol. 11, No. 4, 1989, pp. 355–372.

41. M. Cohen, "Megacities and the Environment," *Finance & Development,* June 1993, p. 46.
42. UNFPA, op. cit. note 2, p. 61.
43. World Bank, op. cit. note 13, p. 67.
44. World Bank, op. cit. note 35, p. 298.
45. UNFPA, op. cit. note 27, p. 9.
46. L.R. Brown and J.L. Jacobson, *The Future of Urbanization: Facing the Ecological and Economic Constraints,* Worldwatch Paper 77 (Washington, D.C.: Worldwatch Institute, 1987), p. 6 ff.
47. World Bank, op. cit. note 13, p. 78.
48. U.N. Development Programme, *Human Development Report 1991* (New York: Oxford University Press, 1991), p. 159.
49. Cohen, op. cit. note 41, p. 45 ff.
50. E.U. von Weizsäcker, *Erdpolitik: Ökologische Realpolitik an der Schwelle zum Jahrhundert der Umwelt* (Darmstadt: Wissenschaftliche Buchgesellschaft, 1989), p. 112.
51. Both examples cited in H.F. French, "Clearing the Air," in L.R. Brown et al., *State of the World 1990* (New York: W.W. Norton & Co., 1990), pp. 100, 103.
52. J.E. Hardoy and D. Satterthwaite, *Squatter Citizen: Life in the Urban Third World* (London: Earthscan Publications, 1989), cited in M.L. Lowe, "Shaping Cities," in L.R. Brown et al., *State of the World 1992* (New York: W.W. Norton & Co., 1992), p. 122.

Part III

1. Often discussed, for example, are the proportion of married women or women living in heterosexual relationships, frequency of sexual intercourse, post-partum abstinence, lactational amenorrhea, contraception, abortion, stillbirths, natural infertility, and infertility due to disease. See J. Bongaarts, O. Frank, and R. Lesthaeghe, "The Proximate Determinants of Fertility," in G.T.F. Acsadi, G. Johnson-Acsadi, and R.A. Bulatao (eds.), *Population Growth and Reproduction in Sub-Saharan Africa: Technical Analysis of Fertility and Its Consequences* (Washington, D.C.: World Bank, 1990), p. 130 ff.
2. See E.A. Hammel, "A Theory of Culture for Demography," *Population and Development Review,* Vol. 16, No. 3, 1990, pp. 455–485, and the bibliographic references cited there.
3. J. Simons, "Culture, Economy, and Reproduction in Contemporary Europe," in D. Coleman and R. Schofield (eds.), *The State of Population Theory: Forward from Malthus* (Oxford: Basil Blackwell, 1986), pp. 256–278.
4. A. Shaw, "Fertility and Child Spacing Among the Urban Poor in a Third World City, The Case of Calcutta, India," *Human Ecology,* Vol. 16, No. 3, 1988, pp. 329–342.
5. K. Davis, "Institutional Patterns Favouring High Fertility in Underdeveloped Areas," *Eugenics Quarterly,* Vol. 2, No. 1, 1955, p. 33 ff. See also H. Leridon and B. Ferry, "Biological and Traditional Restraints on Fertility," in J. Cleland and J. Hobcraft (eds.), *Reproductive Change in Developing Countries: Insights from the World Fertility Survey* (Oxford: Oxford University Press, 1985), pp. 139–164.
6. Ch. Oppong, "Some Aspects of Anthropological Contributions," in G.M. Farooq and G.B. Simmons, *Fertility in Developing Countries: An Economic Perspective on Research and Policy Issues* (New York: MacMillan, 1985), p. 240 ff.
7. See J.C. Caldwell and P. Caldwell, "Cultural Forces Tending to Sustain High Fertility,"

in Acsadi, Johnson-Acsadi, and Bulatao, op. cit. note 1, p. 199 and the references cited there, especially P.A. Talbot, *Some Nigerian Fertility Cults* (Oxford: Oxford University Press, 1927), and J.S. Mbiti, *Concepts of God in Africa* (New York: Praeger, 1970).

8. P.N. Hess, *Population Growth and Socio-Economic Progress in Less Developed Countries: Determinants of Fertility* (New York: Praeger, 1988), Chapters 5 and 6.

9. D.P. Warwick, "The Indonesian Family Planning Program: Government Influence and Client Choice," *Population and Development Review,* Vol. 12, No. 3, 1986, pp. 453–490.

10. S.A. Moustafa, "Problematic Population Phenomena in Arab Countries," *Free Inquiry in Creative Sociology,* May 1988, pp. 45–49.

11. For a general discussion of this, see J.R. Weeks, "The Demography of Islamic Nations," *Population Bulletin,* Vol. 43, No. 4, 1988.

12. Data collected by the Ciba-Geigy Foundation for Cooperation with Developing Countries, Basel, Switzerland.

13. This does not mean there are no latent ideas regarding "adequate numbers of children": the average number of additionally desired children decreases with the number already born and living. In a study of 13 African countries, the number of desired children derived from actual family size was between six (Lesotho and Ghana) and more than eight (Cameroon, Côte d'Ivoire, Mauritania, Nigeria, and Senegal). See Acsadi, Johnson-Acsadi, and Bulatao, op. cit. note 1.

14. M.J. Swartz, "Some Cultural Influences on Family Size in Three East African Societies," *Anthropological Quarterly,* Vol. 42, No. 2, 1969, pp. 73–88. See also A. Oyemade and T.A. Ogunmuyiwa, "Socio-Cultural Factors and Fertility in a Rural Nigerian Community," *Studies in Family Planning,* Vol. 12, No. 3, 1981, p. 109 ff.

15. Caldwell and Caldwell, op. cit. note 7, p. 199; see also G. Kershaw, "The Kikuyu of Central Kenya," in A. Molnos, *Cultural Source Materials for Population Planning in East Africa, Vol 3. Beliefs and Practices* (Nairobi: East African Publishing House, 1973).

16. Kershaw, op. cit. note 15, p. 8 ff. The same is also true, however, of other non-African religions, such as Hinduism.

17. J.C. Caldwell and P. Caldwell, "Cultural Forces Tending to Sustain Fertility in Tropical Africa," PHN Technical Note 85–16, World Bank, Washington, D.C., October 1985, p. 9 ff and 17 ff.

18. G.T.F. Acsadi and G. Johnson-Acsadi, "Demand for Children and Children Spacing," in Acsadi, Johnson-Acsadi, and Bulatao, op. cit. note 1, p. 155 ff.

19. Frank and McNicoll give an excellent description of the traditional factors that regulate fertility in an African country; O. Frank and G. McNicoll, "An Interpretation of Fertility and Population Policy in Kenya," *Population and Development Review,* Vol. 13, No. 2, 1987, pp. 209–243.

20. T.H. Hull, "Cultural Influences on Fertility Decision Styles," in R.A. Bulatao and R.D. Lee (eds.), *Determinants of Fertility in Developing Countries, Vol. 2. Fertility Regulation and Institutional Influences* (New York: Academic Press, 1983), pp. 381–414; I. Schapera, *Married Life in an African Tribe* (Middlesex, U.K.: Pelican, 1940); M.K. Whyte, "Cross-Cultural Codes Dealing With the Relative Status of Women," in H. Barry and A. Schlegel (eds.), *Cross-Cultural Samples and Codes* (Pittsburgh: University of Pittsburgh Press, 1980), pp. 335–361; L.J. Beckman, "Couples' Decision-

Making Processes Regarding Fertility," in K.E. Taueber, L.L. Bumpass, and J.A. Sweet (eds.), *Social Demography* (New York: Academic Press, 1978), pp. 209–231.

21. P.E. Hollerbach, "Power in Families: Communication and Fertility Decision-Making," *Journal of Population,* Vol. 3, No. 2, 1980.

22. Harvey Leibenstein introduced this aspect into the economic theory of population; H. Leibenstein, *Economic Backwardness and Economic Growth* (New York: John Wiley, 1957). For a controversial discussion of this aspect, see Farooq and Simmons, op. cit. note 6, p. 84 ff. De Tray points out that there are important ethnic and regional differences in this respect; D. De Tray, "Children's Work Activities in Malaysia," *Population and Development Review,* Vol. 9, No. 3, 1983, p. 437 ff.

23. S. Cochrane, V. Kozel, and H. Alderman, "Household Consequences of High Fertility in Pakistan," World Bank Discussion Paper No. 111, Washington, D.C., December 1990, p. 27 f. and the referenced bibliography.

24. See the limitations to this in E. Boserup, *Woman's Role in Economic Development* (London: Gower, 1965), p. 10 ff.

25. World Bank, *World Development Report 1984* (New York: Oxford University Press, 1984), p. 59 f.

26. Cochrane, Kozel, and Alderman, op. cit. note 23, p. 27.

27. A.M. Hallouda et al., "Socio-Economic Differentials and Comparative Data from Husbands and Wives," in *The Egyptian Fertility Survey, Vol. III* (Cairo: Central Agency for Public Mobilization and Statistics, 1983), quoted in Cochrane, Kozel, and Alderman, op. cit. note 23, p. 28.

28. Cochrane, Kozel, and Alderman, op. cit. note 23, p. 28.

29. D. Chernichovsky, "Socio-Economic and Demographic Aspects of School Enrollment and Attendance in Rural Botswana," *Economic Development and Cultural Change,* Vol. 11, No. 2, 1985, pp. 319–322.

30. E.M. King and R.E. Evenson, "Time Allocation and Home Production in Philippine Rural Households," in M. Buvinic, M. Lycette, and W.P. McGreevey (eds.), *Women and Povery in the Third World* (Baltimore, Md.: Johns Hopkins University Press, 1983), p. 35 ff.; E.M. King, "The Effects of Family Size on Family Welfare: What Do We Know?" in D.G. Johnson and R.D. Lee (eds.), *Population Growth and Economic Development: Issues and Evidence* (Madison, Wisc.: University of Wisconsin Press, 1987), p. 373 ff.

31. World Bank, op. cit. note 25, p. 59.

32. M.T. Cain, "The Economic Activities of Children in a Village in Bangladesh," *Population and Development Review,* Vol. 3, No. 3, 1977, p. 201; B. White, "The Economic Importance of Children in a Javanese Village," 1973, unpublished, quoted in N. Birdsall, "Population and Poverty in the Developing World," World Bank Staff Working Paper No. 404, Washington, D.C., 1980, p. 50.

33. To complete the picture, it should be noted that low population growth in industrial countries also threatens the social security of the older generations because the burden of financing social security falls on the gainfully employed population and the tolerance for this burden cannot yet be foreseen.

34. J.B. Nugent, "The Old Age Security Motive for Fertility," *Population and Development Review,* Vol. 11, No. 1, 1985, pp. 75–97.

35. J.E. Potter, "Effects of Societal and Community Institutions on Fertility," in Bulatao and Lee, op. cit. note 20, pp. 627–665.

36. World Bank, op. cit. note 25, p. 60.

37. U.D. Rani, "Old Age Security Value of Children and Fertility in Relation to Social Policy," International Sociological Association, Department of Population Studies, Andhra Pradesh, India, 1986.

38. P.E. Hollerbach, "Fertility Decision-Making Processes: A Critical Essay," in Bulatao and Lee, op. cit. note 20, pp. 340–380.

39. J. Bongaarts, "The Measurement of Wanted Fertility," *Population and Development Review,* Vol. 16, No. 3, 1990, p. 487 ff.

40. F. Moore Lappé and R. Schurman, *Taking Population Seriously* (London: Earthscan, 1989), p. 29.

41. See, for example, F. Sultana Begum, "Legal Status of Women in Bangladesh and Its Linkage to Demographic Behavior," *Asia Pacific Women's Studies Journal* (Institute of Women's Studies, Manila), No. 2, 1992, pp. 1–13.

42. R.M. Yehya, "Contraceptive Attitude and Use: The Influence of Contraceptive Knowledge, Availability, Accessibility and Husbands' Attitudes," North Central Sociological Association, Department of Sociology, Bowling, 1989.

43. R. Dixon-Mueller, "Abortion Policy and Women's Health in Developing Countries," *International Journal of Health Services,* Vol. 20, No. 2, 1990, pp. 297–314.

44. See, for example, F. Sultana Begum, "Women's Programmes and Their Impact on Fertility in Bangladesh," *Two Studies on Women, Development and Fertility in Bangladesh,* Population and Development Planning Unit, Planning Commission, Dhaka, Bangladesh, December 1985, p. 46.

45. According to criteria in the Human Development Index in U.N. Development Programme, *Human Development Report 1992* (New York: Oxford University Press, 1992), Table 4, p. 134 f.

Part IV

1. See also the summary of Malthus' biography and the major influences on his thinking in S. Chandrasekhar, "Malthus: Father of Demography," *Population Review,* Vol. 12, No. 1–2, 1969, pp. 76–81.

2. Mark Perlman estimates that the population policy debate began more than 250 years ago. In his research, he came upon "earlier and better explanations of the Malthusian arguments" in Francesco Botero's publication dated 1558, "Delle Cause Della Grandezza Delle Città." See M. Perlman, "Some Economic Growth Problems and the Part Population Policy Plays," *Quarterly Journal of Economics,* May 1975, p. 248. Since Botero, however, has had no effect on the population policy debate, while Malthus has had a strong and lasting influence, Botero's model will not be discussed here.

3. T.R. Malthus, *An Essay on the Principle of Population as It Affects the Future Improvement of Society* (London: 1798). In later editions the title was altered slightly to *An Essay on the Principle of Population or a View on Its Past and Present Effects on Human Happiness* (London: 1803, 1807, 1817, and 1826). The edition quoted here is the one of 1817 ("fifth edition with important additions," 3 Volumes, John Murray), Vol. I, p. 9.

4. See A.J. Coale, "The Use of Modern Analytical Demography by T.R. Malthus," *Population Studies,* July 1979, pp. 329–332.

5. Ibid.

6. He described the reason for this diverging development as the law of diminishing returns or "corn law" in his lesser known economic work. Malthus unleashed there a debate that was carried out with great acrimony. Many of the arguments espoused at that time are still used today in only slightly modified variations to support or counter leading population policy measures.

7. Malthus, op. cit. note 3, pp. 21–22.

8. "It is in the power of each individual to avoid all the evil consequences to himself and society resulting from the principle of population, by the practice of a virtue clearly dictated to him by the light of nature, and expressly enjoined in revealed religions; and as we have reason to think that the exercise of this virtue to a certain degree would tend rather to increase than diminish individual happiness, we can have no reason to impeach the justice of the Deity, because his general laws make this virtue necessary, and punish our offences against it by the evils attended upon vice, and the pains that accompany the various forms of premature death." Malthus, op. cit. note 3, Vol. III, p. 100 f.

9. Malthus, op. cit. note 3, p. 18.

10. Ibid., p. 23.

11. S. Kath, "Alarmist Demography: Power, Knowledge, and the Elderly Population," *Journal of Aging Studies,* Fall 1992, pp. 203–225.

12. Malthus, op. cit. note 3, Vol. III, p. 138. See also J.W. Leasure, "Malthus, Marriage and Multiplication," *Milbank Memorial Fund Quarterly/Health and Society,* October 1963, pp. 419–435; J. Knodel, "Malthus Amiss: Marriage in 19th Century Germany," *Social Science,* Winter 1972, pp. 40–45.

13. L.R. Brown, *The Changing World Food Prospect: The Nineties and Beyond,* Worldwatch Paper 85 (Washington, D.C.: Worldwatch Institute, 1988); P.R. Ehrlich, A.H. Ehrlich, and G.C. Daly, "Food Security, Population and Environment," *Population and Development Review,* Vol. 19, No. 1, pp. 1–32.

14. This is Renate Rott's interpretation in "Bevölkerungskontrolle, Familienplanung, und Geschlechterpolitik," *Peripherie,* Vol. 9, No. 36, 1989, p. 12.

15. Ibid. This is how Rott interprets the second edition of Malthus' work, where he writes "a human who is born into a world already possessed has—if he does not receive any support from his parents, on whom he can make a legitimate demand, and if society does not want his labor—no legal claim on the smallest bite to eat and absolutely no right to his existence."

16. G. Myrdal, *Asian Drama, An Inquiry Into the Poverty of Nations, Vol. III* (Harmondsworth, U.K.: Penquin, 1968), Appendix 3.

17. J.L. Simon, *The Ultimate Resource* (Princeton, N.J.: Princeton University Press, 1981).

18. J.L. Simon, "Population Growth Is Not Bad for Humanity," *National Forum,* Winter 1990, pp. 12–16.

19. C. Clark, "Population Growth and Living Standards," in A.N. Agarwala and S.P. Singh (eds.), *The Economics of Underdevelopment* (Oxford: Oxford University Press, 1958), pp. 32–53. Clark sees, however, the necessity for direct help and foreign markets: "In many cases, where rates of population increase are high and rates of savings in all probability lower, there will be a retrogression of economic standards unless a substantial inflow of external capital is possible." Ibid., p. 52.

20. For instance, World Bank, *Brazil—Human Resources Special Report* (Washington, D.C.: October 1979), Annex II, pp. 32–51.

21. J.L. Simon and R. Gobin, "The Relationship Between Population and Economic Growth in LDCs," in J.L. Simon and J. DaVanzo (eds.), *Research in Population Economics,* Vol. 2 (Greenwich, Conn.: JAI Press, 1979), pp. 215–234; Clark, op. cit. note 19, p. 34 ff.

22. See, for example, World Bank, *World Development Report 1991* and *1992,* as well as U.N. Development Programme (UNDP), *Human Development Report 1991* and *1992.*

23. International Labour Organization, *World Labour Report 1993* (Geneva: 1993).

24. UNDP, *Human Development Report 1993* (New York: Oxford University Press, 1993).

25. A.O. Hirschmann, *The Strategy of Economic Development* (New Haven, Conn.: Yale University Press, 1958), esp. pp. 176–182; J.L. Simon, *The Economics of Population Growth* (Princeton, N.J.: Princeton University Press, 1977), pp. 158–203; E. Boserup, *The Conditions of Agricultural Growth: The Economics of Agrarian Change Under Population Pressure* (Chicago: Aldine Press, 1965); Simon, op cit. note 17.

26. Simon, op. cit. note 25, p. 182.

27. Boserup, op. cit. note 25.

28. Simon and Gobin, op. cit. note 21.

29. K.M. Leisinger and K. Schmitt, *Überleben im Sahel: Eine ökologische und entwicklungspolitische Herausforderung* (Boston: Birkhäuser Verlag, 1992), especially Chapter 6 (to be published in English as *Survival in the Sahel*).

30. Deutscher Bundestag (ed.), *Schutz der Tropenwälder: Eine internationale Schwerpunktaufgabe, Bd. 2* (Bonn: Economica Verlag, 1990) pp. 242–271.

31. Quoted in L. Schmidt, *Das treffende Zitat zu Politik, Recht und Wirtschaft* (Thun: Verlag Ott, 1984), p. 193.

32. D.R. Glover and J.L. Simon, "The Effect of Population Density on Infrastructure: The Case of Road Building," *Economic Development and Cultural Change,* April 1985, pp. 453–468; see also Simon and Gobin, op. cit. note 21.

33. J.L. Simon, "The Positive Effect of Population Growth on Agricultural Saving in Irrigation Systems," *Review of Economic and Statistics,* Vol. 57, 1975, pp. 71–79.

34. Simon gives examples from Ghana, Thailand, Bolivia, Costa Rica, and India where improvements in the transportation infrastructure led to higher prices for agricultural goods; Simon, op. cit. note 25, p. 264 ff. See also J.D. Stryker, "Optimum Population in Rural Areas: Empirical Evidence from the Franc Zone," *Quarterly Journal of Economics,* May 1977, pp. 177–192.

35. R.E. Evenson, "Population Growth, Infrastructure, and Real Incomes in North India," in R.E. Lee et al., (eds.), *Population, Food, and Rural Development* (Oxford: Clarendon Press, 1988), pp. 118–139.

36. UNESCO, *World Education Report 1991* (Paris: 1991), p. 16.

37. World Bank, *World Development Report 1978* (New York: Oxford University Press, 1978), p. 122.

38. UNESCO, op. cit. note 36; UNDP, *Human Development Report 1991* (New York: Oxford University Press, 1991), p. 138 f.

39. World Bank, *World Development Report 1991* (New York: Oxford University Press, 1991), p. 302 f. Although the rate for women here too was lower, it did improve from 5 percent (1965) to 20 percent (1988). For improvements during the last 10 years, see UNESCO, op. cit. note 36, p. 134 f.

40. H. Leibenstein, "The Impact of Population Growth on Economic Welfare: Non-traditional Elements," in National Academy of Sciences, *Rapid Population Growth:*

Consequences and Policy Implications (Baltimore, Md.: 1971); World Bank, *World Development Report 1982* (New York: Oxford University Press, 1982), p. 112 ff.; S. Kuznets, "Population Change and Aggregate Output," in Universities National Bureaus, *Demographic and Economic Change in Developed Countries,* Special Series No. 22 (Princeton, N.J.: 1960), pp. 324–339.

41. UNESCO, op. cit. note 36, p. 34 and Table R-6, p. 126 ff.

42. Kuznets, op. cit. note 40.

43. B. Fritsch, *Mensch-Umwelt-Wissen* (Zürich: Verlag der Fachvereine, 1990), S. 72.

44. Simon, op. cit. note 17.

45. Simon does concede that "short-term" difficulties, which he foresees for a period of 30–80 years, do exist, but maintains that they will eventually be overcome. In our opinion, however, Simon not only underestimates the cumulative negative secondary effects of existing setbacks that Myrdal describes so vividly (see Myrdal, op. cit. note 16, pp. 18–44 ff.), but also ignores the fact that a declining resource base inhibits further economic development or prevents it altogether. If the additional human suffering that Simon foresees for the "short term" can be avoided through appropriate population policy, this alone is of such great intrinsic value—from the point of view of our values—that the measures take on the character of moral requirements.

46. A.C. Kelley, "Economic Consequences of Population Change in the Third World," *Journal of Economic Literature,* December 1988, pp. 1685–1728.

47. S. Cochrane, V. Kozel, and H. Alderman, "Household Consequences of High Fertility in Pakistan," World Bank Discussion Paper No. 111, Washington, D.C., December 1990, pp. 1–5.

48. E. Royston and A.D. Lopez, "On the Assessment of Maternal Mortality," *World Health Statistics Quarterly,* Vol. 40, No. 3, 1987, pp. 214–224; M.O. Seipel Michael, "Promoting Maternal Health in Developing Countries," *Health and Social Work,* August 1992, pp. 200–206.

49. B. Blum and P. Fargues, "Rapid Estimations of Maternal Mortality in Countries with Defective Data: An Application to Bamako (1974–1985) and Other Developing Countries," *Population Studies,* Vol. 44, 1990, pp. 155–171.

50. B. Herz and A.R. Measham, "The Safe Motherhood Initiative," World Bank Discussion Paper No. 9, Washington, D.C., 1987.

51. R. Dixon-Mueller, "Abortion Policy and Women's Health in Developing Countries," *International Journal of Health Services,* Vol. 10, No. 2, 1990, pp. 297–314.

52. J.L. Jacobson, "Improving Women's Reproductive Health," in L. R. Brown et al., *State of the World 1992* (New York: W.W. Norton & Co., 1992), pp. 85–89.

53. D. Maine et al., "Effects of Fertility Change on Maternal and Child Survival," in G.T.F. Acsadi, G. Johnson-Acsadi, and R.A. Bulatao (eds.), *Population Growth and Reproduction in Sub-Saharan Africa: Technical Analysis of Fertility and Its Consequences* (Washington, D.C.: World Bank, 1990), pp. 91–114.

54. B. Winikoff and M. Sullivan, "Assessing the Role of Family Planning in Reducing Maternal Mortality," *Studies in Family Planning,* Vol. 18, No. 3, 1987, pp. 128–143.

55. Z. Sathar, "Seeking Explanations for High Levels of Infant Mortality in Pakistan," *The Pakistan Development Review,* Vol. XXVI, No. 1, 1987, pp. 55–70.

56. For differentiation with respect to income and difficulty of physical labor, see B. Winikoff and M.A. Castle, "The Maternal Depletion Syndrome: Clinical Diagnosis or Eco-Demographic Condition?" Technical Background Paper for the International Con-

ference on Better Health for Women and Children Through Family Planning, quoted in Cochrane, Kozel, and Alderman, op. cit. note 47, p. 7.

57. Cochrane, Kozel, and Alderman, op. cit. note 47, p. 6.

58. A.M. Greenwood and others describe the tragic situation in an African country in "A Prospective Survey of the Outcome of Pregnancy in a Rural Area of The Gambia," *Bulletin of the World Health Organization,* Vol. 65, No. 5, pp. 635–643; see also W.J. Graham, "Maternal Mortality: Levels, Trends, and Data Deficiencies," in R.G. Feachem and D.T. Jamison (eds.), *Disease and Mortality in Sub-Saharan Africa* (Washington, D.C.: World Bank, 1991), pp. 101–116.

59. M. Selowsky, "The Economic Dimension of Malnutrition in Young Children," in S. Doxiadis (ed.), *The Child in the World of Tomorrow* (Oxford: Oxford University Press, 1979), p. 351.

60. H. Alderman et al., "Household Food Security in Pakistan with Reference to the Ration Shop System," Working Paper on Food Studies No. 4, International Food Policy Research Institute, Washington, D.C., May 1988.

61. The West African word kwashiorkor that is now used universally to refer to protein and calorie deficiencies in small children literally means "sickness of the weaned child after the birth of the next child."

62. M.M. Stewart et al., "Ecologic Determinants of Health Problems," III/7, p. 24 ff.; see also V. Sharma and A. Sharma, "Is the Female Child Being Neglected? Immunization in India," *Health Policy and Planning,* September 1991, pp. 287–290.

63. See two well-substantiated case studies: M.M. Teran, "Some Aspects of the Interrelationship Between Fertility Patterns and Health: The Case of Mexico," and A. Chamratrithirong et al., "The Effect of Reduced Family Size on Maternal and Child Health: The Case of Thailand," both in *World Health Statistics Quarterly,* Vol. 40, 1987, pp. 41–62.

64. See J. Wray and D. Maine, "Family Spacing," in UNICEF, *The State of the World's Children 1984* (New York: Oxford University Press, 1984), p. 94 and the references cited there.

65. N. Birdsall, "A Cost of Siblings: Child Schooling in Urban Colombia," in Simon and DaVanzo, op. cit. note 21, p. 117.

66. S.H. Cochrane and D.T. Jamison, "Educational Attainment and Achievement in Rural Thailand," in *New Directions for Testing and Measurement,* Productivity Assessment in Education No. 15, World Bank, Washington, D.C., 1982, pp. 43–59.

67. U.N. Food and Agriculture Organization (FAO), *Land, Food, and People* (Rome: 1984), p. 11 ff.

68. FAO, *Production Yearbook 1990* (Rome: 1991), pp. 3, 19.

69. U.N. Population Fund (UNFPA), *Population, Resources, and the Environment: The Critical Challenges* (New York: 1991), p. 20.

70. P.B.R. Hazell and C. Ramasamy, *The Green Revolution Reconsidered: The Impact of High-Yielding Rice Varieties in South India* (Baltimore, Md.: Johns Hopkins University Press, 1991).

71. W.B. Arthur and G. McNicoll, "An Analytical Survey of Population and Development in Bangladesh," *Population and Development Review,* Vol. 4, No. 1, 1978, pp. 23–80.

72. Ibid., p. 50.

73. The relationship between pastoralists and settled farmers can, under certain circumstances, be positive and mutually advantageous. Where, for example, cattle graze on

fields during the dry season, their excrement fertilizes the soil and increases its productivity during the subsequent planting period. See O. Bennett (ed.), *Greenwar: Environment and Conflict* (London: The Panos Institute, 1991), Chapter 3, pp. 33–52.

74. See Leisinger and Schmitt, op. cit. note 29; Bennett, op. cit. note 73; R.E. Bilsborrow, "Population Pressures and Agricultural Development in Developing Countries: A Conceptual Framework and Recent Evidence," *World Development,* Vol. 15, No. 2, 1987, pp. 183–203.

75. We are using the definition of the Enquete Commission of the 11th German Bundestag: "The term firewood encompasses any wood that is used as a source of energy including that part of the wood that is transformed into charcoal. The term lumber encompasses any round wood that is felled for industrial purposes and is used in the form of sawed timber, timber for mining, veneering, pulp wood, and scrap wood in construction, furniture production, paper production, or for other purposes." [Translated by the authors] Enquete Commission, Vorsorge zum Schutz der Erdatmosphäre, *Schutz der Tropenwälder* (Bonn: Economica Verlag, 1990), p. 271.

76. FAO cited in ibid.

77. World Commission on Environment and Development, *Our Common Future* (New York: Oxford University Press, 1987), pp. 189–192.

78. Enquete Commission, op. cit. note 75, p. 305 [translated by the authors].

79. Ibid.

80. Ibid.

81. Ibid., p. 308.

82. FAO, "An Interim Report on the State of Forest Resources in the Developing Countries," Forestry Department, Rome, 1988.

83. Enquete Commission, op. cit. note 75, p. 305.

84. UNFPA, *The State of World Population 1991* (New York: 1991), pp. 3–4.

85. Ibid.

86. Age structure from World Bank, *World Development Report 1993* (New York: Oxford University Press, 1993), Table 26, p. 288 f. The fact that in countries such as Switzerland senior citizens finance their pensions through their own contributions or pay for their own costs of living with savings or even continue to work is not taken into account here.

87. World Bank, op. cit. note 86.

88. Ibid. This also does not take into account that children in the traditional sector begin to work at an early age in the household and in the fields, and that, due to poverty, older people usually continue to help until they become invalids or until the end of their lives. Here, only the modern sector of the economy, in which monetary income can be earned, is taken into account.

89. S. Hansen, "Absorbing a Rapidly Growing Labor Force, " in Acsadi, Johnson-Acsadi, and Bulatao, op. cit. note 53, pp. 60–73.

90. UNFPA, op. cit. note 69, p. 13.

91. N.H. Leff, "Dependency Rates and Savings Rates," *American Economic Review,* December 1969, p. 887 f.; P. Musgrove, "Determinant of Urban Household Consumption in Latin America: A Summary of Evidence from the ECIEL," *Economic Development and Cultural Change,* April 1978, p. 441 ff.; D. Freedman, "Family Size and Economic Welfare in a Developing Country: Taiwan," Population Studies Center, University of Michigan, Ann Arbor, 1972. For a critical analysis of this theory, see A.

Mason, "Savings, Economic Growth, and Demographic Change," *Population and Development Review,* Vol. 14, No. 1, 1988, pp. 113–144 and references cited there.

92. A. Coale and E.M. Hoover, *Population Growth and Economic Development in Low-Income Countries* (Princeton, N.J.: Princeton University Press, 1958).

93. UNFPA, *The State of World Population 1993* (New York: 1993), p. 8 f.

94. H. Chenery et al., *Redistribution With Growth* (Oxford: Oxford University Press, 3rd ed., 1976), p. 17.

95. See the World Bank case study on Brazil: *Human Resources Special Report* (Washington, D.C.: October 1979), Annex II, pp. 32–52.

96. See the classic article by R. von Barlow, "The Economic Effect of Malaria Eradication," *American Economic Review,* Vol. 54, 1967, pp. 131–148; see also J.E. Meade, "Population Explosion: The Standard of Living and Social Conflict," *The Economic Journal,* June 1967.

97. R.G. Repetto, "The Relation of the Size Distribution of Income to Fertility, and Implications for Development Policy," in World Bank, *Population Policies and Economic Development* (Baltimore, Md.: Johns Hopkins University Press, 1974).

98. Ehrlich, Ehrlich, and Daly, op. cit. note 13, p. 2.

99. The numbers vary considerably. Detailed studies arrive at considerably lower figures with respect to the number of deaths caused by starvation. See J. Seaman, "Famine Mortality in Ethiopia and Sudan," in E. Van der Walle, G. Pison, M. Sala-Diakanda (eds.), *Mortality and Society in Sub-Saharan Africa* (Oxford: Clarendon Press, 1992), pp. 349–366; and J.C. Caldwell and P. Caldwell, "Famine in Africa: A Global Perspective," in ibid., pp. 367–390.

100. See annual FAO publications; FAO, *Food Outlook. Global Information and Early Warning System on Food and Agriculture,* Nos. 8 and 9, 1992, report further decreasing supplies of important grains.

101. J.W. Mellor and S. Gavian, "Famine: Causes, Prevention, and Relief," *Science,* January 30, 1987, p. 539 ff.

102. Ehrlich, Ehrlich, and Daly, op. cit. note 13.

103. UNDP, op. cit. note 24, p. 160 f.

104. FAO, *Agriculture: Toward 2000* (Rome: 1981), p. 57; see also L.R. Brown, "Facing Food Insecurity," in L.R. Brown et al., *State of the World 1994* (New York: W.W. Norton & Co., 1994).

105. Ehrlich, Ehrlich, and Daly, op. cit. note 13, p. 5.

106. Ibid., p. 27.

107. See also R. Repetto, "Population, Resource Pressure and Poverty," in R. Repetto (ed.), *The Global Possible: Resources, Development, and the New Century* (New Haven, Conn.: Yale University Press, 1985), pp. 131–169.

108. World Commission on Environment and Development, op. cit. note 77, p. 8.

109. UNFPA, *The State of World Population 1990* (New York: 1990), p. 13.

110. R.S. McNamara, "A Global Population Policy to Advance Human Development in the 21st Century," Rafael M. Salas Memorial Lecture, New York, December 10, 1991, p. 6 f. He also points out that environmental damage has many causes: "wasteful consumption and wasteful technology, bad management and poor policy. However, the point I wish to emphasize is that, other things being equal, the impact of human activity on the environment is not proportional to changes in population alone,

but rather to the *product* of population levels and consumption per capita, both of which will rise sharply in the future."

111. B. Commoner, "Rapid Population Growth and Environmental Stress," *International Journal of Health Services,* Vol. 21, No. 2, 1991, pp. 199–227.

112. I = P x A x T, where I represents environmental impact, P represents population, A represents per capita consumption determined by income and life-style, and T represents environmentally harmful technology that supplies A. UNFPA, op. cit. note 69, p. 16 f.

113. UNFPA, op. cit. note 109, p. 10.

114. The discussion of this aspect of the environmental impact of rapid population growth relies primarily on three studies: World Resources Institute, *World Resources 1992– 93* (New York: Oxford University Press, 1992); Organisation for Economic Co-operation and Development, *The State of the Environment* (Paris: 1991); and the Enquete Commission of the German Bundestag, Vorsorge zum Schutz der Erdatmosphäre (reports published to date: *Schutz der Tropenwälder, Schutz der Erdatmosphäre,* and *Schutz der Erde,* two volumes, all by Economica Verlag, Bonn).

115. Enquete Commission of the German Bundestag, Vorsorge zum Schutz der Erdatmosphäre, *Schutz der Erde,* Vol. 1 (Bonn: Economica Verlag, 1990), p. 39.

116. Ibid. [translated by the authors].

117. See T.M.L. Wigley and S.C.B. Raper, "Implications for Climate and Sea Level of Revised IPCC Emissions Scenarios," *Nature,* May 28, 1992, pp. 293–300.

118. Enquete Commission, op. cit. note 115, p. 42.

119. J. Jäger, "Climate Change: Floating New Evidence in the CO_2 Debate," *Environment,* Vol. 28, No. 7, 1986, p. 38 ff.

120. "Demographic Dynamics and Sustainability," Chapter 5 (preliminary draft), *Agenda 21,* U.N. Conference on Environment and Development, United Nations, 1992.

121. Ehrlich, Ehrlich, and Daly, op. cit. note 13, p. 18.

122. UNFPA, op. cit. note 69, p. 64. See also D.S. Lazarus, "Environmental Refugees: New Strangers at the Door," *Our Planet,* Vol. 2, No. 3, 1990, pp. 12–14.

123. M. Parry, *Climate Change and World Agriculture* (London: Earthscan, 1990); D. Pimentel et al., "Offsetting Potential Global Climate Change on Food Production," College of Agriculture, Cornell University, Ithaca, N.Y., 1990; B. Smith and L. Ludlow, "Implications of a Global Climatic Warming for Agriculture: A Review and Appraisal," *Journal of Environmental Quality,* Vol. 17, 1988, pp. 519–527.

124. P.R. Ehrlich and G.C. Daly, "An Exploratory Model of the Impact of Rapid Climate Change on The World Food Situation," Morrison Institute for Population and Resource Studies, Stanford University, Stanford, Calif., 1990.

125. W.R. Cline, *Global Warming: The Economic Stakes* (Washington, D.C: Institute for International Economics, 1992), Chapter 3.

126. Enquete Commission, op. cit. note 115, p. 43.

127. Commercial energy here means petroleum, natural gas, and coal, as well as hydroelectric and nuclear energy. Traditional and, for the most part, non-commercialized energy sources such as firewood or dung are not included; they account for 6 percent of world energy consumption—but for 37 percent of energy consumption in Africa, 10 percent in Asia, and 20 percent in South America. World Resources Institute, op. cit. note 114, p. 313.

128. United States, Canada, Japan, Australia, New Zealand, and Western and Eastern Europe (including the former Soviet Union).
129. Enquete Commission, op. cit. note 115, p. 48.
130. World Resources Institute, op. cit. note 114, p. 206.
131. Ibid., p. 346 f.
132. Ibid.
133. UNDP, *Human Development Report 1992* (New York: Oxford University Press, 1992), p. 127.
134. World Resources Institute, op. cit. note 114, p. 348 f.
135. UNFPA, op. cit. note 69, p. 30.
136. *Atmosphere* (Friends of the Earth International), February 1993, p. 7.
137. All data from World Resources Institute, op. cit. note 114, p. 348 f.
138. Intergovernmental Panel on Climate Change, *Climate Change: The IPCC Scientific Assessment* (Cambridge: Cambridge University Press, 1990), quoted in World Resources Institute, op. cit. note 114, p. 208.
139. UNFPA, op. cit. note 69, p. 26.
140. According to the World Resources Institute, the total burden due to CO_2 emissions was 28 billion tons in 1989, of which 77 percent was of industrial origin. The additional burden of 10 billion tons will stem from the assumed growth of the populations of Africa, Asia, and South Amercia by 3 billion between 1990 and 2025, and the assumed doubling of industrial per capita emissions on these continents.
141. B. Gilland, "Population, Economic Growth, and Energy Demand, 1985–2000," *Population and Development Review,* Vol. 14, No. 2, 1988, pp. 233–243.
142. UNFPA, op. cit. note 69, p. 27.
143. Quoted in ibid., p. 28.
144. K.W. Kapp, "Social Costs and Social Benefits—A Contribution to Normative Economics," in E. von Beckerath and H. Giersch (eds.), *Probleme der normativen Ökonomie und der wirtschaftlichen Beratung. Verein für Sozialpolitik* (Berlin: Duncker & Humblot, 1963), pp. 183–210, reprinted in *Hindu Culture, Economic Development and Economic Planning in India* (London: Asia Publishing House, 1963).
145. See also L. Arizpe, R. Constanza, and W. Lutz, "Primary Factors Affecting Population and Natural Resource Use," in International Conference on an Agenda of Science for Environment and Development into the 21st Century, Vienna, November 1991, p. 1–17.
146. D. Meadows, D. Meadows, and J. Randers, *Beyond the Limits* (Post Mills, Vt.: Chelsea Publishing Co., 1992).
147. U.N. Conference on Environment and Development, "Declaration on Environment and Development," Rio de Janeiro, June 13, 1992.
148. K.W. Kapp, *The Social Cost of Private Enterprise* (Cambridge, Mass.: Harvard University Press, 1950), Chapter 8.
149. World Resources Institute, op. cit. note 114, p. 321.
150. Simon, op. cit. note 17, p. 216 ff.
151. A. Chisholm and R. Dumsday (eds.), *Land Degradation: Policies and Problems* (New York: Cambridge University Press, 1987); M.K. Tolba, "Our Biological Heritage Under Siege," *BioScience,* Vol. 39, 1986, p. 725 ff.
152. UNFPA, op. cit. note 109, p. 13.

153. Ehrlich, Ehrlich, and Daly, op. cit. note 13, p. 8; see also A.M. Mannion, *Global Environmental Change* (New York: Longman, 1991), p. 232.
154. D.V.V. Narayana and B. Ram, "Estimation of Soil Erosion in India," *Journal of Irrigation and Drainage Engineering* (New Delhi), Vol. 109, No. 4, 1983.
155. UNFPA, op. cit. note 69, p. 31.
156. Leisinger and Schmitt, op. cit. note 29.
157. UNFPA, op. cit. note 69, p. 31 f. See also R. Repetto, "Soil Loss and Population Pressure on Java," *Ambio,* Vol. 15, No. 1, 1986, pp. 14–18.
158. UNFPA, op. cit. note 69.
159. L.M. Talbot, "Demographic Factors in Resource Depletion and Environmental Degradation in East African Rangeland," *Population and Development Review,* Vol. 12, No. 3, 1986, p. 441 ff.
160. P.M. Mbithi and C. Barnes, *Spontaneous Settlement Problems in Kenya* (Nairobi: East African Literature Bureau, 1975). For a concrete case study, see H.F. Lamprey and H. Yussuf, "Pastoralism and Desert Encroachment in Northern Kenya," *Ambio,* Vol. 10, No. 2–3, 1982, pp. 131–134; see also Leisinger and Schmitt, op. cit. note 29, particularly p. 57 ff.
161. G.O. Barney (ed.), *The Global 2000 Report to the President* (New York: Pergamon, 1980).
162. See in this context Enquete Commission, Vorsorge zum Schutz der Erdatmosphäre, *Schutz der Tropenwälder. Eine internationale Schwerpunktaufgabe,* Vol. 2 (Bonn: Economica Verlag, 1990), particularly Section G, pp. 239–270; see also A.S. Mather, "Global Trends in Forest Resoruces," *Geography,* Vol 72, No. 1, 1987, pp. 1–15, and Mannion, op. cit. note 153, pp. 237 ff, 239, 241 ff.
163. UNFPA, op. cit. note 69, p. 44; the remaining 21 percent is explained by a higher level of food consumption per person (of meat, for example).
164. Ibid., pp. 86–90.
165. H. Hurni, "Towards Sustainable Development in Ethiopia," Geographic Institute of the University of Bern, 1990, p. 1; H. Hurni, "Ecological Issues in the Creation of Famines in Ethiopia," Addis Ababa, 1988.
166. UNFPA, op. cit. note 69, p. 96.
167. Enquete Commission, op. cit. note 162, p. 531.
168. World Resources Institute, op. cit. note 114, p. 111.
169. Ibid., p. 285.
170. Enquete Commission, op. cit. note 162, p. 529.
171. Ibid., p. 530.
172. A. Crump, *Dictionary of Environment and Development* (London: Earthscan, 1991), p. 229.
173. L.R. Brown and J.E. Young, "Feeding the World in the Nineties," in L.R. Brown et al., *State of the World 1990* (New York: W.W. Norton & Co., 1990), p. 61.
174. Enquete Commission, Vorsorge zum Schutz der Erdatmosphäre, *Schutz der Erdatmosphäre* (Bonn: Economica Verlag, 1990), p. 536.
175. Crump, op. cit. note 172, p. 229.
176. Ibid., p. 174.
177. S. Postel and J.C. Ryan, "Reforming Forestry," in L.R. Brown et al., *State of the World 1991* (New York: W.W. Norton & Co., 1991), p. 80 f.

178. U.N. Environment Programme, *The State of the Environment (1972–1992): Saving Our Planet; Challenges and Hopes* (Nairobi: 1992), pp. 49–50.

179. Mannion, op. cit. note 153, p. 153 ff.

180. In this connection, see also D.A. Dunnette and R.J. O'Brien, "The Science of Global Change: The Impact of Human Activities on the Environment," ACS Symposium Series 483, American Chemical Society, Washington, D.C., 1992, especially Chapter 23, "Biogeochemistry of Deforestation and Biomass Burning," p. 426 ff.

181. P.H. Raven, "Disappearing Species: A Global Tragedy," *The Futurist*, Vol. 19, No. 5, 1985, pp. 8–14. For an introduction to this complicated problem, see P.R. Ehrlich, "The Loss of Biodiversity: Causes and Consequences," in E.O. Wilson (ed.), *Biodiversity* (Washington, D.C.: National Academy Press, 1988), p. 21 ff., and "Economics of Biodiversity Loss," *Ambio,* May 1992 (special edition).

182. Enquete Commission, op. cit. note 162, p. 495 ff.

183. The dying out of species has always been part and parcel of evolution, but the speed and extent of this process have increased dramatically as a result of the destruction of forests, growing pollution, and other changes in the habitats of threatened species. It is estimated that in olden times one species was lost every 100 years but that by the beginning of the twentieth century the rate had increased to one species per year and that today we lose up to 10 species a day.

184. World Resources Institute, op. cit. note 114, p. 127.

185. P.R. Ehrlich and A. Ehrlich, "The Value of Biodiversity," *Ambio,* Vol. 21, No. 3, 1992, pp. 219–226.

186. C. Perrings, C. Folke, and K.G. Müller, "The Ecology and Economics of Biodiversity Loss: The Research Agenda," *Ambio,* Vol. 21, No. 3, 1992, p. 205.

187. Enquete Commission, op. cit. note 162, p. 495.

188. P.R. Ehrlich and A.H. Ehrlich, *Bevölkerungswachstum und Umweltkrise* [Population Growth and Environmental Crisis] (Frankfurt a. M.: 1972), p. 84.

189. International Conference on Water and the Environment, "The Dublin Statement and the Report of the Conference," Dublin/Geneva, 1992, p. 3.

190. According to the Report of the Geographic Institute of the University of Bern to the Directorate for Developmental Cooperation and Humanitarian Assistance: Environmental Problems and Developmental Cooperation, Bern, 1987, p. 6.

191. M. Falkenmark, "Global Water Issues Confronting Humanity," *Journal of Peace Research,* Vol. 27, 1990, p. 177 ff.

192. M. Falkenmark, "Rapid Population Growth and Water Scarcity: The Predicament of Tomorrow's Africa," in K. Davis and M.S. Bernstam, *Resources, Environment and Population: Present Knowledge, Future Options, Population and Development Review,* Vol. 16 (Supplement), 1990, pp. 81–94.

193. Leisinger and Schmitt, op. cit. note 29, p. 43 ff.

194. On the benefits and risks of the Green Revolution, see Hazell and Ramaswamy, op. cit. note 70.

195. Sandra Postel, "Saving Water for Agriculture," in Brown et al., op. cit. note 173, p. 40.

196. UNFPA, op. cit. note 69, p. 37.

197. W.R. Gasser, "Survey of Irrigation in Eight Asian Nations," Foreign Agricultural Economic Report No. 165, U.S. Department of Agriculture, Washington, D.C., 1981.

198. M. Falkenmark, "Water-Related Constraints to African Development in the Next Few

Decades," in *Water for the Future: Hydrology in Perspective* (IAHS), cited in UN-FPA, op. cit. note 69, p. 40, footnote 99.

199. Cited in Dossier by Reiner Luyken, *Die Zeit,* December 20, 1991, p. 13 ff.
200. UNDP, op. cit. note 38, Tables 2 and 21.
201. M. Falkenmark and R.A. Suprapto, "Population-Landscape Interactions in Development: A Water Perspective to Environmental Sustainability," *Ambio,* Vol. 21, No. 1, 1992, p. 31 ff.
202. W.S. Thompson, "Population," *American Journal of Sociology,* Vol. 34, No. 6, 1929, pp. 959–975.
203. B. Boubakar, "Uneven Development in Mauritania," in Bennett, op. cit. note 73, p. 85 ff.
204. Nhial Bol Aken, "Civil War in Sudan," in Bennett, op. cit. note 73, p. 100 ff.
205. See also M. Falkenmark, "Fresh Water: Time for a Modified Approach," *Ambio,* Vol. 15, No. 4, 1986, pp. 192–200.
206. Bennett, op. cit. note 73.
207. "Development Wars in Latin America 1945–1989," *International Journal on World Peace,* Vol. VII, No. 2, 1990, pp. 43–58; see also M.A. Ferdowski, "Militant Conflicts in the Third World: Dimensions—Causes—Perspectives," *Aus Politik und Zeitgeschehen,* Vol. 37, Sec. 8, 1987, pp. 27–37, and V. Matthies, *The Third World as a Theater of War* (Munich: Beck'sche Reihe, 1988).
208. N. Choucri, *Population and Conflict: New Dimensions of Population Dynamics,* Policy Development Studies No. 8 (New York: UNFPA, 1983); N. Choucri, "Demographics and Conflict," *Bulletin of the Atomic Scientists,* Vol. 42, 1986, p. 24 ff.
209. N. Myers, "Population, Environment, and Conflict," *Environmental Conservation,* Vol. 14, No. 1, 1987, pp. 15–22.
210. P. Streeten, *First Things First: Meeting Basic Needs in Developing Countries* (New York: Oxford University Press, 1981).
211. UNFPA, op. cit. note 69, p. 105.

Part V

1. Some demographers see a five-phase transition; see, for example, C.P. Blacker, "Stages in Population Growth," *The Eugenics Review,* October 1947, pp. 88–101.
2. When we discuss here "birth and death rates," we mean the figures that demographers call (correctly, but in terms not always clear to the layperson) "crude birth and death rates"—the number of live births and deaths per 1,000 population per year, with no consideration for the age patterns of the society.
3. A.J. Coale, "The Demographic Transition," in IUSSP, *International Population Conference,* Vol. 1 (Liège: 1973), p. 64.
4. E. Fromm, *The Anatomy of Human Destructiveness* (New York: Holt, Rinehart and Winston, 1973).
5. R.A. Easterlin, "Modernization and Fertility: A Critical Essay," in R.A. Bulatao and R.D. Lee (eds.), *Determinants of Fertility in Developing Countries, Vol. 2. Fertility Regulation and Institutional Influences* (New York: Academic Press, 1983), p. 562 ff.
6. Although we talk about a "theory," as far as the developing world is concerned it is a hypothesis whose validity—for example, for sub-Saharan Africa—still needs to be demonstrated. For discussion of the classic theory, see W.S. Thompson, "Population," *American Journal of Sociology,* Vol. 34, No. 6, 1929, p. 959 ff.; F.W. Notestein, "Some

Implications of Population Change for Post-War Europe," *Proceedings of the Amercian Philosophical Society,* August 1943; F.W. Notestein, "Population—The Long View," in T.W. Schultz (ed.), *Food for the World,* Norman Wait Harris Memorial Fund Lectures (Chicago: 1944), pp. 36–57; and F.W. Notestein, "Economic Problems of Population Change," *Proceedings of the Eighth International Conference of Agricultural Economists* (Oxford: Oxford University Press, 1953). Coale points out that there were probably two demographic transitions in Europe: one "Malthusian" transition, preceded by an older age for marriage, a change in sexual ethics, and a larger number of unmarried persons; and a "neo-Malthusian" one, which, as a result of modernization, brought about a smaller number of children per marriage; Coale, op. cit. note 3, pp. 57 and 70.

7. Eight years after publishing on this subject, Notestein himself first risked a general interpretation of the theory of demographic transition; Notestein, "Economic Problems," op. cit. note 6, p. 15 ff.

8. Thompson, op. cit. note 6, p. 960 ff.

9. I.O. Orubuloye, "The Implications of the Demographic Transition Theory for Fertility Change in Nigeria," *International Journal of Sociology of the Family,* Autumn 1991, pp. 161–174.

10. Notestein, "The Long View," op. cit. note 6.

11. Coale, op. cit. note 3, p. 60 ff.; P. Demeny, "Early Fertility Decline in Austria-Hungary: A Lesson in Demographic Transition," *Daedalus,* Vol. 97, 1968, pp. 502–522.

12. M.S.L. Cook and R. Repetto, "The Relevance of the Developing Countries to Demographic Transition Theory: Further Lessons from the Hungarian Experience," *Population Studies,* March 1982, pp. 105–128.

13. P.D. Nolan, "World System Status: Techno-Economic Heritage and Fertility," *Sociological Focus,* Vol. 1, No. 1, 1988, pp. 9–33.

14. A.J. Coale and S. Cotts Watkins (eds.), *The Decline of Fertility in Europe* (Princeton, N.J.: Princeton University Press, 1985); Coale, op. cit. note 3, p. 56 ff.

15. The World Bank estimates that the removal of protectionist measures by industrial countries would alone bring an additional $55 billion in export revenues to developing countries, as much as they now receive in development assistance; World Bank, *World Development Report 1991* (New York: Oxford University Press, 1991), p. 11.

16. There are exceptions to this rule: for example, the Hutterites in Europe and North America, who averaged 11 children per family, and the citizens of seventeenth-century Geneva, who averaged more than 9 children; L. Henry, "Some Data on Natural Fertility," *Eugenics Quarterly,* Vol. 8, No. 2, 1961, p. 84.

17. World Bank, *World Development Report 1984* (New York: Oxford University Press, 1984), p. 58.

18. These figures, from Population Reference Bureau, "World Population Data Sheet 1991," Washington, D.C., 1991, do not take account of potential increases in the death rate from catastrophes such as an endemic spread of AIDS.

19. World Bank, op. cit. note 17, p. 58.

20. A depressing marginal note is the fact that many women from the "Third World" are now enticed to Western Europe for purposes of sexual exploitation.

21. A.R. Zolberg, "The Next Waves: Migration Theory for a Changing World," *International Migration Review,* Fall 1989, pp. 404–430.

22. According to the U.N. High Commissioner for Refugees, about 70 percent of all

refugees were living in developing countries in October 1993; private communication, October 1993.

23. For example, young married couples had to set up their own household and, as a consequence, had to postpone their marriage until they had saved the necessary money. In Ireland, poverty led to late marriages or even none. Marriage was not "legitimated" until the means were at hand to support the family.

24. Demeny, op. cit. note 11, p. 516 ff.

25. J. Cleland and J. Hobcraft (eds.), *Reproductive Changes in Developing Countries: Insights from the World Fertility Survey* (Oxford: Oxford University Press, 1985), p. 69.

26. P. McDonald, "Social Organization and Nuptiality in Developing Societies," in Cleland and Hobcraft, op. cit. note 25, p. 90 ff.

27. See, for example, Demeny, op. cit. note 11, p. 512 ff.

28. These data stem from a very informative overview on the connections between population and development by W.B. Arthur and G. McNicoll, "An Analytical Survey of Population and Development in Bangladesh," *Population and Development Review,* Vol. 4, No. 1, 1978, pp. 23–80.

29. K. Awasabo-Asare, "Interpretations of Demographic Concepts: The Case of Ghana," *Population and Development Review,* Vol. 14, No. 4, 1988, pp. 675–687.

30. World Bank, op. cit. note 17, p. 68.

31. G. Cornia, R. Jolly, and F. Stewart, *Adjustment With a Human Face, Vol. 1* (Oxford: Clarendon Press for UNICEF, 1987). The opposite viewpoint is taken in a study commissioned by the U.S. Government: it found no significant differences between countries subjected to a process of structural adjustment and those that were not; E. Berg and G. Hunter, *Costs of Social Adjustment: The Case of Latin America and the Caribbean* (Bethesda, Md.: DAI, for Agency for International Development, 1992).

32. Notestein, "The Long View," op. cit. note 6, p. 40.

33. Demeny, op. cit. note 11, p. 512.

34. Studies on knowledge, attitudes, and practice (KAP) measure and interpret discrepancies that occur between available knowledge and actual behavior. See, for example, W.P. Mauldin, "Fertility Studies: Knowledge, Attitude and Practice," *Studies in Family Planning,* June 1965; B. Berelson, "KAP Studies on Fertility," in B. Berelson et al. (eds.), *Family Planning and Population Programs* (Chicago: University of Chicago Press, 1966).

35. This should be understood to mean meeting a family's minimum requirements for food, shelter, and clothing and, beyond that, providing vital services such as healthy drinking water, sanitary arrangements, and transportation as well as health and educational facilities.

36. This could not be foreseen by the creators of the theory of demographic transition, so they underestimated the speed with which the mortality rate would drop.

37. Demeny, op. cit. note 11, p. 502.

38. On the various theoretical approaches, see G.M. Farooq and G.B. Simmons, *Fertility in Developing Countries: An Economic Perspective on Research and Policy Issues* (Geneva: MacMillan for ILO, 1985), especially pp. 30–54.

39. J. Knodel and E. van der Walle, "Lessons from the Past: Policy Implications of Historical Fertility Studies," *Population and Development Review,* Vol. 5, 1979, pp. 217–245.

40. C. Hirschmann and P.H. Guest, "The Emerging Demographic Transition of Southeast Asia," *Population and Development Review,* Vol. 16, No. 1, 1990, pp. 121–152.

41. See, for example, S. Enke, "The Economic Aspects of Slowing Population Growth," *The Economic Journal,* March 1966, p. 54.

42. J.L. Simon, "The Effects of Income on Fertility," Carolina Population Center, Chapel Hill, N.C., 1974.

43. J.W. Knight and J.C. Callahan, *Preventing Birth: Contemporary Methods and Related Moral Controversies—Ethics in a Changing World,* Vol. 3 (Salt Lake City: University of Utah Press, 1989), Chapter I.

44. Yet they continue to be important requirements. See K.S. Srikantan, *The Family Planning Program in the Socioeconomic Context* (New York: The Population Council, 1977).

45. See also Y.W. Bradshaw and E.E. Fraser, "City Size, Economic Development, and Quality of Life in China: New Empirical Evidence," *American Sociological Review,* December 1989, pp. 986–1003; "City Size, Birthrates, and Development in China: Evidence of Modernization?" *Journal of Urban Affairs,* Vol. 12, No. 4, 1990, pp. 401–424.

46. But there is no denying that in various cultural and religious circumstances, questions about the number of desired children are met with incomprehension or even rejection. See J.C. Caldwell and P. Caldwell, "Cultural Forces Tending to Sustain High Fertility in Tropical Africa," PHN Technical Note 85–16, World Bank, Washington, D.C., October 1985.

47. Demeny, op. cit. note 11, p. 520.

48. J.C. Caldwell, "Towards a Restatement of Demographic Transition Theory," *Population and Development Review,* Vol. 2, No. 3–4, 1976, pp. 321–366; J.C. Caldwell, "A Theory of Fertility: From High Plateau to Destabilization," *Population and Development Review,* Vol. 4, No. 4, 1978, pp. 553–577.

49. Notestein, "The Long View," op. cit. note 6, p. 37.

50. T. Bengtsson "Lessons from the Past: The Demographic Transition Revised," *Ambio,* Vol. 21, No. 1, 1992, p. 24 ff.; N. Keyfitz, "Completing the Worldwide Demographic Transition: The Relevance of Past Experience," *Ambio,* Vol. 21, No. 1, 1992, pp. 26–30.

51. Cleland and Hobcraft, op. cit. note 25, p. 233.

52. Notestein, "The Long View," op. cit. note 6, p. 52.

Part VI

1. See D. Callahan, "Ethics and Population Limitation," in M.D. Bayles (ed.), *Ethics and Population* (Cambridge, Mass.: Schenkman Publishing Company, 1976), pp. 19–40.

2. J.G. Patterson and N.R. Shresta, "Population Growth and Development in the Third World: The Neocolonial Context," *Studies in Comparative International Development,* Vol. 23, No. 2, 1988, pp. 3–32.

3. A. Schweitzer, *Das Christentum und die Weltreligionen* [Christianity and the World Religions] (Munich: 1978), p. 86 ff [translation by the authors].

4. The International Human Rights Conference in Teheran in 1968 proclaimed the right of all people "to decide, freely, responsibly and in an informed way on the number of their children and the amount of time between births." UN document St/Hr/1, 1973,

p. 18. The World Population Conferences in Bucharest (1974) and Mexico City (1984) confirmed this right.

5. United Nations, *The International Bill of Human Rights* (New York: 1993).

6. Callahan, op. cit. note 1, p. 28.

7. K. Hardee-Cleaveland and J. Banister, "Fertility Policy and Implementation in China, 1986–1988," *Population and Development Review,* Vol. 14, No. 2, 1988, especially p. 255 ff.

8. H.Y. Tien et al., "China's Demographic Dilemmas," *Population Bulletin,* June 1992, p. 39.

9. Jan Narveson, for example, believes that moral questions presuppose the existence of human beings and that because those not yet born (or conceived) do not meet this condition, there is no moral reason for concern over their integrity. J. Narveson, "Moral Problems of Population," in Bayles, op. cit. note 1, pp. 59–80.

10. Arguing, for example, that humans do not have a right of disposal over human life because this life, resulting from the creative intervention of God, is holy (see HV II.13) and that all human beings must therefore conduct themselves in such a way as not to endanger present or future life.

11. See, in this context, R. Lee and T. Miller, "Population Policy and Externalities to Childbearing," *Annals of the American Academy of Political and Social Science,* July 1990, pp. 17–32.

12. G. Hardin, "The Tragedy of the Commons," in Bayles, op. cit. note 1, pp. 7–8.

13. Ibid., p. 8.

14. Ibid., p. 12.

15. This term has been used by Daniel Callahan.

16. Callahan, op. cit. note 1, p. 35.

17. Y. Yu, "China's One-Child Policy: The Unacknowledged Negatives for Women," American Sociological Association, 1992.

18. M.D. Bayles, "Limits to a Right to Procreate," in Bayles, op. cit. note 1, pp. 41–55.

19. Callahan, op. cit. note 1, p. 35.

20. Ibid., pp. 35–36.

21. K.M. Leisinger, "Health Policy for Least Developed Countries," available from Ciba-Geigy Foundation for Cooperation with Developing Countries, Basel, Switzerland; see also B. Winikoff, "The Effects of Birth Spacing on Child and Maternal Health," *Studies in Family Planning,* Vol. 14, 1983, pp. 231–245.

22. A. Ong Tsui, "The Rise of Modern Contraception," in J. Cleland and J. Hobcraft (eds.), *Reproductive Changes in Developing Countries* (Oxford: Oxford University Press, 1985), p. 119; see also F.T. Sai and J. Nassim, "The Role of International Agencies, Governments, and the Private Sector in the Diffusion of Modern Contraception," *Technology in Society,* Vol. 3–4, No. 9, 1987, pp. 497–520.

23. K. Trent, "Teenage Childbearing: Structural Determinants in Developing Countries," *Journal of Biosocial Science,* Vol. 22, No. 3, pp. 281–292; V.K. Pillai, "Teenage Fertility in Developing Countries," *Studies in Comparative International Development,* Vol. 23, No. 4, 1988, pp. 3–14.

24. Social marketing is a strategy for changing behavior in society. It combines the best elements of traditional and modern communications and marketing techniques in order to gain greater acceptance of a social idea or form of social behavior. See H. Kotler and E.L. Roberto, *Social Marketing: Strategies for Changing Public Behavior* (New York:

The Free Press, 1989); J.T. Bertrand, J. Stover, and R. Porter, "Methodologies for Evaluating the Impact of Contraceptive Social Marketing Programs," *Evaluation Review,* Vol. 13, No. 4, 1989, pp. 323–345.

25. S.M. Wishak and J.T. Bertrand, "Field Supervision for Quality Control of Local Family Planning Workers in Developing Countries," *International Quarterly of Community Health Education,* Vol. 11, No. 2, 1991, pp. 111–122; Population, Health and Nutrition Division, "Effective Family Planning Programs," World Bank, Washington, D.C., November 6, 1991 (prepublication draft).

26. U.N. Population Fund (UNFPA), *The State of World Population 1991* (New York: 1991).

27. J.A. Ross, "Birth Control Methods and Their Effects on Fertility," in R.A. Bulatao and R.D. Lee (eds.), *Determinants of Fertility in Developing Countries, Vol. 2. Fertility Regulation and Institutional Influences* (New York: Academic Press, 1983), p. 55.

28. P.N. Hess, *Population Growth and Socioeconomic Progress in Less Developed Countries: Determinants of Fertility Transition* (New York: Praeger, 1988), p. 6 and Chapter 5.

29. K.G. Foreit, "Private Sector Approaches to Effective Family Planning," Policy Research Working Papers, Population, Health, and Nutrition Division, WPS No. 940, World Bank, Washington, D.C., 1992.

30. Hess, op. cit. note 28, p. 6 and Chapter 5.

31. Ibid.

32. Population, Health, and Nutrition Division, "Effective Family Planning Programs," World Bank, Washington, D.C., 1993, p. 13 ff.

33. UNFPA, *The State of World Population 1988* (New York: 1988), p. 1.

34. W.P. Mauldin and J.A. Ross, "Contraceptive Use and Commodity Costs in Developing Countries 1990–2000," *International Family Planning Perspectives,* Vol. 18, No. 1, 1992, p. 6.

35. Ibid.

36. Ibid.

37. J. Bongaarts, "The KAP Gap and the Unmet Need for Contraception," *Population and Development Review,* Vol. 17, No. 2, 1991, pp. 293–313.

38. Population Crisis Committee, "Access to Affordable Contraception: 1991 Report on World Progress Towards Population Stabilization," Washington, D.C., 1991.

39. Ross, op. cit. note 27, p. 58 ff.

40. J. Kaufman et al., "Family Planning Policy and Practice in China: A Study of Four Rural Counties," *Population and Development Review,* Vol. 15, No. 4, 1989, pp. 707–729.

41. Ross, op. cit. note 27, p. 63.

42. J.W. Knight and J.C. Callahan, *Preventing Birth: Contemporary Methods and Related Moral Controversies. Ethics in a Changing World, Vol. 3* (Salt Lake City: University of Utah Press, 1989), p. 287.

43. H.P. David, "Abortion: Its Prevalence, Correlates and Costs," in Bulatao and Lee, op. cit. note 27, pp. 193–244.

44. Ibid., p. 193.

45. C. Tietze, *Induced Abortion: A World Review 1981* (New York: Population Council, 4th ed., 1981).

46. S.C. Huber, "World Survey of Family Planning Services and Practice," in International Planned Parenthood Federation, *Survey of World Needs in Population* (New York: 1974).

47. S.K. Henshaw, *Induced Abortions: A World Review 1990* (New York: Alan Guttmacher Institute, 1990).

48. Worst, in terms of our own values, not only because of the severe risks to health that are associated with abortion—especially when it is clandestine—but also because abortion ought not to be used as a routine means of family planning.

49. Interested readers might like to refer to Knight and Callahan, op. cit. note 42.

50. This means availability to couples when they actually need them. In the literature (but not here) a distinction is made between administrative, economic, subjective, and objective availability. See J. Foreit, "Community-based and Commercial Contraception Distribution: An Inventory Appraisal," Population Report, Series J, No. 19, Population Information Program, Johns Hopkins University, Baltimore, Md., 1978.

51. In Kerala, it was about 40 percent in 1968–78; K.D. Zachariah, "The Anomaly of the Fertility Decline in India's Kerala State," Population and Development Series No. 25, World Bank, Washington, D.C., 1984, pp. 168–174. See also K.C. Zachariah and S. Patel, "Determinants of Fertility Decline in India," Population and Development Series No. 14, World Bank, Washington, D.C., 1984; R. Rofman, "How Reduced Demand for Children and Access to Family Planning Accelerated the Fertility Decline in Colombia," Policy Research Working Papers, Population, Health and Nutrition Division, WPS No. 924, World Bank, Washington, D.C., 1992.

52. T.W. Merrick, "Recent Fertility Declines in Brazil and Mexico," Population and Development Series No. 17, World Bank, Washington, D.C., 1985, p. 19 ff.

53. C. Westoff, L. Moreno, and N. Goldman, "The Demographic Impact of Changes in Contraceptive Practice in Third World Populations," *Population and Development Review,* Vol. 15, No. 1, 1989, p. 93.

54. J. Bongaarts, "The Measurement of Wanted Fertility," *Population and Development Review,* Vol. 16, No. 3, 1990, pp. 487–506.

55. Operations Evaluation Department, "Population and the World Bank: A Review of Activities and Impacts From Eight Case Studies," World Bank, Washington, D.C., October 22, 1991.

56. UNFPA, op. cit. note 26, p. 6 f.

57. Owing to the special circumstances of population policy in China, that country is not comparable to others; experience there is of only limited significance for other countries.

58. UNFPA, op. cit. note 26, p. 11; see also A. Rosenfield et al., "Thailand's Family Planning Program: An Asian Success Story," *International Family Planning Perspectives,* June 1982, pp. 43–51.

59. N. Birdsall et al. (eds.), "The Effects of Family Planning Programs on Fertility in the Developing World," World Bank Staff Working Papers No. 67, Washington, D.C., 1985.

60. W.B. Arthur and G. McNicoll, "An Analytical Survey of Population and Development in Bangladesh," *Population and Development Review,* Vol. 4, No. 1, 1978, p. 64.

61. Sai and Nassim, op. cit. note 22.

62. Hess, op. cit. note 28, p. 76 ff.

63. See World Bank, *Governance and Development* (Washington, D.C.: 1992).

64. United Nations, *The World's Women: Trends and Statistics 1970–1990* (New York: 1991).
65. J.C. Caldwell, "A Theory of Fertility: From High Plateau to Destabilization," *Population and Development Review,* Vol. 4, No. 4, 1978, p. 556.
66. Ibid. See also J.C. Caldwell, "Cultural and Social Factors Influencing Mortality Levels in Developing Countries," *Annals of the American Academy of Political and Social Science,* July 1990, pp. 44–59.
67. C.O.N. Moser, "Gender Planning in the Third World: Meeting Practical and Strategic Gender Needs," *World Development,* Vol. 17, No. 11, 1989, pp. 1799–1925.
68. World Bank, *The Population, Agriculture and Environment Nexus in Sub-Saharan Africa* (Washington, D.C., December 1991), p. 6.
69. W. Maathai, "The Green Belt Movement: Sharing the Approach and the Experience," Environmental Liaison Center International, Nairobi, 1988.
70. M.T. Cain, S.R. Khanam, and S. Nahar, "Class, Patriarchy, and Women's Work in Bangladesh," *Population and Development Review,* Vol. 5, No. 3, pp. 405–438; see also M.T. Cain, "Risk and Insurance: Perspectives on Fertility and Agrarian Change in India and Bangladesh," *Population and Development Review,* Vol. 7, No. 3, 1981, pp. 435–474.
71. Cain, Khanam, and Nahar, op. cit. note 70, pp. 417 and 432.
72. See, for example, M. Das Gupta, "Selective Discrimination Against Female Children in India," *Population and Development Review,* Vol. 13, No. 1, 1987, pp. 77–101; P.K. Muhuri and S.H. Preston, "Effects of Family Composition on Mortality Differentials by Sex Among Children in Matlab, Bangladesh," *Population and Development Review,* Vol. 17, No. 3, 1991, pp. 415–434; A. Haupt, "The Shadow of Female Infanticide," *Intercom,* Vol. 11, No. 1/2, 1983, pp. 13–14; T.H. Hull, "Recent Trends in Sex Ratios at Birth in China," *Population and Development Review,* Vol. 16, No. 1, 1990, pp. 63–83.
73. S. Johansson and O. Nygren, "The Missing Girls of China: A New Demographic Account," *Population and Development Review,* Vol. 17, No. 1, 1991, pp. 35–51.
74. Knight and Callahan, op. cit. note 42, p. 79 ff.
75. E. Boserup, "Economic and Demographic Interrelationships in Sub-Saharan Africa," *Population and Development Review,* Vol. 11, No. 3, 1985, pp. 383–397.
76. H. Leibenstein, "Beyond Economic Man: Economics, Politics, and the Population Problem," *Population and Development Review,* Vol. 3, No. 3, 1977, pp. 183–199.
77. K. Awusabo-Asare, "Interpretations of Demographic Concepts: The Case of Ghana," *Population and Development Review,* Vol. 14, No. 4, pp. 675–687.
78. E.R. Faphohunda and M.P. Todaro, "Family Structure, Implicit Contracts, and the Demand for Children in Southern Nigeria," *Population and Development Review,* Vol. 14, No. 4, 1988, pp. 571–594.
79. M. Cain, "The Household Life Cycle and Economic Mobility in Rural Bangladesh," *Population and Development Review,* Vol. 4, No. 3, 1978, pp. 421–455; Cain, op. cit. note 70; Cain, Khanam, and Nahar, op. cit. note 70; M. Cain, "Women's Status and Fertility in Developing Countries: Preference and Economic Security," World Bank Population and Development Series No. 7, Washington, D.C., 1984.
80. For example, the Encyclicals "Mater et Magistra" in 1961, "Populorum Progressio" in 1967, and "Humanae Vitae" in 1969, as well as the pastoral constitution of the

Second Vatican Council on the church in today's world, "Gaudium et Spes," in 1965.

81. This would not be appropriate for social scientists. But, as Arthur Utz points out, modern society cannot expect a moral philosopher to approve only those measures that are convenient for the morally degraded. They are the people, in his view, who separate sexuality from marriage and the family. A.F. Utz, "Das Wachstum der Weltbevölkerung und die natürlichen Resourcen," *Institut für Gesellschaftswissenschaften, Walerberg (Hrsg.): Die neue Ordnung.* 46 Jg. Heft 1, 1992, p. 51 ff.

82. The original text of "Humanae Vitae" expresses concern along these lines in connection with the availability of artificial means of birth control: "Another effect that gives cause for alarm is that a man who grows accustomed to the use of contraceptive methods may forget the reverence due to a woman, and, disregarding her physical and emotional equilibrium, reduce her to being a mere instrument for the satisfaction of his own desires, no longer considering her as his partner whom he should surround with care and affection." HV II.17.

83. J.C. Caldwell, "Mass Education as a Determinant of the Timing of Fertility," *Population and Development Review,* Vol. 6, No. 2, 1980; U.N. Population Division, *Relationships Between Fertility and Education* (New York: 1983); S.H. Cochrane, *Fertility and Education: What Do We Really Know?* (Baltimore, Md.: Johns Hopkins University Press, 1979).

84. S. Singh and J. Casterline, "The Socio-Economic Determinants of Fertility," in Cleland and Hobcraft, op. cit. note 22, p. 204 ff.

85. S.H. Cochrane, "Effects of Education and Urbanization on Fertility, " in Bulatao and Lee, op. cit. note 27, p. 613.

86. R.A. LeVine et al., "Women's Schooling and Child Care in the Demographic Transition: A Mexican Case Study," *Population and Development Review,* Vol. 17, No. 3, 1991, pp. 459–496; D. Kabagarama and C.L. Mulford, "The Relationship Between Women's Education, Nutrition, Fertility, GNP Per Capita and Infant Mortality: Implications for the Role of Women in Development," *International Journal of Contemporary Sociology,* Vol. 26, No. 3–4, pp. 189–200.

87. Hess, op. cit. note 28, p. 64 ff. and p. 133.

88. A.I. Hermalin, "Fertility Regulation and Its Costs: A Critical Essay," in Bulatao and Lee, op. cit. note 27, p. 16 ff.; G.M. Farooq, "Household Fertility Decision-Making in Nigeria," in G.M. Farooq and G.B. Simmons, *Fertility in Developing Countries: An Economic Perspective on Research and Policy Issues* (Geneva: MacMillan for ILO, 1985), p. 341 ff.; M.T.R. Sarma, "Demand for Children in Rural India," in ibid., p. 351–364.

89. Cochrane, op. cit. note 85; J. Cleland and G. Rodriguez, "The Effect of Parental Education on Marital Fertility in Developing Countries," *Population Studies,* Vol. 42, No. 3, pp. 419–442.

90. Singh and Casterline, op. cit. note 84, p. 199 ff.

91. United Nations, op. cit. note 64.

92. Ibid., p. 31.

93. Ibid., p. 32.

94. C.B. Lloyd, "Understanding the Relationship Between Women's Work and Fertility," in Population Council, *The Contribution of the World Fertility Surveys,* Research Division Working Papers No. 9 (New York: 1990).

95. M. Osawa, "Working Mothers: Changing Patterns of Employment and Fertility in Japan," *Economic Development and Cultural Change,* July 1988, pp. 623–650.

96. UNFPA, *The State of World Population 1992* (New York: 1992), p. 10 ff.

97. E. Kennedy and L. Haddad, "Food Security and Nutrition 1971–1991: Lessons Learned and Future Priorities," *Food Policy,* Vol. 17, No. 1, 1992, pp. 2–6; M. Garcia, "Impact of Female Sources of Income on Food Demand Among Rural Households in the Philippines," *Quarterly Journal of International Agriculture,* Vol. 30, No. 2, 1991, pp. 109–124; E. Kennedy and P. Peters, "Household Food Security and Child Nutrition: The Interaction of Income and Gender of Household Head," *World Development.* Vol. 20, No. 8, 1992, pp. 1077–1085.

98. J.C. Caldwell, "Towards a Restatement of Demographic Transition Theory," *Population and Development Review,* Vol. 2, No. 3/4, 1976, pp. 321–366; Caldwell, op. cit. note 65, pp. 553–577.

99. Caldwell, op. cit. note 98, p. 337.

100. Caldwell, op. cit. note 65, pp. 553–577.

101. Caldwell, op. cit. note 98, p. 340.

102. Ibid., p. 341.

103. M. Cain, "The Economic Activities of Children in a Village in Bangladesh," *Population and Development Review,* Vol. 3, No. 3, pp. 201–227.

104. Caldwell, op. cit. note 98.

105. Caldwell, op. cit. note 98, p. 342 f; Caldwell, op. cit. note 83.

106. Caldwell, op. cit. note 83.

107. P.W. Turke, "Evolution and the Demand for Children," *Population and Development Review,* Vol. 15, No. 1, pp. 61–90.

108. P.W. Turke, "Theory and Evidence on Wealth Flows and Old-Age Security: A Reply to Fricke," *Population and Development Review,* Vol. 17, No. 4, pp. 687–702.

109. Leibenstein, op. cit. note 76, p. 196.

110. M. Cain, "Perspectives on Family and Fertility in Developing Countries," *Population Studies,* July 1982, pp. 159–175; Boserup, op. cit. note 75.

111. V.N. Thadani, "The Logic of Sentiment: The Family and Social Change," *Population and Development Review,* Vol. 4, No. 3, pp. 457–499.

112. Cain, Khanam, and Nahar, op. cit. note 70.

113. Caldwell, op. cit. note 65.

114. Ibid., p. 557.

115. G.T. Acsadi and G. Johnson-Acsadi, "Demand for Children and Spacing in Sub-Saharan Africa," PHN Technical Note No. 85–6, World Bank, Washington, D.C., July 1985.

116. Caldwell, op. cit. note 65, p. 568.

117. R.S. McNamara, "A Global Population Policy to Advance Human Development in the 21st Century," Rafael M. Salas Memorial Lecture, New York, December 10, 1991, p. 19.

118. Birdsall and Jamison point out, using China as an example, that in these cases as well economic growth would, at the least, be helpful. N. Birdsall and D.T. Jamison, "Income and Other Factors Influencing Fertility in China," *Population and Development Review,* Vol. 9, No. 4, 1983, pp. 651–675.

119. M. Vasold, "Der Herr hat's gegeben, der Herr hat's genommen. Säuglingssterblichkeit in Deutschland von 1800 bis heute" [The Lord hath Given, The

Lord hath Taken Away: Infant Mortality in Germany from 1800 to the Present], *Die Zeit,* February 28, 1992, p. 46 [translation by the authors].

120. A.T. Flegg, "The Role of Inequality of Income in the Determination of Birth Rates," *Population Studies,* November 1979, pp. 457–477; R. Repetto, *Economic Equality and Fertility in Developing Countries* (Baltimore, Md.: Johns Hopkins University Press, 1979); M.S.L. Cook and R. Repetto, "The Relevance of the Developing Countries to Demographic Transition Theory: Further Lessons from the Hungarian Experience," *Population Studies,* March 1982, pp. 105–128; R. Repetto, *Economic Equality and Fertility in Developing Countries* (Baltimore, Md.: Johns Hopkins University Press, 1979), p. 29 ff.; R. Repetto, "The Interaction of Fertility and the Size Distribution of Income," *Journal of Development Studies,* July 1978, p. 32 ff.; J.E. Hocher, *Rural Development, Income Distribution and Fertility Decline* (New York: 1975); D. Morawetz, "Basic Needs Policies and Population Growth," *World Development,* Vol. 6., No. 11/12, 1978, p. 1253. For an opposing view, see C.R. Weingarden, "Can Income Redistribution Reduce Fertility?" in Farooq and Simmons, op. cit. note 88, p. 462 ff. Weingarden does not exclude the possibility that income redistribution can have the effect of lowering birth rates but he discusses a series of arguments that make the case for a more complex relationship.

121. B. Boulier, "Income Redistribution and Fertility Decline: A Skeptical View," *Population and Development Review,* Vol. 8 (Supplement), 1982, pp. 159–173; S. Menard, "Inequality and Fertility," *Studies in Comparative International Development,* Spring 1985, pp. 83–97.

122. B. Russett et al., "Health and Population Patterns as Indicators of Income Inequality," *Economic Development and Cultural Change,* July 1981, pp. 759–779.

123. M.W. Kusnic and J. DaVanzo, "Who are the Poor in Malaysia? The Sensitivity of Poverty Profiles to Definition of Income," *Population and Development Review,* Vol. 8 (Supplement), 1982, pp. 17–34.

124. H.M. Rajyaguru, "Relative Status of Women and Family Planning," *Indian Journal of Social Work,* July 1981, pp. 141–148.

125. Zachariah, op. cit. note 51; Zachariah and Patel, op. cit. note 51.

126. T. Neil, "Land, Fertility, and the Population Establishment," *Population Studies,* November 1991, pp. 379–397.

127. B. Rogers, "Land Reform: The Solution or the Problem," *Human Rights Quarterly,* Spring 1981, pp. 96–102.

128. African Development Bank, *Economic Report 1984* (Abidjan: 1984).

129. H. de Soto, *The Other Path* (New York: Harper & Row, 1989).

130. U.N. Development Programme (UNDP), *Human Development Report 1991* (New York: Oxford University Press, 1991).

131. Vienna Institute for Questions of Development and Cooperation, *The World Ten Years After the Brandt Report* (Vienna: 1989), p. 65.

132. World Bank, *World Development Report 1990* (New York: Oxford University Press, 1990).

133. UNDP, op. cit. note 130, Table 19.

134. Isopublic, "Entwicklungspolitik" [Development Policy], Zurich, 1989; Deutsche Welthungerhilfe [German Assistance Against World Hunger], "Die Europäer und die Entwicklungszusammenarbeit" [The Europeans and Development Assistance],

Bonn, March 1988; BMZ [Federal German Ministry for Economic Cooperation], "BMZ Informationen" [BMZ Information], No. 5, Bonn, July 1986.

135. U. Lele, "Sustainable Development: A Critical Review," *World Development,* Vol. 19, No. 6, 1991, pp. 607–621.

136. H. Daly, "Sustainable Development: From Concept and Theory to Operational Principles," in K. Davis and M.S. Bernstam, *Resources, Environment and Population: Present Knowledge, Future Options, Population and Development Review* Vol. 16 (Supplement), 1990, pp. 25–43; "Sustainable Development: From Theory to Practice," *Journal of the Society for International Development,* No. 2/3, 1989.

137. In parts of the Sahel, for example, infant and child mortality began to climb again in the last 15 years, as a result of both drought-induced famine and the effects of war; see the mortality statistics in World Bank reports for various years.

138. International Monetary Fund, *World Economic Outlook,* October 1990 and issues from earlier years.

139. G.A. Cornia, R. Jolly, and F. Stewart, *Adjustment With a Human Face, Vol. 1* (Oxford: Clarendon Press for UNICEF, 1987), p. 21 ff.

140. Today, for example, Brazil and Kenya have to export two to three times as many sacks of coffee to buy one Jeep as they did 20 years ago.

141. K.M. Leisinger, *Wege aus der Not* [Avenues of Escape from Peril] (Frankfurt am Main: 1990), especially pp. 103–122.

142. On food subsidies, see also P. Pinstrup-Andersen (ed.), *Consumer-Oriented Food Subsidies: Costs, Benefits, and Policy Options for Developing Countries* (Baltimore, Md.: Johns Hopkins University Press, 1987).

143. World Bank, *World Development Report 1991* (New York: Oxford University Press, 1991), Table 11, p. 266; Cornia, Jolly, and Stewart, op. cit. note 139, p. 29 ff.

144. Cornia, Jolly, and Stewart, op. cit. note 139, pp. 29–34.

145. Ibid.

146. R. McNamara, "Address to the Board of Governors," World Bank, Nairobi, September 24, 1973.

147. International Labour Organization, *Employment, Growth and Basic Needs: A Worldwide Problem* (Geneva: 1976), p. 7 f.

148. P. Streeten, *First Things First: Meeting Basic Human Needs in Developing Countries* (New York: Oxford University Press, 1981).

149. For a precise calculation of the Human Development Index, see UNDP, op. cit. note 130, p. 88 ff.

150. C.E.A. Winslow, "The Cost of Sickness and the Price of Health," World Health Organization, Geneva, 1951, p. 9.

151. World Bank, *World Development Report 1993* (New York: Oxford University Press, 1993), p. 1.

152. Ibid., p. 25.

153. R. Chambers, "Rural Poverty Unperceived: Problems and Remedies," *World Development,* Vol. 9, No. 1, 1981, pp. 1–19.

154. J.P. Vaughan, "Health Personnel Development in Sub-Saharan Africa," Population, Health, and Nutrition Department, Policy Research Working Papers WPS 914, World Bank, Washington, D.C., 1992.

155. This section is based on Leisinger, op. cit. note 21.

156. Department of International Economic and Social Affairs, *Family Building by Fate or Design: A Study of Relationships Between Child Survival and Fertility* (New York: United Nations, 1987).

157. Programme Manager, Maternal and Child Health/Family Planning, WHO, Geneva, private communication, January 21, 1992.

158. This relationship has been proved for many years: United Nations, *The Determinants and Consequences of Population Trends* (New York: 1953); H. Frederikson, "Determinants and Consequences of Mortality and Fertility Trends," *Public Health Reports,* Vol. 81, 1986, p. 755 ff.; S. Friedlander and M. Silver, "A Quantitative Study of the Determinants of Fertility Behavior," *Demography,* Vol. 4, No. 1, 1967, p. 36; D. Heer and D.O. Smith, "Mortality Level, Desired Family Size and Population Increase," *Demography,* Vol. 5, No. 1, 1968, p. 105.

159. C.E. Taylor, J.S. Newman, and N.U. Kelly, "Interactions Between Health and Population," *Studies in Family Planning,* Vol. 7, No. 4, 1976, p. 98.

160. Ibid., p. 97.

161. S.H. Preston, "Health Programs and Population Growth," *Population and Development Review,* Vol. 1, No. 2, 1975, p. 191 ff.

162. C.B. Lloyd and S. Ivanov, *The Effect of Improved Child Survival on Family Planning Practice and Fertility* (New York: United Nations, 1987).

163. Heer and Smith, op. cit. note 178, pp. 107–109.

164. A.I. Hermalin, "Empirical Research in Taiwan on Factors Underlying Differences in Fertility," in A.J. Coale (ed.), *Economic Factors in Population Growth* (London: MacMillan, 1976), p. 248.

165. There is a great deal of empirical material on this; see R.H. Gray, "Birth Intervals, Post-Partum Sexual Abstinence and Child Health," in H.J. Page and R. Lesthaeghe (eds.), *Child Spacing in Tropical Africa: Traditions and Change* (London: 1981), p. 100 ff.

166. UNICEF, *The State of the World's Children 1984* (New York: Oxford University Press, 1984), p. 25.

167. Harvard Institute for International Development, *Nutrition Intervention in Developing Countries* (Cambridge, Mass.: Gunn & Hain, 1981).

168. N.E. Johnson, "Women's Status and Child Health in LDCs," Rural Sociology Society, Michigan State University, East Lansing, Mich., 1989.

169. UNICEF, op. cit. note 166, p. 33.

170. According to WHO, there can be as many as 10 episodes of diarrhea a year; Programme for the Control of Diarrhoeal Disease, "Eighth Programme Report 1990–1991," WHO, Geneva, 1992, p. 85 ff.

171. WHO/UNICEF, "The Management of Diarrhoea and Use of Oral Rehydration Therapy," Geneva, 1983.

172. J.K. Ginneken and A.W. Teunissen, "Morbidity and Mortality from Diarrhoeal Diseases in Children Under Age Five in Sub-Saharan Africa," in E. Van der Walle, G. Pisons, and M. Sala-Diakanda (eds.), *Mortality and Society in Sub-Saharan Africa* (Oxford: Clarendon Press, 1992), pp. 176–203.

173. World Bank, *Bangladesh—Strategies for Enhancing the Role of Women in Economic Development,* a World Bank Country Study (Washington, D.C., 1990), p. 80.

174. J. Dobbing (ed.), *Infant Feeding: Anatomy of a Controversy 1973–1984* (New York: Springer, 1988).

175. UNICEF, op. cit. note 166, p. 257 ff.

176. Vasold, op. cit. note 119, p. 45. The contents of these bottles was generally a mixture of flour paste, sugar water, milk pap, prechewed bread, and the like. Cow's milk offered no guarantee of healthy nourishment before pasteurization was introduced, and the tap water of the time was even less to be trusted.

177. B. Janowitz and D.J. Nicols, "The Determinants of Contraceptive Use, Reproductive Goals and Birth Spacing in Relation to Mortality, Breastfeeding and Previous Contraceptive Behavior," International Fertility Research Program, Research Triangle Park, N. Car., 1980. Regarding the biological basis, see A.S. McNeilly, "Effects of Lactation of Fertility," *British Medical Journal,* Vol. 35, 1979, pp. 151–154; A. Palloni and G. Kephart, "The Effects of Breastfeeding and Contraception on the Natural Rate of Increase: Are There Compensating Effects?" *Population Studies,* Vol. 43, 1989, pp. 455–478; J.P. Habicht et al., "The Contraceptive Role of Breastfeeding," *Population Studies,* Vol. 39, 1985, pp. 213–232.

178. J. Leridon and B. Ferry, "Biological and Traditional Restraints on Fertility," in Cleland and Hobcraft, op. cit. note 22, p. 152 ff.

179. K.I. Kennedy and C.M. Visness, "Contraceptive Efficacy of Lactational Amenorrhoea," *The Lancet,* January 25, 1992, pp. 227–230.

180. Arthur and McNicoll, op. cit. note 60, p. 50.

181. K. Newland, *Infant Mortality and the Health of Societies,* Worldwatch Paper 47 (Washington, D.C.: Worldwatch Institute, 1981), p. 42.

182. J.M. Mondot-Bernard, *Relationships Between Fertility, Child Mortality and Nutrition in Africa* (Paris: Organisation for Economic Co-operation and Development, 1977), pp. 17–31.

183. B. Ferry and D.P. Smith, "Breastfeeding Differentials," in WFS Comparative Studies No. 23, 1983, cited in Leridon and Ferry, op. cit. note 178, p. 149.

184. S.L. Huffman, "Determinants of Breastfeeding in Developing Countries: Overview and Policy Implications," *Studies in Family Planning,* July-August 1984, pp. 170–183; M.-A. Savané, "Yes to Breast Feeding, But . . . How?" *Assignment Children,* Spring 1980, pp. 81–87.

185. M.A. Koenig, V. Fauveau, and B. Wojtyniak, "Mortality Reductions from Health Interventions: The Case of Immunization in Bangladesh," *Population and Development Review,* Vol. 17, No. 1, 1991, pp. 87–104.

186. Stockholm International Peace Research Institute (SIPRI), *SIPRI Yearbook 1991* (Oxford: Oxford University Press, 1991), p. 164 ff.

187. According to the first Brandt report, $450 billion was spent annually for military purposes during the early eighties, almost 2 billion Swiss francs a day; Independent Commission on International Development Issues, *North-South—A Programme for Survival* (London: Pan Books, 1980). For a comparison of military and social expenses, see S. Deger and S. Sen, "Arms and the Child," Staff Working Paper No. 9, UNICEF/SIPRI, New York, 1991.

188. On the importance of evaluating immunization programs, see J.A. Meredith, "Transmission and Control of Childhood Infectious Diseases: Does Demography Matter?" *Population Studies,* Vol. 44, No. 2, p. 195 ff.

189. Appropriate Health Resources & Technologies Action Group, "Health Basics: Immunization" (Supplement), *Dialogue on Diarrhoea,* September 1987.

190. V. Sharma and A. Sharma, "Is the Female Child Being Neglected? Immunization in India," *Health Policy and Planning*, September 1991, pp. 287–290.
191. UNDP, "The Immunization Success Story," *Development Forum*, January/February 1988, p. 1 ff.
192. UNICEF, *The State of the World's Children 1992* (New York: Oxford University Press, 1992), p. 21 ff.
193. Especially in Africa south of the Sahara. See, for example, O. Leroy and M. Garenne, "The Two Most Dangerous Days of Life: A Study of Neonatal Tetanus in Senegal Niakhar," in Van der Walle, Pisons, and Sala-Diakanda, op. cit. note 172, pp. 160–175.
194. UNICEF, op. cit. note 166, p. 59.
195. N.P. Stromquist, "Gender Inequality in Education: Accounting for Women's Subordination," *British Journal of Sociology in Education*, Vol. 2, No. 11, 1990, pp. 137–153.
196. Most people in developing countries live in rural areas or in marginal shantytowns. Their energies have largely been directed toward producing export-oriented plantation or agroindustrial crops, or toward subsistence agriculture and sporadic employment. Often overlooked in evaluations of these people is the role women and children play. Charged with the bulk of the labor and maintenance in these agrarian societies, they are integral funtionaries in the system. Projects designed to upgrade agricultural practices in many developing countries still offer agricultural education to men, as they are viewed as "breadwinners," largely at the expense of the family-oriented agriculturalists, the women. Thus men frequently have access to techniques, chemicals, and tools to enhance crop production, while women tending small family plots seldom have access to either equipment or expertise. J.G. Carew, "A Note on Women and Agricultural Technology in the Third World," *Labour and Society*, September 1981, pp. 279–285.
197. Paulo Freire, *Pedagogy of the Oppressed* (New York: Herder & Herder, 1971).
198. For a specific example in Benin, see Institute Nationale de la Statistique et de l'Analyse Economique, "Enquete Fecondite au Benin," Benin City, 1983.
199. D. Maine, "Family Planning: Its Impact on the Health of Women and Children," Columbia University, New York, 1981; W. Rinehart, A. Kols, and S.H. Moorse, "Healthier Mothers and Children Through Family Planning," *Population Report*, May/June 1984, pp. J-675–J-696.
200. Leridon and Ferry, op. cit. note 178, p. 155 ff.
201. Acsadi and Johnson-Acsadi, op. cit. note 115, p. 87 ff. and Table p. 94.
202. J. Bongaarts, O. Franck, and R. Lesthaeghe, "Fertility Determinants in Sub-Saharan Africa," *Population and Development Review*, Vol. 10, No. 3, 1984, p. 522 ff.
203. R.G. Castadot et al., "The International Postpartum Family Planning Program: Eight Years of Experience," *Report on Population/Family Planning*, November 1975.
204. The World Fertility Survey found that people in developing countries also use traditional methods such as those used in premodern Europe (coitus interruptus, vaginal douches, temporary abstinence, and so on); Leridon and Ferry, op. cit. note 178, pp. 139–164.
205. K.P. Shah, "Food Supplements," in UNICEF, op. cit. note 166, p. 101 ff.
206. Ibid., p. 102.

207. J. Leslie, "Women's Nutrition: The Key to Improving Family Health in Developing Countries?" *Health and Policy Planning,* March 1991, pp. 1–19; Caldwell, op. cit. note 66.

208. World Bank, *The Gambia: Basic Needs in The Gambia* (Washington, D.C.: 1981), p. 85 ff.

209. In the Encyclicals "Humanae Vitae" and "Gaudium et Spes" (GS 87).

210. To clarify the effect on population policy of a possible change in Church teaching on this matter, this includes a small part of the so-called Third World. Only about 2.7 percent of the 3.2 billion inhabitants of Asia and about 14 percent of the 650 million inhabitants of Africa are Catholic. It is only in Latin America, with 450 million inhabitants, that support for the Catholic Church is strong (87 percent). *L'Osservatore Romano,* August 14, 1992.

211. *Humanae Vitae,* II.16.

212. "Another effect that gives cause for alarm is that a man who grows accustomed to the use of contraceptive methods may forget the reverence due to a woman, and, disregarding her physical and emotional equilibrium, reduce her to being a mere instrument for the satisfaction of his own desires, no longer considering her as his partner whom he should surround with care and affection." *Humanae Vitae* II.17.

213. Clandestine or unsafe induced abortion is estimated to result in the deaths of nearly 500,000 women in developing countries annually and 25–50 percent of all maternal deaths in Latin America; R. Dixon-Mueller, "Abortion Policy and Women's Health in Developing Countries," *International Journal of Health Services,* Vol. 10, No. 2, 1990, pp. 297–314. See also J. McCarthy and D. Maine, "A Framework for Analyzing the Determinants of Maternal Mortality," *Studies in Family Planning,* January–February 1992, pp. 23–33; WHO, "Abortion: A Tabulation of Available Data on the Frequency and Mortality of Unsafe Abortion," Geneva, 1990.

214. D. Maine, "Mothers in Peril," *People,* Vol. 12, No. 2, 1985, p. 6 ff.

215. C. Woodroffe, "Medical Abortion and the Availability of RU486—Are Women's Rights Being Ignored in Developing Countries?" *Health Policy and Planning,* March 1992, pp. 77–81.

216. Ibid.

217. These are a few statements by South African men on the condom; A. Nasadi, "Men and Women Sharing the Challenge," in Global Programme on AIDS, World AIDS Day Feature No. 2, WHO, Geneva, 1991, p. 2.

218. United Nations, op. cit. note 64.

219. J. Leslie, "Women's Time: A Factor in the Use of Child Survival Technologies?" *Health Policy and Planning,* March 1989, pp. 1–16; B.G. McSweeney, "Time to Learn, Time for a Better Life: The Women's Education Project in Upper Volta," *Assignment Children,* Spring 1980, pp. 109–126.

220. G. Sen and C. Grown, "Development, Crisis, and Alternative Visions: Third World Women's Perspectives," Development Alternatives with Women for a New Era, Stavanger, Norway, 1985.

Part VII

1. Population data from Population Reference Bureau, *1993 World Population Data Sheet* (Washington, D.C.: 1993).

2. N. Sadik, "World Population Continues to Rise," *The Futurist,* March/April 1991, p. 9.

3. A. King and B. Schneider, *The First Global Revolution: A Report by the Council of the Club of Rome—The World Twenty Years After the "Limits to Growth"* (London: Simon & Schuster, 1991), p. xx.

Bibliography

Abdullah T.A./Zeidenstein S.A.: Village Women of Bangladesh. Prospects for Change. Pergamon Press, New York 1982.

Acsadi G.T.F./Johnson-Acsadi G./Bulatao R.A. (eds.): Population Growth and Reproduction in Sub-Saharan Africa. Technical Analysis of Fertility and Its Consequences. World Bank, Washington, D.C. 1990.

Acsadi G.T.F./Johnson-Acsadi G.: Demand for Children and Child Spacing. In: Acsadi G.T.F/Johnson-Acsadi G./Bulatao R.A. (eds.): Population Growth and Reproduction in Sub-Saharan Africa. Technical Analysis of Fertility and Its Consequences. World Bank, Washington, D.C. 1990, p. 155ff.

African Development Bank: Economic Report 1984. Abidjan 1984.

Agarwala A.N./Singh S.P. (eds.): The Economics of Underdevelopment. Oxford University Press, Oxford 1958.

Alderman H. et al.: Household Food Security in Pakistan with Reference to the Ration Shop System. In: International Food Policy Research Institute: Working Paper on Food Subsidies, No. 4, May 1988.

Ambio: Journal of the Human Environment: Economics of Biodiversity Loss. Special Edition, Vol. XXI, No. 3, May 1992.

Arizpe L./Costanza R./Lutz W.: Primary Factors Affecting Population and Natural Resource Use. In: International Conference on An Agenda of Science for Environment and Development Into the 21st Century. Wien, November 1991, pp. 1–17.

Armstrong J.: Socio-Economic Implications of AIDS in Developing Countries. In: Finance and Development, December 1991, pp. 14–17.

Arntz W.E./Fahrbach E.: El Niño. Klimaexperiment der Natur. Birkhäuser, Basel/Berlin/Boston 1991.

Arrhenius E.: Population, Development and Environmental Disruption. An Issue on Efficient Natural Resource Management. In: Ambio, Vol. 21, No. 1, 1992, pp. 9–13.

Arthur W.B./McNicoll G.: An Analytical Survey of Population and Development in Bangladesh. In: Population and Development Review, Vol. 4, No. 1, 1978, pp. 23–80.

Awusabo-Asare K.: Interpretations of Demographic Concepts: The Case of Ghana. In: Population and Development Review, Vol. 14, No. 4, 1988, pp. 675–687.

Bankowski Z./Barzellatto J./Capron A.M. (eds.): Ethics and Human Values in Family Planning. XXII CIOMS Conference, June 1988. CIOMS, Geneva 1989.

Barney G.O./Council on Environmental Quality (ed.): The Global 2000. Report to the President of the U.S. Pergamon, New York 1980.

Bayles Michael D. (ed.): Ethics and Population. Schenkman Publishing Company Inc., Cambridge, Massachusetts 1976.

Bayles Michael D.: Limits to a Right to Procreate. In: Bayles Michael D. (ed.): Ethics and Population. Schenkman Publishing Company Inc., Cambridge, Massachusetts 1976, pp. 41–55.

Beauchamp T.L./Walters L.(eds.): Contemporary Issues in Bioethics. Third Edition. Wadsworth Publishing Company, Belmont, California 1989.

Beckman L.J.: Couple's Decision-Making Processes Regarding Fertility. In: Taeuber K.E./Bumpass L.L./Sweet J.A. (eds.): Social Demography, Academic Press, New York 1978, pp. 209–231.

Behrendt R.F.: Soziale Strategie für Entwicklungsländer. Frankfurt am Main 1965.

Bengtsson T.: Lessons From the Past: The Demographic Transition Revised. In: Ambio, Vol. 21, No. 1, 1992, pp. 24–25.

Benneh G.: Population Growth and Development in Ghana. Legon, Ghana 1987.

Bennett O. (ed.): Greenwar: Environment and Conflict. The Panos Institute, London 1991.

Berelson B. et al. (eds.): Family Planning and Population Programs. University of Chicago Press, Chicago 1966.

Berger P.L./Luckmann Th.: Die gesellschaftliche Konstruktion der Wirklichkeit. Eine Theorie der Wissenssoziologie. Fischer, Frankfurt am Main 1980.

Bertrand J.T./Stover J./Porter R.: Methodologies for Evaluating the Impact of Contraceptive Social Marketing Programs. In: Evaluation Review, Vol. 13, No. 4, 1989, pp. 323–354.

Bilsborrow R.E.: Population Pressures and Agricultural Development in Developing Countries: A Conceptual Framework and Recent Evidence. In: World Development, Vol. 15, No. 2, 1987, pp. 183–203.

Binswanger H.P./Pingali P.L.: Population Growth and Technological Change in Agriculture. In: Davis T.J. (ed.): Proceedings of the Fifth Agriculture Sector Symposium: Population and Food. World Bank, Washington, D.C. 1985, p. 62ff.

Birdsall N./Boulier B./Mauldin W.P./Lapham R.J./Wheeler D. (eds.): The Effects of Family Planning Programs on Fertility in the Developing World. World Bank Staff Working Papers No. 677, Washington, D.C., 1985.

Birdsall N./Jamison D.T.: Income and Other Factors Influencing Fertility in China. In: Population and Development Review, Vol. 9, No. 4, 1983, pp. 651–675.

Birdsall N.: A Cost of Sibling: Child Schooling in Urban Colombia. In: Simon J.L. (ed.): Research in Population Economics. Vol. 2, Greenwich 1980, p. 117ff.

Birdsall N.: Population and Poverty in the Developing World. World Bank Staff Working Paper No. 404, Washington, D.C. 1980.

Birg H.: Der Konflikt zwischen Space Ethics und Lifeboat Ethics und die Verantwortung der Bevölkerungstheorie für die Humanökologie. In: Deutsche Gesellschaft für die Vereinten Nationen (ed.): Dokumentationen, Informationen, Meinungen—Zur Diskussion gestellt. Nr.40, Bonn, November 1991.

Birg H.: Die demographische Zeitenwende. In: Spektrum der Wissenschaft, Januar 1989, pp. 40–49.

Blacker C.P.: Stages in Population Growth. In: The Eugenics Review, Vol. 39, No. 3, October 1947, pp. 88–101.

Bloch E.: Das Prinzip Hoffnung. Suhrkamp, Frankfurt 1959.

Bloom D.E./Freeman R.B.: Economic Development and the Timing and Components of Population Growth. In: Journal of Policy Modeling, Vol. 10, No. 1, 1988, pp. 57–81.

Bloom D.E./Freeman R.B.: The Effects of Rapid Population Growth on Labor Supply and Employment in Developing Countries. In: Population and Development Review, Vol. 12, No. 3, 1986, p. 381ff.

Blum A./Fargues Ph.: Rapid Estimations of Maternal Mortality in Countries with Defective Data. An Application to Bamako (1974–85) and Other Developing Countries. In: Population Studies, Vol. 44, Cambridge, UK 1990, pp. 155–171.

Blum R.: Marktwirtschaft, soziale. In: Handwörterbuch der Wirtschaftswissenschaft, Bd.5., J.C.B. Mohr, Tübingen 1980, pp. 153–166.

Böckle F./Hemmer H.R./Kötter H.: Armut und Bevölkerungsentwicklung in der Dritten Welt. Wissenschaftliche Arbeitsgruppe für weltkirchliche Aufgaben der Deutschen Bischofskonferenz (ed.), Bonn 1990.

Bongaarts J./Franck O./Lesthaeghe R.: Fertility Determinants in Sub-Saharan Africa. In: Population and Development Review, Vol. 10, No. 3, 1984, p. 522ff.

Bongaarts J./Frank O./Lesthaeghe R.: The Proximate Determinants of Fertility. In: Acsadi G.T.F/Johnson-Acsadi G./Bulatao R.A. (eds.): Population Growth and Reproduction in Sub-Saharan Africa. Technical Analysis of Fertility and Its Consequences. World Bank, Washington, D.C. 1990, p. 133ff.

Bongaarts J.: The KAP-Gap and the Unmet Need for Contraception. In: Population and Development Review, Vol. 17, No. 2, 1991, pp. 293–313.

Bongaarts J.: The Measurement of Wanted Fertility. In: Population and Development Review, Vol. 16, No. 3, 1990, pp. 487–506.

Bos E./Vu M.T./Levin A./Bulatao R.A.: World Population Projections. 1992–1993 Edition. Estimates and Projections with Related Demographic Statistics. Washington D.C. (World Bank) 1993.

Boserup E.: Die ökonomische Rolle der Frau in Afrika, Asien, Lateinamerika. Edition Cordelier, Stuttgart 1982.

Boserup E.: The Conditions of Agricultural Growth. The Economics of Agrarian Change under Population Pressure. Chicago 1965.

Bossel H.: Umweltwissen. Daten, Fakten, Zusammenhänge. Springer, Berlin 1990.

Boubakar B.: Uneven Development in Mauretania. In: Bennett O. (ed.): Greenwar: Environment and Conflict. The Panos Institute, London 1991, p. 85ff.

Bradshaw Y.W./Fraser E.E.: City Size, Birthrates, and Development in China: Evidence of Modernization? In: Journal of Urban Affairs, Vol. 12, No. 4, 1990, pp. 401–424.

Bradshaw Y.W./Fraser E.E.: City Size, Economic Development, and Quality of Life in China: New Empirical Evidence. In: American Sociological Review, Vol. 54, December 1989, pp. 986–1003.

Brown L./Jacobson J.L.: The Future of Urbanization: Facing the Ecological and Economic Constraints. Worldwatch Institute Paper No. 77, Washington, D.C. 1987.

Brown L.R. et al.: State of the World 1990. A Worldwatch Institute Report on Progress Toward a Sustainable Society. Norton, New York 1990.

Brown L.R.: Zur Lage der Welt 88/89. Worldwatch Institute Report, S. Fischer Verlag, Frankfurt am Main 1988.

Brown L.R.: Zur Lage der Welt 91/92. Daten für das Überleben unseres Planeten. Worldwatch Institute Report, S. Fischer Verlag, Frankfurt 1991.

Bulatao R.A./Lee R.D. (eds.): Determinants of Fertility in Developing Countries. Vol. 2, Fertility Regulation and Institutional Influences. Academic Press, New York, London 1983.

Bundesminister für Wirtschaft (ed.): Wirtschaftsordnung, sozio-ökonomische Entwicklung und weltwirtschaftliche Integration in den Entwicklungsländern. Bonn 1982.

Bundesminister für wirtschaftliche Zusammenarbeit: Umweltwirkungen von Entwicklungsprojekten. Bonn, Oktober 1987.

Buvinic M./Lycette M./McGreevey W.P.: Women and Poverty in the Third World. Johns Hopkins University Press, Baltimore 1983.

Cain M.T.: The Economic Activities of Children in a Village in Bangladesh. In: Population and Development Review, Vol. 3, No. 3, 1977, p. 201ff.

Cain M.T.: Women's Status and Fertility in Developing Countries. Preference and Economic Security. World Bank Population and Development Series No. 7, Washington, D.C. 1984.

Caldwell J.C./Caldwell P.: Cultural Forces Tending to Sustain High Fertility in Tropical Africa. PHN Technical Note 85–16. World Bank, Washington, D.C., October 1985.

Caldwell J.C./Caldwell P.: Cultural Forces Tending to Sustain High Fertility. In: Acsadi G.T.F/Johnson-Acsadi G./Bulatao R.A. (eds.): Population Growth and Reproduction in Sub-Saharan Africa. Technical Analysis of Fertility and its Consequences. World Bank, Washington, D.C. 1990.

Caldwell J.C./Caldwell P.: Famine in Africa: A Global Perspective. In: Van der Walle E./Pison G./Sala-Diakanda M. (eds.): Mortality and Society in Sub-Saharan Africa. Clarendon Press, Oxford 1992.

Caldwell J.C./Caldwell P.: High Fertility in Sub-Saharan Africa. In: Scientific American, May 1990, pp. 82–89.

Caldwell J.C.: A Theory of Fertility: From High Plateau to Destabilization. In: Population and Development Review, Vol. 4, No. 4, 1978, pp. 553–577.

Caldwell J.C.: Education as a Factor of Mortality Decline. An Examination of Nigerian Data. In: Population Studies, Vol. 33, No. 3, November 1979, pp. 395–413.

Caldwell J.C.: Mass Education as a Determinant of the Timing of Fertility Decline. In: Population and Development Review, Vol. 6, No. 2, 1980, pp. 225–255.

Caldwell J.C.: Toward a Restatement of Demographic Transition Theory. In: Population and Development Review, Vol. 2, No. 3/4, 1976, pp. 321–366.

Callahan D.: Ethics and Population Limitation. In: Bayles Michael D. (ed.): Ethics and Population. Schenkman Publishing Company Inc., Cambridge, Massachusetts 1976, pp. 19–40.

Callahan S.: The Role of Emotion in Ethical Decisionmaking. In: Hastings Center Report, Vol. 18, No. 1, February/March 1988, pp. 9–15.

Cassen R.H.: Population and Development: A Survey. In: Population and Development Review, Vol. 4, No. 10/11, 1976, pp. 785–830.

Castadot R.G. et al.: The International Postpartum Family Planning Program. Eight Years of Experience. In: Report on Population/Family Planning, No. 18, November 1975.

Chambers R.: Rural Poverty Inperceived. Problems and Remedies. In: World Development, Vol. 9, 1981, pp. 1–19.

Chamratrithirong A. et al.: The Effect of Reduced Familiy Size on Maternal and Child Health: The Case of Thailand. In: WHO: World Health Statistics Quarterly, Vol. 40, Genf 1987, pp. 41–62.

Chenery H. et al.: Redistribution with Growth. Oxford University Press, London/Oxford, 3. Auflage 1976.

Chernichovsky D.: Socio-Economic and Demographic Aspects of School Enrollment and Attendance in Rural Botswana. In: Economic Development and Cultural Change, 1985, pp. 319–322.

Chisholm A./Dumsday R. (eds.): Land Degradation. Policies and Problems. Cambridge University Press, New York 1987.

Choucri N.: Demographics and Conflict. In: Bulletin of the Atomic Scientists, Vol. 42, 1986, p. 24ff.

Choucri N.: Population and Conflict. New Dimensions of Population Dynamics. In: UN-FPA (ed.): Policy Development Studies, No. 8, New York 1983.

Clark C.: Population Growth and Living Standards. In: Agarwala A.N./ Singh S.P. (eds.): The Economics of Underdevelopment. Oxford University Press, Oxford 1958, pp. 32–53.

Cleland J./Hobcraft J. (eds.): Reproductive Change in Developing Countries. Insights from the World Fertility Survey. Oxford University Press, Oxford/New York 1985.

Cleland J./Rodriguez G.: The Effect of Parental Education on Marital Fertility in Developing Countries. In: Population Studies, Vol. 42, No. 3, 1988, pp. 419–442.

Cleland J./Sathar Z.: The Effect of Birth Spacing on Childhood Mortality in Pakistan. In: Population Studies, Vol. 38, No. 3, 1984, pp. 401–418.

Cline W.R.: The Economics of Global Warming. Institute for International Economics, Washington, D.C. 1992.

Club of Rome: The First Global Revolution. A Report by the Council of the Club of Rome. Simon & Schuster, London 1991.

Coale A./Hoover E.M.: Population Growth and Economic Development in Low-Income Countries. Princeton University Press, Princeton 1958.

Coale A.J./Cotts Watkins S. (eds.): The Decline of Fertility in Europe. Princeton University Press, New York 1985.

Coale A.J.: Population Trends in China and India. A Review. In: Proceedings of the National Academy of Science, Vol. 80, 1983, pp. 1757–1763.

Coale A.J.: The Demographic Transition. In: IUSSP (ed.): International Population Conference, Liège 1973, Vol. 1, p. 56ff.

Cochrane S./Kozel V./Alderman H.: Household Consequences of High Fertility in Pakistan. World Bank Discussion Paper No. 111, Washington, D.C., December 1990.

Cochrane S./Sai F.T.: Excess Fertility. Health Sector Priorities Review No. 9, World Bank, Washington, D.C. 1991.

Cochrane S.H./Farid S.M.: Fertility in Sub-Saharan Africa. Analysis and Explanation. World Bank Discussion Paper No. 43, Washington, D.C. 1989.

Cochrane S.H./Jamison D.T.: Educational Attainment and Achievement in Rural Thailand. In: New Directions for Testing and Measurement: Productivity Assessment in Education No. 15, Washington, D.C. 1982, pp. 43–59.

Cochrane S.H./O'Hara D.J./Leslie J.: The Effects of Education on Health. World Bank Staff Working Paper No. 405, Washington, D.C. 1980.

Cochrane S.H./Zachariah K.C.: Infant and Child Mortality as a Determinant of Fertility. World Bank Staff Working Paper No. 550, Washington, D.C. 1983.

Cochrane S.H.: Effects of Education and Urbanization on Fertility. In: Bulatao R.A./Lee R.D.: Determinants of Fertility in Developing Countries. Vol. 2, Fertility Regulation and Institutional Influences. Academic Press, New York, London 1983.

Cochrane S.H.: Fertility and Education: What Do We Really Know? World Bank Staff Occasional Papers No. 26, Baltimore 1979.

Cohen C.: Sex, Birth Control and Human Life. In: Ethics. An International Journal of Social, Political, and Legal Philosophy. Vol. 79, No. 4, University of Chicago Press, July 1969, pp. 251–262.

Coleman D./Schofield R.: The State of Population Theory. Forward from Malthus. Basil Blackwell, Oxford 1986.

Commoner B.: Rapid Population Growth and Environmental Stress. In: International Journal of Health Services, Vol. 21, No. 2, 1991, pp. 199–227.

Cornia G.A./Jolly R./Stewart F.: Adjustment with a Human Face. Protecting the Vulnerable and Promoting Growth. Vol. 1 and 2, UNICEF (ed.), Clarendon Press, Oxford 1988.

Croll E./Davin D./Kane P.: China's One-Child Family Policy. Macmillan, London 1985.

Cross E.J.: Production Versus Reproduction: A Threat to China's Development Strategy. In: World Development, Vol. 7, No. 1, March 1981, pp. 85–97.

Crump A.: Dictionary of Environment and Development. People, Places, Ideas and Organizations. Earthscan Publications Ltd., London 1991.

Daily G.C./Ehrlich P.R.: An Exploratory Model of the Impact of Rapid Climate Change on the World Food Situation. Morrison Institute for Population and Resource Studies, Stanford University, Stanford, CA 1990.

Daly H.E.: Sustainable Development: From Concept and Theory to Operational Principles. In: Davis K./Bernstam M.S.: Resources, Environment and Population. Present Knowledge, Future Options. A Supplement to Population and Development Review, Vol. 16, 1990, pp. 25–43.

Das Gupta M.: Selective Discrimination Against Female Children in India. In: Population and Development Review, Vol. 13, No. 1, 1987, pp. 77–101.

Dave J.M.: Policy Options for Development in Response to Global Atmospheric Changes. Case Study for India for Greenhouse Effect Causes. Nehru University, New Delhi 1988.

David H.P.: Abortion: Its Prevalence, Correlates and Costs. In: Bulatao R.A/Lee R.D. (eds.): Determinants of Fertility in Developing Countries. Vol. 2, Fertility Regulation and Institutional Influences. Academic Press, New York/London 1983.

Davis K./Bernstam M.S./Sellers H.M.: Population and Resources in a Changing World. Current Reading. Morrison Institute for Population and Resource Studies, Stanford, CA 1989.

Davis K./Bernstam M.S.: Resources, Environment and Population. Present Knowledge, Future Options. A Supplement to Population and Development Review, Vol. 16, 1990.

Davis K.: Institutional Patterns Favouring High Fertility in Underdeveloped Areas. In: Eugenics Quarterly, Vol. 2, No. 1, 1955, p. 33ff.

Davis K.: Population Policy: Will Current Programs Succeed? In: Science, Vol. 158, November 1967, pp. 730–739.

Davis K.: The Theory of Change and Response in Modern Demographic History. In: Population Index, Princeton, Vol. 29, No. 4, 1963, pp. 345–366.

De Soto H.: Marktwirtschaft von unten. Die unsichtbare Revolution in Entwicklungsländern. Orell Füssli, Zürich/Köln 1992. (Original: Hernando de Soto et al.: El otro sendero. Lima 1985/Caracas 1987).

De Tray D.: Children's Work Activities in Malaysia. In: Population and Development Review, Vol. 9, No. 3, 1983, p. 437ff.

Deger S./Sen S.: Arms and the Child. A SIPRI Report for UNICEF on the Impact of Military Expenditure in Sub-Saharan Africa on the Survival, Protection and Development of Children. UNICEF/SIPRI Staff Working Papers No. 9, New York 1991.

Del Mundo F./Ines-Cuyegkenk E./Aviado D.M. (eds.): Primary Maternal and Neonatal Health. A Global Concern. New York 1983.

Demeny P.: A Perspective on Long-Term Population Growth. In: Population and Development Review, Vol. 10, No. 1, March 1984.

Demeny P.: Early Fertility Decline in Austria-Hungary: A Lesson in Demographic Transition. In: Daedalus, Vol. 97, 1968, p. 520ff.

Deutsche Gesellschaft für die Vereinten Nationen/Bevölkerungsfonds der Vereinten Nationen (ed.): Weltbevölkerungsbericht 1988. Die Zukunft Sichern. Bonn 1988.

Deutsche Gesellschaft für die Vereinten Nationen/Bevölkerungsfonds der Vereinten Nationen (ed.): Weltbevölkerungsbericht 1989. Vorrang für Frauen: Der Schwerpunkt für die neunziger Jahre. Bonn 1989.

Deutsche Welthungerhilfe (ed.): Die Europäer und die Entwicklungs-Zusammenarbeit. Bonn, März 1988.

Dobbing J. (ed.): Infant Feeding: Anatomy of a Controversy 1973–1984. London/New York 1988.

Dolan J.V.: *Humanae Vitae* and Nature. In: Thought, No. 44, 1979, pp. 358–376.

Donner-Reichle C./Klemp L. (eds.): Frauenwort für Menschenrechte. Sozialwissenschaftliche Studien zu internationalen Problemen. Bd.46, Breitenbach Verlag, Saarbrücken/Fort Lauderdale 1990.

Dorfman R.: Protecting the Global Environment. An Immodest Proposal. In: World Development, Vol. 19, No. 1, 1991, pp. 103–110.

Dunnette D.A./O'Brien R.J.: The Science of Global Change. The Impact of Human Activities on the Environment. ACS Symposium Series 483, American Chemical Society, Washington, D.C. 1992.

Easterlin R.A.: Modernization and Fertility: A Critical Essay. In: Bulatao R.A./Lee R.D.: Determinants of Fertility in Developing Countries. Vol. 2, Fertility Regulation and Institutional Influences. Academic Press, New York/London 1983.

Ehrlich P.R./Ehrlich A.H.: Bevölkerungswachstum und Umweltkrise. S. Fischer, Frankfurt 1972.

Ehrlich P.R./Ehrlich A.H.: Population, Resources, Environment: Issues in Human Ecology. Freeman, San Francisco 1970.

Ehrlich P.R./Ehrlich A.H.: The Population Explosion. From Global Warming to Rain Forest Destruction, Famine, and Air and Water Pollution. Why Overpopulation is Our #1 Environmental Problem. Simon and Schuster, New York/London 1990.

Ehrlich P.R./Ehrlich A.H.: The Value of Biodiversity. In: Ambio, Vol. 2, No. 3, 1992, pp. 219–226.

Ehrlich P.R.: Die Bevölkerungsbombe. Piper, München 1971.

Ehrlich P.R.: The Loss of Biodiversity: Causes and Consequences. In: Wilson E.O. (ed.): Biodiversity. National Academy Press, Washington, D.C. 1988, 21 pp.

Elguea J.A.: Development Wars in Latin America 1945–1989. In: International Journal on World Peace, Vol. VII, No. 2, Mexico, D.F. 1990, pp. 43–58.

Enke St. et al.: Economic Benefits of Slowing Population Growth. Tempe, Santa Barbara 1970.

Enke St.: The Economic Aspects of Slowing Population Growth. In: The Economic Journal, Vol. 76, No. 1, March 1966.

Enquete-Kommission *Vorsorge zum Schutz der Erdatmosphäre* des Deutschen Bundestages (ed.): Schutz der Erdatmosphäre. Eine internationale Herausforderung. 3.erw.Aufl., Economica Verlag/Verlag C.F. Müller, Bonn/Karlsruhe 1990.

Enquete-Kommission *Vorsorge zum Schutz der Erdatmosphäre* des Deutschen Bundestages (ed.): Schutz der Erde. Eine Bestandsaufnahme mit Vorschlägen zu einer neuen Energiepolitik. Teilbände I und II, Economica Verlag/Verlag C.F. Müller, Bonn/Karlsruhe 1991.

Enquete-Kommission *Vorsorge zum Schutz der Erdatmosphäre* des Deutschen Bundestages (ed.): Schutz der Tropenwälder. Eine Internationale Schwerpunktaufgabe. Economica Verlag/Verlag C.F. Müller, Bonn/Karlsruhe 1990.

Ernst C./Angst J.: Birth Order. Its Influence on Personality. New York 1983.

Evenson R.E.: Population Growth, Infrastructure, and Real Incomes in North India. In: Lee R.E. et al. (eds.): Population, Food and Rural Development. Clarendon Press, Oxford 1988, pp. 118–140.

Falkenmark M./Suprapto R.A.: Population-Landscape Interactions in Development: A Water Perspective to Environmental Sustainability. In: Ambio, Vol. 21, No. 1, 1992, p. 31ff.

Falkenmark M.: Fresh Water. Time for A Modified Approach. In: Ambio, Vol. 15, No. 4, 1986, pp. 192–200.

Falkenmark M.: Global Water Issues Confronting Humanity. In: Journal of Peace Research, Vol. 27, 1990, p. 177ff.

Falkenmark M.: Rapid Population Growth and Water Scarcity: The Predicament of Tomorrow's Africa. In: Davis K./Bernstam M.S.: Resources, Environment and Population. Present Knowledge, Future Options. A Supplement to Population and Development Review, Vol. 16, 1990, pp. 81–94.

FAO: Land, Food and People. Rome 1984.

FAO: Second Interim Report on the State of Tropical Forests. Rom 1991. In: Farooq G.M./Simmons G.B. (eds.): Fertility in Developing Countries. An Economic Perspective on Research and Policy Issues. MacMillan/ILO, Genf 1985.

Farooq G.M./MacKellar F.L.: Demographic, Employment and Development Trends: The Need for Integrated Planning. In: International Labour Review (ILO), Vol. 129, No. 3, 1990, pp. 301–315.

Feachem R.G./Jamison D.T. (eds.): Disease and Mortality in Sub-Saharan Africa. World Bank, Washington, D.C. 1991.

Ferdowski M.A.: Militante Konflikte in der Dritten Welt. Dimensionen—Ursachen—Perspektiven. In: Aus Politik und Zeitgeschehen, Vol. 37, Bd.8, 1987, pp. 27–37.

Foreit J. et al.: Community-Based and Commercial Contraception Distribution. An Inventory Appraisal. In: Population Information Programme: Population Reports Series J, No. 19, Johns Hopkins University, Baltimore 1978.

Foreit K.G.: Private Sector Approaches to Effective Family Planning. In: World Bank, Population, Health, and Nutrition Department: Policy Research Working Papers WPS 940. Washington, D.C. 1992.

Frank O./McNicoll G.: An Interpretation of Fertility and Population Policy in Kenya. In: Population and Development Review, Vol. 13, No. 2, 1987, pp. 209–243.

Frederikson H.: Derminants and Consequences of Mortality and Fertility Trends. In: Public Health Reports, Vol. 81, 1986, p. 755ff.

Freedman D.: Family Size and Economic Welfare in a Developing Country. Taiwan. Population Studies Center, University of Michigan 1972.

Friedlander S./Silver M.: A Quantitative Study of the Determinants of Fertility Behavior. In: Demography, Vol. 4, No. 1, Chicago 1967.

Fritsch B: Mensch—Umwelt—Wissen. Evolutionsgeschichtliche Aspekte des Umweltproblems. Verlag der Fachvereine, Zürich 1990.

Garcia M.: Impact of Female Sources of Income on Food Demand Among Rural Households in the Philippines. In: Quarterly Journal of International Agriculture, Vol. 30, No. 2, 1991, pp. 109–124.

Gasser W.R.: Survey of Irrigation in Eight Asian Nations. Foreign Agricultural Economic Report No. 165. US Department of Agriculture, Washington, D.C. 1981.

Gbenyon K./Locoh T.: Mortality Differences in Childhood by Sex in Sub-Saharan Africa. In: Van der Walle E. et al.: Mortality and Society in Sub-Saharan Africa. Clarendon Press, Oxford 1992, pp. 230–252.

Gesellschaft für entwicklungspolitische Bildungsarbeit e.V. Hamburg (ed.): Menschen zweiter Klasse. Bevölkerungspolitik in der Dritten Welt. Entwicklungspolitische Korrespondenz, 22.Jg., No. 3, Hamburg 1991.

Gilland B.: Population, Economic Growth, and Energy Demand, 1985–2020. In: Population and Development Review, Vol. 14, No. 2, 1988, pp. 233–243.

Gillick V.: Confidentiality and Young People. In: Ethics & Medicine, Vol. 4, No. 2, 1988, pp. 21–23.

Glover D.R./Simon J.L.: The Effect of Population Density on Infrastructure: The Case of Road Building. In: Economic Development and Cultural Change, Vol. 23, No. 3, April 1985, pp. 453–468.

Goldemberg J.: Energy, Technology, Development. In: Ambio, Vol. 21, No. 1, 1992, p. 14ff.

Gray R.H.: Birth Intervals, Post-Partum Sexual Abstinence and Child Health. In: Page H.J./Lesthaeghe R. (eds.): Child Spacing in Tropical Africa. Traditions and Change. London 1981, p. 100ff.

Greenwood A.M. et al.: A Prospective Survey of the Outcome of Pregnancy in a Rural Area of the Gambia. In: Bulletin of the World Health Organization, Vol. 65, No. 5, 1987, pp. 635–643.

Gwatkin D.: Mortality Reduction, Fertility Decline, and Population Growth. World Bank Population and Development Series No. 11, Washington, D.C. 1984.

Gwatkin D.R./Brandel S.K.: Life Expectancy and Population Growth in the Third World. In: Scientific American, Vol. 246, No. 5, 1982, pp. 57–65.

Gwatkin D.R.: Why Bother? Gobi-FF. Population Growth, and Human Well-Being. Overseas Development Council, Washington, D.C., July 1983.

Habicht J.P./DaVanzo J./Butz B./Meyers L.: The Contraceptive Role of Breastfeeding. In: Population Studies, Vol. 39, Cambridge 1985, pp. 213–232.

Hallouda A.M. et al.: Socio-Economic Differentials and Comparative Data from Husbands and Wives. In: The Egyptian Fertility Survey, Vol. III, Central Agency for Public Mobilization and Statistics, Cairo 1983.

Hammel E.A.: A Theory of Culture for Demography. In: Population and Development Review, Vol. 16, No. 3, 1990, pp. 455–485.

Hansen St.: Absorbing a Rapidly Growing Labor Force. In: Acsadi G.T.F./Johnson-Acsadi G./Bulatao R.A.: Population Growth and Reproduction in Sub-Saharan Africa. Technical Analysis of Fertility and Its Consequences. World Bank, Washington, D.C. 1990, pp. 60–73.

Hardee-Cleaveland K./Banister J.: Fertility Policy and Implementation in China, 1986–88. In: Population and Development Review, Vol. 14, No. 2, 1988, pp. 245–286.

Hardin G.: The Tragedy of the Commons. In: Bayles Michael D. (ed.): Ethics and Population. Schenkman Publishing Company Inc., Cambridge, Massachusetts 1976, pp. 3–18.

Hartfiel G./Hillmann K.-H.: Würterbuch der Soziologie. 3. Aufl., Kr—ner, Stuttgart 1982.

Harvard Institute for International Development: Nutrition Intervention in Developing Countries. Gunn & Hain, Cambridge 1981.

Haub C.: Understanding Population Projections. In: Population Bulletin, Vol. 42, No. 4, December 1987.

Hauff V. (ed.): Unsere gemeinsame Zukunft. Der Brundtland-Bericht der Weltkommission für Umwelt und Entwicklung. Eggenkamp Verlag, Greven 1987.

Haupt A.: The Shadow of Female Infanticide. In: Intercom, Vol. 11, No. 1/2, 1983, pp. 13–14.

Hauser J.A.: Bevölkerungs- und Umweltprobleme der Dritten Welt, Bd.1u.2, UTB/Haupt, Stuttgart/Bern 1991.

Hauser J.A.: Von der demographischen zur demo-ökologischen Transformation. Ein essayistischer Beitrag. In: Zeitschrift für Bevölkerungswissenschaft, 15.Jg., No. 1, 1989, pp. 13–37.

Hauser J.A.: Zur Theorie der demographischen Transformation. Ihre Bedeutung für die Länder der Dritten Welt. In: Zeitschrift für Bevölkerungswissenschaft, 7.Jg., No. 2, 1981, pp. 255–271.

Hazell P.B.R./Ramasamy C.: The Green Revolution Reconsidered. The Impact of High Yielding Rice Varieties in South India. Johns Hopkins University Press, Baltimore 1991.

Heer D./Smith D.O.: Mortality Level, Desired Family Size and Population Increase. In: Demography, Vol. 5, No. 1, 1968, pp. 104–121.

Hemmer H.-R.: Bevölkerungspolitik unter anderen Vorzeichen. In: E+Z Entwicklung und Zusammenarbeit, No. 12, Frankfurt am Main 1991.

Henry L.: Some Data on Natural Fertility. In: Eugenics Quarterly, Vol. 8, No. 2, 1961, p. 84ff.

Henshaw S.K.: Induced Abortions. A World Review 1990. Alan Guttmacher Institute, New York 1990.

Hermalin A.I.: Empirical Research in Taiwan on Factors Underlying Differences in Fertility. In Coale A.J.: Economic Factors in Population Growth. MacMillan, London 1976.

Hermalin A.I.: Fertility Regulation and Its Costs. A Critical Essay. In: Bulatao R.A./Lee R.D. (eds.): Determinants of Fertility in Developing Countries. Vol. 2, Fertility Regulation and Institutional Influences. Academic Press, New York 1983, p. 16ff.

Herz B./Measham A.R.: The Safe Motherhood Initiative. World Bank Discussion Paper No. 9, Washington, D.C. 1987.

Hess P.N.: Population Growth and Socio-Economic Progress in Less Developed Countries. Determinants of Fertility. Praeger, New York/London 1988.

Hirschman A.O.: The Strategy of Economic Development. New Haven 1958.

Hirschman Ch./Guest Ph.: The Emerging Demographic Transition of Southeast Asia. In: Population and Development Review, Vol. 16, No. 1, 1990, pp. 121–152.

Hobcraft J.N./McDonald J.W./Rutstein S.O.: Demographic Determinants of Infant and Early Child Mortality: A Comparative Analysis. In: Population Studies, Vol. 39, No. 3, 1985, pp. 363–386.

Hocher J.E.: Rural Development, Income Distribution and Fertility Decline. New York 1975.

Hollerbach P.E.: Fertility Decision-Making Processes. A Critical Essay. In: Bulatao R.A./Lee R.D. (eds.): Determinants of Fertility in Developing Countries. Vol. 2, Fertility Regulation and Institutional Influences. Academic Press, New York/London 1983, pp. 340–380.

Hollerbach P.E.: Power in Families. Communication and Fertility Decision-Making. In: Journal of Population, Vol. 3, No. 2, 1980.

Hösle V.: Philosophie der ökologische Krise. C.H. Beck, München 1991.

Huber S.C.: World Survey of Family Planning Services and Practice. In: International Planned Parenthood Federation (ed.): Survey of World Needs in Population. New York 1974.

Hull T.H.: Cultural Influences on Fertility Decision Styles. In: Bulatao R.A./Lee R.D. (eds.): Determinants of Fertility in Developing Countries. Vol. 2, Fertility Regulation and Institutional Influences. Academic Press, New York/London 1983.

Hull T.H.: Recent Trends in Sex Ratios at Birth in China. In: Population and Development Review, Vol. 16, No. 1, 1990, pp. 63–83.

Hurni H.: Ecological Issues in the Creation of Famines in Ethiopia. Addis Ababba 1988.

Hurni H.: Towards Sustainable Development in Ethiopia. Geographisches Institut der Universität Bern 1990.

Independent Commission on International Development Issues (ed.): North-South. A Programme for Survival. London 1980.

Intergovernmental Panel on Climate Change (IPCC): Climate Change. The IPCC Scientific Assessment. Cambridge University Press, Cambridge, U.K. 1990.

International Conference on Water and the Environment: Development Issues for the 21st Century. The Dublin Statement and the Report of the Conference. Dublin/Geneva 1992.

International Planned Parenthood Federation (ed.): Survey of World Needs in Population. New York 1974.

Internationales Arbeitsamt (ILO): Beschäftigung, Wachstum und Grundbedürfnisse. Ein weltweites Problem. Genf 1976. Auf englisch erschienen als ILO: Employment, Growth and Basic Needs. A One-World Problem. Genf 1976.

Isopublic (ed.): Entwicklungspolitik. Zürich 1989.

Jacobi C.: Die menschliche Springflut. Ullstein, Frankfurt a. M./Wien 2.Aufl.1970.

Jäger J.: Climate Change: Floating New Evidence in the CO_2-Debate. In: Environment, Vol. 28, No. 7, 1986, p. 38ff.

Janowitz B./Nicols D.J.: The Determinants of Contraceptive Use, Reproductive Goals and Birth Spacing in Relation to Mortality, Breastfeeding and Previous Contraceptive Behavior. International Fertility Research Program, Research Triangle Park, North Carolina 1980.

Jersild P.T./Johnson D.A. (eds.): Moral Issues and Christian Response. Fourth Edition. Holt/Rinehart/Winston Inc., New York 1988.

Johansson S./Nygren O.: The Missing Girls of China: A New Demographic Account. In: Population and Development Review, Vol. 17, No. 1, 1991, pp. 35–51.

Jonas H./Mieth D.: Was für morgen lebenswichtig ist. Unentdeckte Zukunftswerte. Herder, Freiburg i. Br. 1983.

Kant I.: Grundlegung zur Metaphysik der Sitten. Felix Meiner Verlag, Hamburg 1965.

Kapp K.W.: Social Costs and Social Benefits. A Contribution to Normative Economics. Zuerst erschienen in: von Beckerath E./Giersch H. (eds.): Probleme der normativen ëkonomik und der wirtschaftlichen Beratung. Verein für Socialpolitik, Duncker & Humblot, Berlin 1963, pp. 183–210.

Kapp K.W.: Economic Development in a New Perspective: Existential Minima and Substantive Rationality. In: Kyklos, Vol. XVII, No. 1, 1965.

Kapp K.W.: Für eine ökosoziale Ökonomie. Entwürfe und Ideen. Ausgewählte Aufsätze. fischer alternativ, Frankfurt am Main 1987.

Kaufman J. et al.: Family Planning Policy and Practice in China. A Study of Four Rural Counties. In: Population and Development Review, Vol. 15, No. 4, 1989, pp. 707–729.

Kelley A.C.: Economic Consequences of Population Change in the Third World. In: Journal of Economic Literature, Vol. XXVI, December 1988, pp. 1685–1728.

Kelley A.C./Nobbe Ch.E.: Kenya at the Demographic Turning Point? Hypothesis and A Proposed Research Agenda. World Bank Discussion Papers No. 107, Washington, D.C. 1990.

Kennedy E./Haddad L.: Food Security and Nutrition, 1971–91. Lessons Learned and Future Priorities. In: Food Policy, Vol. 17, No. 1, 1992, pp. 2–6.

Kershaw G.: The Kikuyu of Central Kenya. In: Molnos A. (ed.): Cultural Source Materials for Population Planning in East Africa. Vol. 3, Beliefs and Practices. East African Publishing House, Nairobi 1973.

Keyers L./Smyth I.: Familienplanung: Mehr als Fruchtbarkeitskontrolle. In: Peripherie, Nr.36, 1989, pp. 61–77.

Keyfitz N.: The Limits of Population Forecasting. In: Davis K./Bernstam M.S./Sellers H.M.: Population and Resources in a Changing World. Current Readings. Morrison Institute for Population and Resources Studies, Stanford University 1989.

Keyfitz N.: The Growing Human Population. In: Scientific American, No. 261, September 1989, pp. 119–126.

Keyfitz N.: Completing the Worldwide Demographic Transition: The Relevance of Past Experience. In: Ambio, Vol. 21, No. 1, 1992, pp. 26–30.

Keyfitz N.: Population and Development within the Ecosphere: One View of the Literature. In: Focus (Carrying Capacity Network), Winter 1992, pp. 12–25.

Keysers L./Smyth I.: Familienplanung: Mehr als Fruchtbarkeitskontrolle? In: Peripherie, No. 36, 1989, pp. 61–77.

Kielman A.A. et al.: Integrated Nutrition and Health Care. Johns Hopkins University Press, Baltimore 1984.

Kilian S.J.: The Question of Authority in *Humanae Vitae* In: Thought, No. 44, Herbst 1979, pp. 327–342.

Kilner J.J.: Who Shall be Saved? An African Answer. In: The Hastings Center Report, June 1984, pp. 18–22.

King Th.: Population Policies and Economic Development. Johns Hopkins University Press, Baltimore 1974.

King E.M./Evenson R.E.: Time Allocation and Home Production in Philippine Rural Households. In: Buvinic M./Lycette M./McGreevey W.P.: Women and Poverty in the Third World. Johns Hopkins University Press, Baltimore 1983.

King E.M.: Consequences of Population Pressure in the Family's Welfare. National Research Council, Washington, D.C. 1985.

King E.M.: The Effects of Family Size on Family Welfare: What do We Know? In: Johnson D.G./Lee R.D. (eds.): Population Growth and Economic Development: Issues and Evidence. The University of Wisconsin Press, Madison 1987, p. 373ff.

Klingshirn A.: Frauen und ländliche Entwicklung in Afrika. Erschienen als Forschungsberichte des Bundesministeriums für wirtschaftliche Zusammenarbeit, Bd. 32, Weltforum Verlag, München 1982.

Knight J.W./Callahan J.C.: Preventing Birth. Contemporary Methods and Related Moral Controversies. Ethics in a Changing World. University of Utah Press, Salt Lake City 1989.

Knodel J./van der Walle E.: Lessons from the Past: Policy Implications of Historical Fertility Studies. In: Population and Development Review, Vol. 5, 1979, pp. 217–245.

Koenig M.A./Fauveau V./Wojtyniak B.: Mortality Reductions from Health Interventions: The Case of Immunization in Bangladesh. In: Population and Development Review, Vol. 17, No. 1, 1991, pp. 87–104.

Kotler Ph./Roberto E.L.: Social Marketing. Strategies for Changing Public Behavior. The Free Press, New York 1989.

Kumar V./Datta.: Home-Based Mothers's Health Records. In: World Health Forum, Vol. 9, Geneva 1988, pp. 107–110.

Kunz G.: Medizinische Experimente mit der Antibabypille. Ein Rückblick auf die ersten Versuche an puertoricanischen Frauen. In: Zeitschrift für Sexualforschung, 2.Jg., Hft.2, Enke Verlag, Stuttgart, Juni 1989, pp. 119–131.

Kuznets S.: Population Change and Aggregate Output. In: Universities National Bureaus Special Series No. 22: Demographic and Economic Change in Developed Countries. Princeton 1960, pp. 324–339.

Kuznets S.: Population, Capital and Growth. Norton, New York 1973.

Lamprey H.F./Yussuf H.: Pastoralism and Desert Encroachment in Northern Kenya. In: Ambio, Vol. 10, No. 2–3, 1982, pp. 131–134.

Lazarus D.S.: Environmental Refugees: New Strangers at the Door. In: Our Planet, Vol. 2, No. 3, 1990, pp. 12–14.

Lee R.E. et al. (eds.): Population, Food and Rural Development. Clarendon Press, Oxford 1988.

Lee R.D.: Long-Run Global Population Forecasts. A Critical Appraisal. In: Davis K./Bernstam M.S.: Resources, Environment and Population. Present Knowledge, Future Options. A Supplement to Population and Development Review, Vol. 16, 1990, pp. 44–71.

Leff N.H.: Dependency Rates and Saving Rates. In: The American Economic Review, Vol. LIX, December 1969, pp. 887f.

Leibenstein H.: Economic Backwardness and Economic Growth. Wiley, New York 1957.

Leibenstein H.: The Impact of Population Growth on Economic Welfare. Nontraditional Elements. In: National Academy of Science: Rapid Population Growth. Consequences and Policy Implications. Baltimore 1971.

Leisinger K.M.: Arbeitslosigkeit, Direktinvestitionen und angepasste Technologie. Haupt, Bern/Stuttgart 1975.

Leisinger K.M.: Health Policy for Least Developed Countries. Available through Ciba-Geigy Stiftung für Zusammenarbeit mit Entwicklungsländern, Postfach, 4002 Basel/Schweiz.

Leisinger K.M.: Die *Grüne Revolution* im Wandel der Zeit: Technologische Variablen und soziale Konstanten. Erschienen als Leisinger K.M./Trappe P. (eds.): Social Strategies Forschungsberichte, Vol. 2, No. 2, Soziologisches Seminar der Universität Basel 1987.

Leisinger K.M.: Gentechnik für die Dritte Welt? Birkhäuser Verlag, Basel/Berlin/Boston 1991.

Leisinger K.M.: Nutzen und Risiken der Entwicklungszusammenarbeit. In: Gesundheitshilfe Dritte Welt/German Pharma Health Fund e.V. (ed.): Hilfe zur Selbsthilfe. Modellprojekte in Ländern der Dritten Welt. Frankfurt am Main 1991.

Leisinger K.M./Schmitt K. (eds.): Überleben im Sahel. Eine ökologische und entwicklungspolitische Herausforderung. Birkhäuser Verlag, Basel/Berlin/Boston 1992.

Lele S.M.: Sustainable Development. A Critical Review. In: World Development, Vol. 19, No. 6, pp. 607–621.

Leridon H./Ferry B.: Biological and Traditional Restraints on Fertility. In: Cleland J./Hobcraft J. (eds.): Reproductive Change in Developing Countries. Insights from the World Fertility Survey. Oxford University Press, London/New York 1985, pp. 139–164.

Leroy O./Garenne M.: The Two Most Dangerous Days of Life. A Study of Neonatal Tetanus in Senegal Niakhar. In: Van der Walle E./Pisons G./Sala-Diakanda M. (eds.): Mortality and Society in Sub-Saharan Africa. Clarendon Press, Oxford 1992, pp. 160–175.

Lloyd C.B./Ivanov S.: The Effects of Improved Child Survival on Family Planning Practice and Fertility. United Nations, New York 1987.

Lloyd C.B.: Understanding the Relationship Between Women's Work and Fertility. The Contribution of the World Fertility Surveys. In: The Population Council: Research Division Working Papers No. 9, New York 1990.

Maathai W.: The Green Belt Movement. Sharing the Approach and the Experience. Environmental Liaison Centre International, Nairobi 1988.

Mackenroth G.: Bevölkerungslehre. Theorie, Soziologie und Statistik der Bevölkerung. Springer-Verlag, Berlin/Göttingen/Heidelberg 1953.

Maine D. et al.: Effects of Fertility Change on Maternal and Child Survival. In: Acsadi G.T.F./Johnson-Acsadi G./Bulatao R.A.: Population Growth and Reproduction in Sub-Saharan Africa. Technical Analysis of Fertility and Its Consequences. World Bank, Washington, D.C. 1990.

Maine D.: Family Planning: Its Impact on the Health of Women and Children. Columbia University, New York 1981.

Maine D.: Mothers in Peril. The Heavy Toll of Needless Death. In: People, Vol. 12, No. 2, 1987, p. 6ff.

Malthus T.R.: An Essay on the Principle of Population as It Affects the Future Improvement of Society. London 1798.

Mamlouk M.: Knowledge and Use of Contraception in Twenty Developing Countries. In: Population Reference Bureau (ed.): Reports on the World Fertility Survey, No. 3, Washington, D.C. 1982.

Mannion A.M.: Global Environmental Change. A Natural and Cultural Environmental History. Longman, London 1991.

Mason A.: Saving, Economic Growth, and Demographic Change. In: Population and Development Review, Vol. 14, No. 1, 1988, pp. 113–144.

Mather A.S.: Global Trends in Forest Resources. In: Geography, Vol. 72, No. 1, 1987, pp. 1–15.

Matthies V.: Kriegsschauplatz Dritte Welt. Beck'sche Reihe, München 1988.

Maturana H.R.: Erkennen: Die Organisation und Verkörperung von Wirklichkeit. Vieweg, Braunschweig/Wiesbaden, 2.Aufl.1985. Schriften der Carl Friedrich von Siemens Stiftung: Einführung in den Konstruktivismus. Oldenbourg Verlag, München 1985.

Mauldin W.P./Ross J.A.: Contraceptive Use and Commodity Costs in Developing Countries 1990–2000. In: International Family Planning Perspectives, Vol. 18, No. 1, 1992, p. 6ff.

Mauldin W.P.: Fertility Studies. Knowledge, Attitude and Practice. In: Studies in Family Planning, Vol. 1, No. 7, June 1965.

Mbithi P.M./Barnes C.: Spontaneous Settlements Problems in Kenya. East African Literature Bureau, Nairobi 1975.

Mbiti J.S.: Concepts of God in Africa. Praeger, New York 1970.

McCallion D.J.: Human Population and Birth Control. In: Canadian Journal of Theology, Vol. VI, No. 3, 1960, pp. 170–178.

McDonald P.: Social Organization and Nuptiality in Developing Societies. In: Cleland J./Hobcraft J. (eds.): Reproductive Changes in Developing Countries. Insights from the World Fertility Survey. Oxford University Press, London 1985, p. 90ff.

McNamara R.S.: A Global Population Policy to Advance Human Development in the 21st Century. Rafael M. Salas Memorial Lecture, New York, December 1991.

McNamara R.S.: Accelerating Population Stabilization through Social and Economic Progress. Overseas Development Council, Development Paper No. 24., Washington, D.C. August 1977.

McNamara R.S.: Address to the Board of Governors. World Bank, Washington, D.C., 30 September 1968.

McNamara R.S.: Africa's Development Crisis: Agricultural Stagnation, Population Explosion, and Environmental Degradation. Address to the African Leadership Forum. Ota, Nigeria, 21. June 1990.

McNamara R.S.: Time Bomb or Myth. The Population Problem. In: Foreign Affairs, Summer 1984, pp. 1107–1131.

McNeilly A.S.: Effects of Lactation on Fertility. In: British Medical Journal, Vol. 35, 1979, pp. 151–154.

McNicoll G./Cain M. (eds.): Rural Development and Population. A Supplement to Population and Development Review, Vol. 15, 1989.

Meade J.E.: Population Explosion. The Standard of Living and Social Conflict. In: The Economic Journal, Vol. LXXVII, London, June 1967.

Meadows D./Meadows D./Randers J.: Beyond the Limits. Chelsea Green Publishing Company, Post Mills, Vermont 1992.

Mellor J.W./Gavian S.: Famine. Causes, Prevention and Relief. In: Science, Vol. 235, 30. January 1987, p. 539ff.

Meredith J.A.: Transmission and Control of Childhood Infectious Diseases: Does Demography Matter? In: Population Studies, Vol. 44, No. 2, Cambridge, UK 1990, pp. 195–215.

Merrick T.W.: Recent Fertility Declines in Brazil and Mexico. Published as World Bank Population and Development Series No. 17, Washington, D.C. 1985.

Mertens H.: Bevölkerungspolitik und das Recht der Frauen auf Selbstbestimmung. Die verschlungenen Pfade der Solidarität. In: Peripherie, No. 32, 1988, pp. 41–52.

Mertens, H.: Familienplanung als Entwicklungsstrategie. In: Peripherie, No. 36, 1989, pp. 41–60.

Messerli B. et al.: Umweltprobleme und Entwicklungszusammenarbeit. Entwicklungspolitik in weltweiter und langfristig ökologischer Sicht. Bericht des Geographischen Instituts der Universität Bern zu Handen der Direktion für Entwicklungszusammenarbeit und humanitäre Hilfe. Bern 1987.

Milhaven J.G.: The Grounds of the Opposition to *Humanae Vitae* In: Thought, No. 44, Fall 1979, pp. 343–357.

Mondot-Bernard J.M.: Relationships between Fertility, Child Mortality and Nutrition in Africa. OECD, Paris 1977.

Morawetz D.: Basic Needs Policies and Population Growth. In: World Development, Vol. 6, No. 11/12, 1978, p. 1253ff.

Morris M.D.: Measuring the Condition of the World's Poor. The Physical Quality of Life Index. Pergamon, New York 1979.

Moustafa S.A.: Problematic Population Phenomena in Arab Countries. In: Free Inquiry in Creative Sociology, Vol. 16, No. 1, May 1988.

Muhuri P.K./Preston S.H.: Effects of Family Composition on Mortality Differentials by Sex among Children in Matlab, Bangladesh. In: Population and Development Review, Vol. 17, No. 3, 1991, pp. 415–434.

Müller-Armack A.: Wirtschaftsordnung und Wirtschaftspolitik. Studien und Konzepte zur sozialen Marktwirtschaft und zur europäischen Integration. Freiburg i.Br. 1966.

Musgrove P.: Determinants of Urban Household Consumption in Latin-America: A Summary of Evidence from the ECIEL. In: Economic Development and Cultural Change, Vol. 26, No. 3, April 1978, p. 441ff.

Myers N.: Population, Environment, and Conflict. In: Environmental Conservation, Vol. 14, No. 1, 1987.

Myrdal G.: Asian Drama. An Inquiry Into the Poverty of Nations. Penguin Books, Harmondsworth 1968.

Myrdal G.: Das Wertproblem in der Sozialwissenschaft. Schriftenreihe des Forschungsinstituts der Friedrich-Ebert-Stiftung, Bd.40. Verlag Neue Gesellschaft, Bonn-Bad Godesberg, 2.Aufl. 1975.

Myrdal G.: Das politische Element in der national-ökonomischen Doktrinbildung. Schriftenreihe des Forschungsinstituts der Friedrich-Ebert-Stiftung, Bd.24. Verlag Neue Gesellschaft, Bonn-Bad Godesberg, 2.Aufl.1976.

Narayana D.V.V./Ram B.: Estimation of Soil Erosion in India. In: Journal of Irrigation and Drainage Engineering, Vol. 109, No. 4, New Delhi, 1983.

Narveson J.: Moral Problems of Population. In: Bayles Michael D. (ed.): Ethics and Population. Schenkman Publishing Company, Cambridge 1976, pp. 59–80.

Narveson J.: Semantics, Future Generations, and the Abortion Problem. In: Social Theory and Practice, Vol. 3, No. 1, Spring 1974, pp. 461–485.

Nerlove M./Razin A./Sadka E.: Household and Economy. Welfare Economics of Endogenous Fertility. Academic Press, Boston 1987.

Newland K.: Infant Mortality and the Health of Societies. Erschienen als Worldwatch Paper No. 47, Washington, D.C. December 1981.

Nhial Bol Aken: Civil War in Sudan. In: Bennett O. (ed.): Greenwar: Environment and Conflict. The Panos Institute, London 1991, p. 100ff.

Nolan P.D.: World System Status, Techno-Economic Heritage and Fertility. In: Sociological Focus, Vol. 21, No. 1, 1988, pp. 9–33.

Notestein F.W.: Some Implications of Population Change for Post-War Europe. In: Proceedings of the American Philosophical Society, Vol. 87, No. 2, August 1943.

Notestein F.W.: Population—The Long View. In: Schultz T.W. (ed.): Food for the World. Norman Wait Harris Memorial Fund Lectures, Chicago 1944, pp. 36–57.

Notestein F.W.: Economic Problems of Population Change. In: Proceedings of the Eighth International Conference of Agricultural Economists, Oxford University Press, London 1953, p. 15ff.

Nugent J.B.: The Old Age Security Motive for Fertility. In: Population and Development Review, Vol. 11, No. 1, 1985, pp. 75–97.

OECD: Zusammenarbeit im Dienst der Entwicklung. Bericht 1990. Paris 1990.

OECD: The State of the Environment. Paris 1991.

OECD: Migration. The Demographic Aspects. Paris 1991.

Ong Tsui A: The Rise of Modern Contraception. In: Cleland J./Hobcraft J. (eds.): Reproductive Change in Developing Countries. Insights from the World Fertility Survey. Oxford University Press, Oxford/New York 1985.

Oppong Ch.: Some Aspects of Anthropological Contributions. In: Farooq G.M./Simmons G.B.: Fertility in Developing Countries. An Economic Perspective on Research and Policy Issues. MacMillan/ILO, London/Geneva 1985, p. 240ff.

Overseas Development Administration of the U.K. Government: Population, Environment and Development. An Issues Paper for the Third UNCED Preparatory Committee. London 1992.

Oyemade A./Ogunmuyiwa T.A.: Socio-Cultural Factors and Fertility in a Rural Nigerian Community. In: Studies in Family Planning, Vol. 12, No. 3, 1981, p. 109ff.

Page H.J./Lesthaeghe R. (eds.): Child Spacing in Tropical Africa. Traditions and Change. London 1981.

Palloni A./Kephart G.: The Effects of Breastfeeding and Contraception on the Natural Rate of Increase: Are There Compensating Effects? In: Population Studies, Vol. 43, Cambridge, UK 1989, pp. 455–478.

Parry M.: Climate Change and World Agriculture. Earthscan Publications, London 1990.

Patterson J.G./Shresta N.R.: Population Growth and Development in the Third World. The Neocolonial Context. In: Studies in Comparative International Development, Vol. 23, No. 2, New Brunswig, 1988, pp. 3–32.

Perrings C. et al.: The Ecology and Economics of Biodiversity Loss: The Research Agenda. In: Ambio, Vol. 21, No. 3, 1992, p. 205ff.

Peter H.-B. et al.: Kreative Entschuldung. Diskussionsbeiträge des Instituts für Sozialethik des schweizerischen evangelischen Kirchenbundes, Bern 1990.

Pillai V.K.: Teenage Fertility in Developing Countries. In: Studies in Comparative International Development, Vol. 23, No. 4, Winter 1988, pp. 3–14.

Pimentel D. et al.: Offsetting Potential Global Climate Change on Food Production. Cornell University (College of Agriculture), Ithaca 1990.

Pinn I./Nebelung M.: Das Menschenbild in der Bevölkerungstheorie und Bevölkerungspolitik. Deutsche Traditionslinien vom *klassischen* Rassismus bis zur Gegenwart. In: Peripherie, No. 37, pp. 21–50.

Pinstrup-Andersen P. (ed.): Consumer-Oriented Food Subsidies. Costs, Benefits, and Policy Options for Developing Countries. Johns Hopkins, Baltimore 1987.

Pitaktepsombati P./Janowitz B.: Sterilization Acceptance and Regret. In: Contraception, Vol. 44, 1991, p. 623ff.

Pollock C.: The Garbage Glut. Mining Urban Wastes: The Potential for Recycling. Worldwatch Institute Paper No. 76, Washington, D.C. 1987.

Population Crisis Committee: Access to Affordable Contraception. 1991 Report on World Progress Towards Population Stabilization, Washington, D.C. 1991.

Population Reference Bureau (ed.): World Population Data Sheet 1992, Washington, D.C., June 1992.

Postel S./Heise L.: Wiederaufforstung. Die Welt braucht Wälder. In: Brown L.R.: Zur Lage der Welt 88/89. Worldwatch Institute (ed.), Fischer, Frankfurt am Main 1988, p. 129ff.

Potter J.E.: Effects of Societal and Community Institutions on Fertility. In: Bulatao R.A./Lee R.D. (eds.): Determinants of Fertility in Developing Countries. Vol. 2, Fertility Regulation and Institutional Influences. Academic Press, New York/London 1983.

Preiswerk R.: Kulturelle Identität, Self-Reliance und Grundbedürfnisse. In: Das Argument, Vol. 22, 1980.

Preston S.H.: Health Programs and Population Growth. In: Population and Development Review, Vol. 1, No. 2, 1975, p. 191ff.

Puffer R.R./Serrano C.V.: Patterns of Mortality in Childhood. PanAmerican Health Organization (PAHO), Washington, D.C. 1973.

Raven P.H.: Disappearing Species. A Global Tragedy. In: The Futurist Vol. 19, No. 5, 1985, pp. 8–14.

Repetto R.: The Relation of the Size Distribution of Income to Fertility, and Implications for Development Policy. In: World Bank: Population Policies and Economic Development, Johns Hopkins University Press, Baltimore 1974.

Repetto R.: The Interaction of Fertility and the Size Distribution of Income. In: Journal of Development Studies, Vol. 24, No. 4, July 1978.

Repetto R.: Economic Equality and Fertility in Developing Countries. Johns Hopkins, Baltimore 1979.

Repetto R.: Soil Loss and Population Pressure on Java. In: Ambio, Vol. 15, No. 1, 1986, p. 14ff.

Repetto R. (ed.): The Global Possibles. Resources, Development and the New Century. World Resources Institute, New Haven 1985.

Retherford R.D./Rele J.R.: A Decomposition of Recent Fertility Changes in South Asia. In Population and Development Review, Vol. 15, No. 4, 1989, pp. 739–747.

Rich W.: Smaller Families through Social and Economic Progress. Overseas Development Council, Washington, D.C. 1973.

Richards P./Gooneratne W.: Basic Needs, Poverty and Government Policies in Sri Lanka, Geneva (ILO) 1980.

Richardson H.W.: The Big, Bad City. Mega-City Myth? In: Third World Planning Review, Vol. 11, No. 4, Liverpool 1989, pp. 355–372.

Rinehart W./Kols A./Moorse S.H.: Healthier Mothers and Children through Family Planning. In: Population Reports J-27, May/June 1984, pp. J-675–J-696.

Rodgers G.: Poverty and Population. Approaches and Evidence. ILO, Geneva 1984.

Rodriguez G./Cleland J.: Socio-Economic Determinants of Marital Fertility in Twenty Countries. A Multivariate Analysis. In: World Fertility Survey Conference 1980: Record of Proceedings Vol. 2, New York 1981.

Rofman R.: How Reduced Demand for Children and Access to Family Planning Accelerated the Fertility Decline in Colombia. In: Policy Research Working Papers/Population, Health, and Nutrition (WPS 924),World Bank, Washington, D.C. 1992.

Rosenfield A./Bennett A./Varakim S./Lauro D.: Thailand's Family Planning Program. An Asian Success Story. In: International Family Planning Perspectives, Vol. 8., No. 2, June 1982, pp. 43–51.

Ross J.A.: Birth Control Methods and Their Effects on Fertility. In: Bulatao R.A./Lee R.D. (eds.): Determinants of Fertility in Developing Countries. Vol. 2, Fertility Regulation and Institutional Influences. Academic Press, New York/London 1983.

Rott R.: Bevölkerungskontrolle, Familienplanung und Geschlechterpolitik. In: Peripherie, Vol. 9, Nr.36, 1989, p. 12ff.

Rouyer A.R.: The Effects of Political Structure on Fertility in Poor Countries. In: Scandinavian Journal of Development Alternatives, Vol. 8, No. 3, 1989, pp. 19–36.

Royston E./Lopez A.D.: On the Assessment of Maternal Mortality. In: World Health Statistics Quarterly, Vol. 40, No. 3, 1987, pp. 214–224.

Sadik N.: Population, Resources and the Environment. The Critical Challenges. United Nations Population Fund, London, October 1991.

Sadik N.: The State of World Population 1989. UNFPA, New York 1989.

Sadik N.: The State of World Population 1990. UNFPA, New York 1990.

Sadik N.: The State of World Population 1991. UNFPA, New York 1991.

Sadik N.: The State of World Population 1992. UNFPA, New York 1992.

Sathar Z.: Seeking Explanations for High Levels of Infant Mortality in Pakistan. In: The Pakistan Development Review, Vol. XXVI, No. 1, 1987, pp. 55–70.

Saure S.: Frauenbildung. In: Donner-Reichle C./Klemp L. (eds.): Frauenwort für Menschenrechte. Sozialwissenschaftliche Studien zu internationalen Problemen, Bd.46. Breitenbach Verlag, Saarbrücken/Fort Lauderdale 1990.

Schapera I.: Married Life in an African Tribe. Pelican, Middlesex 1940.

Schipper L./Meyers St.: World Energy. Building a Sustainable Future. Stockholm Environment Institute 1992.

Schmidheiny St./Business Council for Sustainable Development: Changing Course. A Global Business Perspective on Development and the Environment. Cambridge, Mass.: The MIT Press 1992.

Schmidt S.J. (ed.): Der Diskurs des Radikalen Konstruktivismus. Suhrkamp, Frankfurt a. M. 1991.

Schockenhoff E.: Genug Platz für alle? Bevölkerungswachstum, Welternährung und Familienplanung. Schwabenverlag, Ostfildern 1992.

Schönwiese Ch.-D.: Klima im Wandel. Tatsachen-Irrtümer-Risiken. DVA, Stuttgart 1992.

Schultz P.T.: Retrospective Evidence of a Decline in Fertility and Child Mortality in Central East Pakistan. In: Demography, Vol. 9, August 1972.

Schultz T.W. (ed.): Food for the World. Chicago 1945.

Schumacher E.F.: Small is beautiful. A Study of Economics as if People Mattered. London 1973.

Schweitzer A.: Das Christentum und die Weltreligionen. München 1978.

Seaman J.: Famine Mortality in Ethiopia and Sudan. In: Van der Walle E./Pison G./Sala-Diakanda M. (eds.): Mortality and Society in Sub-Saharan Africa. Clarendon Press, Oxford 1992, pp. 349–366.

Selowsky M.: The Economic Dimension of Malnutrition in Young Children. In: Doxiadis S. (ed.): The Child in the World of Tomorrow. Oxford 1979, p. 351ff.

Serageldin I.: Development Partners: Aid and Cooperation in the 1990s. SIDA/World Bank, Washington D.C. 1993.

Shah K.P.: Food Supplements. In: UNICEF: The State of the World's Children 1984. New York 1983, pp. 101ff.

Shaw A.: Fertility and Child Spacing Among the Urban Poor in a Third World City. The Case of Calcutta, India. In: Human Ecology, Vol. 16, No. 3, 1988, pp. 329–342.

Simon J.L./daVanzo J. (eds.): Research in Population Economics, Vols.1 and 2, JAI Press, Greenwich 1979.

Simon J.L./Gobin R.: The Relationship between Population and Economic Growth in LDC's. In: Simon J.L./daVanzo J. (eds.): Research in Population Economics Vol. 2, JAI Press, Greenwich 1979.

Simon J.L./Gobin R.: The Relationship between Population and Economic Growth in LDC's. In: Simon J.L./daVanzo J. (eds.): Research in Population Economics Vol. 2, Greenwich 1980, pp. 215–234.

Simon J.L./Pilarski A.M.: The Effect of Population Growth Upon the Quantity of Education Children Receive. In: Review of Economics and Statistics, Vol. 61, 1979, pp. 572–584.

Simon J.L.: The Economics of Population Growth. Princeton University Press, Princeton 1977.

Simon J.L.: The Effects of Income on Fertility. Carolina Population Center, Chapel Hill 1974.

Simon J.L.: The Positive Effect of Population Growth on Agricultural Saving in Irrigation Systems. In: The Review of Economics and Statistics, Vol. 57, 1975, pp. 71–79.

Simon J.L.: The Ultimate Resource. Princeton University Press, Princeton 1981.

Simons J.: Culture, Economy and Reproduction in Contemporary Europe. In: Coleman D./Schofield R.: The State of Population Theory. Forward from Malthus. Basil Blackwell, Oxford 1986, pp. 256–278.

Singh S./Casterline J.: The Socio-Economic Determinants of Fertility. In: Cleland J./Hobcraft J. (ed): Reproductive Change in Developing Countries. Insights from the World Fertility Survey. Oxford University Press, Oxford/New York 1985.

SIPRI: Yearbook 1991. World Armaments and Disarmament. Oxford University Press, Oxford 1991.

SIPRI: Yearbook 1992. World Armaments and Disarmament. Oxford University Press, Oxford 1992.

Skinner C.: Population Myth and the Third World. In: Social Policy, Vol. 19, No. 1, 1988, pp. 57–62.

Smit B./Ludlow L.: Implications of a Global Climatic Warming for Agriculture: A Review and Appraisal. In: Journal of Environmental Quality, Vol. 17, 1988, pp. 519–527.

Srikantan K.S.: The Family Planning Program in the Socioeconomic Context. The Population Council, New York 1977.

Srinivasan T.N.: Population Growth and Food: An Assessment of Issues, Models and Projections, In: Lee R.E. et al. (eds.): Population, Food and Rural Development. Clarendon Press, Oxford 1988, pp. 11–39.

Stavenhagen G./von Wiese L.: Malthus und der Malthusianismus. In: Handwörterbuch der Sozialwissenschaften, Bd.7, Fischer/J.C.B.Mohr, Stuttgart/Tübingen 1961, pp. 101–105.

Streeten P. et al.: First Things First. Oxford University Press, Oxford/New York 1981.

Streeten P.: Adjustment with a Human Face. UNICEF, New York 1989.

Stryker J.D.: Optimum Population in Rural Areas: Empirical Evidence from the Franc Zone. In: Quarterly Journal of Economics, Vol. XCI, No. 2, May 1977, pp. 177–192.

Swartz M.J.: Some Cultural Influences on Family Size in Three East African Societies. In: Anthropological Quarterly, Vol. 42, No. 2, 1969.

Tabah L.: Population Growth and Economic Development in the Third World. IUSSP, Liège 1975.

Talbot P.A.: Some Nigerian Fertility Cults. Oxford University Press, London 1927.

Talbot L.M.: Demographic Factors in Resource Depletion and Environmental Degradation in East African Rangeland. In: Population and Development Review, Vol. 12, No. 3, 1986, p. 441ff.

Taylor C.E./Hall M.-F.: Health, Population, and Economic Development. In: Science, Vol. 157, 11 August 1967, pp. 651–657.

Taylor C.E./Newman J.S./Kelly N.U.: The Child Survival Hypothesis. In: Population Studies, Vol. 30, No. 2, 1976, pp. 263–277.

Taylor C.E./Newman J.S./Kelly N.U.: Interactions between Health and Population. In: Studies in Family Planning, Vol. 7, No. 4, New York 1976.

Taylor C.E. et al.: Integrated Family Planning and Health Care. Johns Hopkins University Press, Baltimore 1984.

Teran M.M.: Some Aspects of the Interrelationship between Fertility Patterns and Health. The Case of Mexico. In: WHO: World Health Statistics Quarterly, Vol. 40, Geneva 1987, pp. 41–62.

Thompson W.S.: Population. In: The American Journal of Sociology, Vol. 34, No. 6, 1929, pp. 959–975.

Tietze C.: Induced Abortion. A World Review. 4th Edition. 1981, Population Council, New York 1981.

Tinker I./Raynolds L.T.: Integrating Family Planning and Women's Enhancement Activities: Theory and Practice. Equity Policy Center, Washington, D.C. 1983.

Tolba M.K.: Our Biological Heritage under Siege. In: Bio Science, Vol. 39, 1986, p. 725ff.

Trent K.: Teenage Childbearing. Structural Determinants in Developing Countries. In: Journal of Biosocial Science, Vol. 22, No. 3, Cambridge 1990, pp. 281–292.

Trussel J./Rebley A.R.: The Potential Impact of Changes in Fertility on Infant, Child and Maternal Mortality. Princeton 1984.

UNDP: Human Development Report 1991. Oxford University Press, New York 1991.

UNDP: Human Development Report 1992. Oxford University Press, New York 1992.

UNESCO: World Education Report 1991. Paris 1991.

UNICEF: Within Human Reach. A Future for Africa's Children. New York 1985.

UNICEF: The State of the World's Children 1990. Oxford University Press, New York 1990.

UNICEF: The State of the World's Children 1991. Oxford University Press, New York 1991.

UNICEF: The State of the World's Children 1992. Oxford University Press, New York 1992.

UNICEF: The State of the World's Children 1993. Oxford University Press, New York 1993.

United Nations Conference on Environment and Development/UNCED: Agenda 21. Geneva, August 1992.

United Nations Department of International Economic and Social Affairs: Family Building by Fate or Design. A Study of Relationships between Child Survival and Fertility. New York 1987.

United Nations Development Programme: Human Development Report 1991. Oxford University Press, New York 1991.

United Nations Development Programme: Human Development Report 1992. Oxford University Press, New York 1992.

United Nations Environment Programme/WHO: Assessment of Urban Air Quality. Nairobi 1988.

United Nations Environment Programme: The State of the Environment (1972–1992): Saving our Planet. Challenges and Hopes. Nairobi 1992.

United Nations Population Division: Long-Range Global Population Projections Based on Data as Assembled in 1978. ESA/P/WP.75. New York 1981.

United Nations Population Division: Relationships between Fertility and Education. New York 1983.

United Nations Population Fund (UNFPA): Population, Resources and the Environment. The Critical Challenges. New York 1991.

United Nations Population Fund (UNFPA): The State of World Population 1990. New York 1990.

United Nations Population Fund (UNFPA): The State of World Population 1991. New York 1991.

United Nations Population Fund (UNFPA): The State of World Population 1992. New York 1992.

United Nations Population Fund (UNFPA): The State of World Population 1993. New York 1993.

United Nations: The Determinants and Consequences of Population Trends. New York 1953.

United Nations: The Prospects of World Urbanization. Revised as of 1984–85. United Nations Population Division, New York 1987.

United Nations: The World Population. Situation in 1970. New York 1971.

United Nations: The World's Women. Trends and Statistics 1970–1990. New York 1991.

Uthoff A./Gonzales G.: A Comparative Study of Costa Rica and Mexico. In: Farooq G.M./Simmons G.B. (eds.): Fertility in Developing Countries. An Economic Perspective on Research and Policy Issues. MacMillan/ILO, Genf 1985.

Van der Walle E./Foster A.D.: Fertility Decline in Africa. Assessment and Prospects. World Bank Technical Paper No. 125, Washington, D.C. 1990.

Van der Walle E./Pison G./Sala-Diakanda M. (eds.): Mortality and Society in Sub-Saharan Africa. Clarendon Press, Oxford 1992.

Van Ginneken J.K./Teunissen A.W.: Morbidity and Mortality from Diarrhoeal Diseases in Children under Age Five in Sub-Saharan Africa. In: Van der Walle E./Pisons G./Sala-Diakanda M. (eds.): Mortality and Society in Sub-Saharan Africa. Clarendon Press, Oxford 1992, pp. 176–203.

Vasold M.: Der Herr hat's gegeben, der Herr hat's genommen. Säuglingssterblichkeit in Deutschland von 1800 bis heute. In: DIE ZEIT, Nr.10, 28. Februar 1992.

Vaughan J.P.: Health Personnel Development in Sub-Saharan Africa. In: Policy Research Working Papers/Population, Health, and Nutrition WPS 914. World Bank, Washington, D.C. 1992.

Von der Ohe W. et al.: Die Bedeutung sozio-kultureller Faktoren in der Entwicklungstheorie und -praxis. Weltforum Verlag, Köln 1982.

Von Weizsäcker E.U.: Erdpolitik. ökologische Realpolitik an der Schwelle zum Jahrhundert der Umwelt. Wissenschaftliche Buchgesellschaft, Darmstadt 1989.

Waldron I.: Patterns and Causes of Excess Female Mortality among Children in Developing Countries. In: World Health Statistics Quarterly, Vol. 40, No. 3, 1987, pp. 194–210.

Wander H.: Bevölkerungspolitik. Möglichkeiten und Grenzen der Förderung sozioökonomischen Fortschritts. In: Opitz P.J. (ed.): Grundprobleme der Entwicklungsländer. Beck, München 1991.

Warwick D.P.: The Indonesian Family Planning Program: Government Influence and Client Choice. In: Population and Development Review, Vol. 12, No. 3, 1986, pp. 453–490.

Warwick D.P.: The Moral Message of Bucharest. In: Hastings Center Report 12, December 1974, pp. 8–9.

Weber M.: Gesammelte Aufsätze zur Religionssoziologie. Bd.1, Mohr/UTB, Tübingen, 9.Aufl.1988.

Weeks J.R.: The Demography of Islamic Nations. In: Population Bulletin, Vol. 43, No. 4, December 1988.

Westley R.J.: Some Reflections on Birth Control. In: Listening, Vol. 12, 1977, pp. 43–61.

Westoff Ch./Moreno L./Goldman N.: The Demographic Impact of Changes in Contraceptive Practice in Third World Populations. In: Population and Development Review, Vol. 15, No. 1, 1989, p. 90ff.

Westoff Ch.F.: Is the KAP-Gap Real? In: Population and Development Review, Vol. 14, No. 2, 1988, pp. 225–232.

Whyte M.K.: Cross-Cultural Codes Dealing with the Relative Status of Women. In: Barry H./Schlegel A. (eds.): Cross-Cultural Samples and Codes. University of Pittsburg Press, Pittsburg 1980.

Wichterich Ch.: Die allseitig verwendbare Persönlichkeit. Frauenförderung in der Entwicklungshilfe. In: Kommune 6, 1987.

Wicke L.: Umweltökonomie. Eine praxisorientierte Einführung. Verlag Franz Vahlen, München 1982.

Wiener Institut für Entwicklungsfragen und Zusammenarbeit (ed.): The World Ten Years after the Brandt-Report. A Conference Report. Wien 1989.

Wigley T.M.L./Raper S.C.B.: Implications for Climate and Sea Level of Revised IPCC Emissions Scenarios. In: Nature, Vol. 357, pp. 293–300.

Winegarden C.R.: Can Income Redistribution Reduce Fertility? In: Farooq G.M./Simmons G.B. (eds.): Fertility in Developing Countries. An Economic Perspective on Research and Policy Issues. MacMillan/ILO, Geneva 1985.

Winikoff B.: The Effects of Birth Spacing on Child and Maternal Health. In: Studies in Family Planning, Vol. 14, 1983, pp. 231–245.

Winikoff B./Sullivan M.: Assessing the Role of Family Planning in Reducing Maternal Mortality. In: Studies in Family Planning, Vol. 18, No. 3, 1987, pp. 128–143.

Winslow C.E.A.: The Cost of Sickness and the Price of Health, WHO, Geneva 1951.

Wishik S.M./Bertrand J.T.: Field Supervision for Quality Control of Local Family Planning Workers in Developing Countries. In: International Quarterly of Community Health Education, Vol. 11, No. 2, 1991, pp. 111–122.

World Bank: World Development Report 1984. Washington D.C. 1984.

World Bank: World Development Report 1990. Oxford University Press, New York. 1990.

World Bank: World Development Report 1991. Oxford University Press, New York. 1991.

World Bank: World Development Report 1992. Oxford University Press, New York. 1992.

World Bank: World Development Report 1993. Oxford University Press, New York. 1993.

World Bank (Operations Evaluation Department): Population and the World Bank. A Review of Activities and Impacts from Eight Case Studies. Washington, D.C. 22. October 1991.

World Bank Population and Human Resources (ed.): Europe, Middle East, and North Africa Region Population Projections. 1990–91 Edition (WPS 601).

World Bank: Accelerated Development in Sub-Saharan Africa. An Agenda for Action. Washington, D.C. 1981.

World Bank: Effective Family Planning Programs. Washington, D.C., Draft, 6. November 1991.

World Bank: Population Change and Economic Development. Reprinted from World Development Report 1984. Washington, D.C. 1985.

World Bank: Population Growth and Policies in Sub-Saharan Africa. Washington, D.C. 1986.

World Bank: Sub-Saharan Africa. From Crisis to Sustainable Growth. A Long-Term Perspective Study. Washington, D.C. 1989.

World Bank: The Population, Agriculture and Environment Nexus in Sub-Saharan Africa. Washington, D.C. (revised draft) 6. December 1991.

World Bank: Governance and Development. Washington, D.C. 1991.

World Bank: Effective Family Planning Programs. Washington, D.C. 1993.

World Commission on Environment and Development: Our Common Future. Oxford University Press, New York 1987.

World Health Organization (WHO): Programme for Control of Diarrhoeal Diseases. Eighth Programme Report 1990–1991. Geneva 1992.

World Health Organization (WHO): Research in Human Reproduction. Biennial Report 1988–1989. Geneva 1990.

World Health Organization (WHO): World Health Statistics Quarterly, Vol. 40, Geneva 1987.

World Health Organization, Maternal and Child Health & Family Planning: Abortion. A Tabulation of Available Data on the Frequency and Mortality of Unsafe Abortion. Dok.WHO/MCH/90.14, Geneva 1990.

World Health Organization/UNICEF: The Management of Diarrhoea and Use of Oral Rehydration Therapy. Geneva 1983.

World Resources Institute (ed.): World Resources 1992–93. A Guide to the Global Environment. Washington, D.C. 1992.

Worldwatch Institute Report: Zur Lage der Welt 90/91. S. Fischer Verlag, Frankfurt am Main 1990.

Wray J./Maine D.: Family Spacing. In: UNICEF: The State of the World's Children 1984, New York 1984.

Yi Z./Ping T./Liu G./Ying X.: A Demographic Decomposition of the Recent Increase in Crude Birth Rates in China. In: Population and Development Review, Vol. 17, No. 3, 1991, pp. 435–458.

Yuan Tien H. et al.: China's Demographic Dilemmas. In: Population Reference Bureau (ed.): Population Bulletin, Vol. 47, No. 1, Washington, D.C. June 1992.

Zachariah K.C./Patel S.: Determinants of Fertility Decline in India. World Bank Population and Development Series No. 24, Washington, D.C. 1984.

Zachariah K.C.: The Anomaly of the Fertility Decline in India's Kerala State. World Bank Population and Development Series No. 25, Washington, D.C. 1984.

Zentralkomitee der deutschen Katholiken (ZdK): Neuorientierung der deutschen Entwicklungspolitik. Offensive für die Armen. Dokumentation, 2.Aufl., Bonn, Dezember 1990.

Zolberg A.R.: The Next Waves. Migration Theory for a Changing World. In: International Migration Review, Vol. 23, No. 3, Fall 1989, pp. 404–430.

Index

Island Press Board of Directors

SUSAN E. SECHLER, CHAIR, Director, Pew Global Stewardship Initiative, The Aspen Institute

HENRY REATH, VICE-CHAIR, President, Collector's Reprints, Inc.

DRUMMOND PIKE, SECRETARY, President, The Tides Foundation

ROBERT E. BAENSCH, Consulting Partner, Scovill, Paterson Inc.

PETER R. BORRELLI, Executive Vice President, Open Space Institute

CATHERINE M. CONOVER

PAUL HAWKEN, Author

LINDY HESS, Director, Radcliffe Publishing Program

JEAN RICHARDSON, Director, Environmental Programs in Communities (EPIC), University of Vermont

CHARLES C. SAVITT, President, Center for Resource Economics/Island Press

PETER R. STEIN, Managing Partner, Lyme Timber Company

RICHARD TRUDELL, Executive Director, American Indian Resources Institute